The 7th Manchesters
at War

The 7th Manchesters at War

Two linked accounts of the First World War
on the Middle Eastern & Western Fronts

With Manchesters in the East
Gerald B. Hurst

The Seventh Manchesters
S. J. Wilson

LEONAUR

The 7th Manchesters
at War
Two linked accounts of the First World War
on the Middle Eastern & Western Fronts
With Manchesters in the East by Gerald B. Hurst
The Seventh Manchesters by S. J. Wilson

First published under the titles
With Manchesters in the East
and
The Seventh Manchesters

Leonaur is an imprint of Oakpast Ltd

Copyright in this form © 2010 Oakpast Ltd

ISBN: 978-0-85706-118-8 (hardcover)
ISBN: 978-0-85706-117-1 (softcover)

http://www.leonaur.com

Publisher's Notes

Contents

With Manchesters in the East   7

The Seventh Manchesters   83

With Manchesters in the East

Gerald B. Hurst

THE BATTALION OFFICERS ON MOBILIZATION, AUGUST 1914

FRONT ROW, LEFT TO RIGHT—REV. E.T. KERBY, CHAPLAIN; CAPT. C. NORBURY; CAPT. H.G. DAVIES; CAPT. AND ADJ. P.H. CREAGH; MAJOR G.B. HURST; LIEUT.-COL. H.E. GRESHAM; MAJOR J.H. STAVEACRE; MAJOR J. SCOTT; CAPT. J.N. BROWN; CAPT. H. SMEDLEY.

MIDDLE ROW, LEFT TO RIGHT——; LIEUT. F. HAYES; CAPT. J.F. FARROW (R.A.M.C.); LIEUT. G. CHADWICK; LIEUT. W.G. FREEMANTLE; LIEUT. C.H. WILLIAMSON; CAPT. A.T. WARD JONES; LIEUT. W.F. CREERY; CAPT. C.E. HIGHAM.

BACK ROW, LEFT TO RIGHT—CAPT. T.W. SAVATARD; LIEUT. B. NORBURY; CAPT. D. NELSON; LIEUT. D. NORBURY; LIEUT. E. TOWNSON; LIEUT. G.S. LOCKWOOD; LIEUT. J.H. THORPE; LIEUT. G.C. HANS HAMILTON; LIEUT. H.D. THEWLIS; LIEUT. A.H. TINKER.   ABSENT—CAPT. R.V. RYLANDS.

Contents

Eastward Ho!   13

The Sudan   21

Gallipoli   28

The August Battles at Cape Helles   35

Trench Warfare on Gallipoli   43

The Strain   50

The Limit   57

Last Words On Gallipoli   61

Revival in Egypt   64

On the Suez Canal   68

Sinai   73

The Territorial Idea   78

Appendix   81

FORMER PUBLISHERS' NOTE

DURING THE PASSAGE OF THIS BOOK THROUGH THE PRESS,
THE AUTHOR HAS BEEN ENGAGED OVERSEAS ON ACTIVE SERVICE,
AND HAS BEEN UNABLE TO DEVOTE THE NECESSARY ATTENTION TO
THE CORRECTION OF THE PROOFS, ETC.

DUE ALLOWANCE MUST THEREFORE BE MADE FOR SUCH ERRORS
AS HAVE CREPT INTO THE PAGES.

THE PUBLISHERS HAVE FELT OBLIGED TO DELETE THE NUMBERS OF
THE TERRITORIAL BATTALIONS MENTIONED IN THE BOOK,
A FACT WHICH ACCOUNTS FOR OCCASIONAL VAGUENESS
IN TERMINOLOGY.

CHAPTER 1

Eastward Ho!

Our battalion of the Manchesters was typical of the old Territorial Force, whose memory has already faded in the glory of the greater Army created during the War, but whose services in the period between the retreat from Mons and the coming into action of "Kitchener's Men" claim national gratitude.

Their earlier history hardly emerges from parochialism. Founded in 1859 and recruited mainly from the southerly suburbs of Manchester, the battalion lived through the common vicissitudes of the English Volunteer unit. It knew the ridicule and disparagement of the hypercritical and cosmopolitan, the too easy praise of the hurried inspecting general, the enthusiasm of the camp fire, the chill of the wet afternoon on a wintry rifle range at Crowden. The South African War gave many a chance of active service, and infused more serious and systematic training in the routine of the yearly Whitsuntide camps.

At that time everything depended on the Regular officer who acted as adjutant, and officers and men owed much to the inspiring energy of Captain (now Colonel) W.P.E. Newbigging, C.M.G., D.S.O., of the Manchesters, whose adjutancy (1902-1907) meant a great step in their efficiency. The letter "Q," which signifies success in all examinations required by the War Office, figured in the Army List after most of our officers' names during this vivid and strenuous phase. For the rest, the pre-War period turned mainly on the fortnightly camps and occasional Regimental exercises. Salisbury Plain, the Isle of Man, Aldershot and a few North Country areas are full of memories of manoeuvre and recreation in a peaceful age. Regimental exercises filled weekends in Cheshire or the West Riding.

Volunteering served many purposes in England. It kept alive in luxurious times a sense of discipline and a cultivation of endurance.

13

Its comradeship brought classes together so closely that the easy relationship between officers and men in the 1st line Territorial unit of 1914-1915 was the despair of the more crusted Regular martinet. Its joyous amateurism freed it from every trace of the mental servitude which is the curse of militarism, and stimulated initiative and individuality. Long before the War, most Territorials believed in universal training, not so much on account of the German peril, which to too many Englishmen seemed a mere delusion, as on account of its social value. It is pleasant to remember how solidly Lord Roberts received local Territorial support when he made the most prophetic of all his speeches in the Free Trade Hall, Manchester, on the 22nd October 1912.

Lord Haldane's conversion of the Volunteers into the Territorial Force of 1907 meant little change in the internal economy or in the personnel of this battalion. Its mounted infantry company, 140 strong, and its cyclists were lost in the interest of uniformity. Nevertheless, the change made us better fitted for war by incorporating us in the larger Divisional organisation essential in European war. Volunteer units supplied select companies for South Africa in 1899 and 1900. The East Lancashire Territorial Division was ready to take the field *en bloc* against the Germans in 1914.

The story to be told in these pages is so largely that of one battalion that a word can be said of its leaders in August, 1914, without making any claim to special pre-eminence, for our old and honourable rivalries with other local battalions faded long ago in mutual confidence.

Lieutenant-Colonel H.E. Gresham, who had commanded since 1912, was an ideal C.O.—a Territorial of long service and sound judgment, a fine shot, and in civil life a distinguished engineer. In Major J.H. Staveacre, the junior Major, we had an incomparable enthusiast, with a zest for every kind of sport, a happy gift of managing men and an almost professional aptitude for arms which had been enriched by his experiences in the Boer War. Captain P.H. Creagh of the Leicestershire Regiment was a fine adjutant, whose ability and character were to win him recognition in wider fields. His management of our mobilisation was beyond praise. The quartermaster, Major James Scott, was an old Manchester Regiment man, with a record of good work at Ladysmith and Elandslaagte. Of the company officers and N.C.O.'s, there is no need to add here to the tribute which will be theirs in any detailed history of Gallipoli. Nothing was more characteristic

LIEUTENANT-COLONEL H. E. GRESHAM

than their readiness to volunteer for foreign service as soon as we mobilised—long before the immensity of the War was understood, and considerably before the day of the lurid poster and the recruiting meeting.

The Manchester Territorial Infantry Brigade was embodied on the 4th August 1914, and on the 20th marched out through Rochdale to a camp on the Littleborough moors near Hollingworth Lake, where they were asked to offer themselves for service abroad. Twenty-six officers and 808 men of our battalion (roughly, 90 *per cent.* of our strength) volunteered. A wise pledge, afterwards unavoidably broken, was given by the authorities that no man should be transferred from his own unit against his will.

We dropped down the Channel on the evening of the 10th September 1914 in a convoy of fourteen transports and one ammunition ship, with H.M.S. *Minerva* as escort—the first Territorial Division that ever left England on active service. We sailed in a ship with a few East Lancashire details and the Headquarters Staff of the Brigade. General Noel Lee, the Brigadier, was an old Manchester Territorial officer, who understood the Territorial spirit to a nicety, and his death from wounds received in the battle of the 4th June 1915 was our irreparable loss. The Brigade Major was a tower of strength when on Gallipoli.

Of our battalion, who enjoyed during those shining autumn days their first vision of Gibraltar "grand and grey," with its covey of German prizes in harbour, and of the Mediterranean, then free of the submarine, and who half feared that the War would be over while they were still buried in the African desert, only a small number survive unscathed. Many sleep amid the cliffs and *nullahs* of Gallipoli.

The virtues and capacities of these my comrades will always haunt my imagination. Their psychology was extraordinarily interesting. They were unlike the Regulars, who preceded them in the field, and to some extent unlike the New Army, which gathered in their wake.

They had very little of the professional soldier. Only 45 among them had ever served in the Regular Army. Their homes and callings and the light amusements of a great city filled their minds in the same way as the Regimental tradition and routine filled those of the old British Regular Army. With a few exceptions, the feeling of duty was a far stronger motive to their soldiering than any love of adventure. These Manchester men had little of the Crusader or Elizabethan but his valour. They were, in fact, almost arrogantly civilian, coming from a country which had dared ineptly to look down on its defenders.

The Northerner is not an enthusiast by nature. His politics are usually limited to concrete questions of work and wages, prices and tariffs, and he knows no history.

The Germans in August, 1914, were still "Lancashire's best customers"—not a warlike race bent on winning world-empire by blood and iron. The social traditions of the middle-class urban population, from which the Territorials were drawn, had never fostered the military spirit, nor the power to recognise and understand that spirit in others. In such circumstances the sober zeal with which middle-aged sergeants forsook their families and businesses at the very outset of the War, without a moment's hesitation, is a signal proof of their character. No men were ever greater lovers of peace. Some philosophers have seen or tried to see in the War a judgment on the luxury and frivolity of pre-War England, on her neglect of defence, and her absorption in opulence.

Were this the case, it would be ironical to reflect how the North Country homes, first and most cruelly scourged by the War, were homes to which the so-called "sins of society" were least known and most repugnant, and where military training had been long pursued in the teeth of public ridicule and at the sacrifice of leisure. Long afterwards the father of a very talented private (Arthur Powell), who was killed in Turkey, wrote of his son: "We never intended him for the rude alarums of war, but his sense of duty and the horrors of Belgium fired his imagination, so that with hundreds of thousands of high-spirited young Englishmen, he placed himself in his country's service." This cast of thought is uncommon in the ranks of a Regular army.

Officers and N.C.O.'s were obviously and admittedly amateurs, and never acquired the distinctive dash of the old army. Soldiering was not their profession. Yet Territorials like the Manchesters possessed a range of talent in many ways beyond the normal standard of the army. They had the manual arts and crafts of the industrial North. These volunteers were in civil life builders and joiners; railwaymen, tramwaymen, engineers; clerks, shorthand-writers, draughtsmen, warehousemen, packers; carters and fitters; telephonists, chemists. When half of C Company was suddenly converted into the British Camel Corps at Khartum it was discovered to contain the camel-keeper of Bostock's menagerie.

We found piano-tuners for the *Sirdar's* Palace, gardeners for the Barrack plantations, and in later days expert mechanics for anti-aircraft gunnery. Skilled clerks like Sergeants J.C. Jones and Beaumont were marked out by Nature for the orderly room. Many men well qualified to hold commissions served in the ranks and died before the nation recognised their quality. Lastly, we could turn out more barristers than all the other East Lancashire units put together. It would be hard to imagine better officers than our three ex-Juniors of the Northern Circuit—N. H.P.Whitley, J.H.Thorpe and Hans Hamilton.

With the New Army, that was destined to do so much to save the cause of civilisation, our men had more in common than with the Regulars. In 1914, however, we had inevitably a less thorough training in technique than that which fell to their lot in the ensuing years. Only a few of our officers had gone the round of "schools of instruction" and "courses." We had fewer specialists, and our equipment was probably inferior. During all our Eastern experiences we used the long rifle only. It was, however, a real advantage to have had nearly sixty years' record as a Volunteer unit behind us, with all sorts of Regimental traditions, which lie at the roots of comradeship and ensure happy relations between officers and men. Another distinctive virtue of the Territorial system about Manchester was that all ranks, from Brigadier-General to private, came from one neighbourhood, and viewed life from much the same angle. They ran to type, and their interest in soldiering, obviously spontaneous in the first instance, had been fostered by common experiences in time of peace.

We saw Malta in the far distance on the evening of the 21st September, and next day, in mid-afternoon, our convoy unexpectedly met an Indian Division on its way from Bombay to Marseilles. Their transports, mainly British Indian liners, passed ours and exchanged escorts with us, thrilling the least imaginative with pride in the Empire and a sense of the illimitable issues at stake in Europe. We had left England ringing with the legendary passage of the Russians from Archangel, the snow still clinging to their furs, just as the British Army in Spain, in 1812, had been cheered by a similar mirage of Russians streaming to their aid through Corunna. The first paper that we read on reaching Egypt announced in giant headlines the arrival of 250,000 no less shadowy Japanese at Antwerp. But the Indians were real. Their appearance was a true touch of the World War and they reached the firing line in Flanders on the 19th October.

We eventually arrived at Alexandria on the 25th September 1914. B Company, under Captain (afterwards Lieutenant-Colonel) J.N. Brown, was dropped here, half of it under Captain E.Townson going on to Cyprus, which they garrisoned until the eve of its annexation.

Eventually the whole Company, then under Captain (afterwards Major) D. Nelson, was reunited to the rest of the battalion when it left for the Dardanelles. The remaining part of the Division also disembarked at Alexandria, in order to relieve the Regular garrisons of Alexandria and Cairo. The Battalion passed on to Port Said. As we neared the harbour, our men hailed watchers on the quay for the latest news. Antwerp was then at its last gasp, and the *Aboukir, Hague* and *Cressy* had been torpedoed in the North Sea. The first cry from the ship was "How is City getting on?" League football was still the first interest of Young England in the second month of the Great War.

We sailed down the Canal on a scorching Sunday morning to Suez and the Red Sea. A few Indians guarded its banks. Onward through the misty heat, under escort of a destroyer, with a wind blowing hot from Arabia, to Port Sudan, where we put in at 11 a.m. on the 30th September. The temperature was 105° F. in the shade. Here half of C Company, under Captain T. W. Savatard (afterwards killed on Gallipoli) were left to garrison and construct defences for the place. Once a desolate coral reef, it is now a great harbour with the promise of a greater future. This first night of Africa we rowed happily across its starlit lagoon in the full glamour of the East to enjoy British hospitality.

Next morning we started, with Major Boyle of the Egyptian Army Staff as a *"cicerone,"* on the long railway track from the sea to Atbara and Khartum, past scattered villages peopled by staring Fuzzy Wuzzies with erect and luxuriant black hair, and across hot stretches of desert and rock. At a quarter past eleven on the morning of the 2nd October 1914 we arrived at Khartum North, where we detrained and were met by the *Sirdar*, General Sir Reginald Wingate, then Governor-General of the Sudan, and his Staff. We marched over the Blue Nile Bridge to the spacious British barracks, the only spot in the Sudan where the Union Jack flies unaccompanied by the flag of Egypt, and relieved the Suffolk Regiment. In the afternoon our band played them out of the cantonment, and we cheered them on the first stage of their long journey to the blood-stained battle-fields of Flanders.

ARRIVAL AT KHARTUM, 2ND OCTOBER, 1914

CHAPTER 2

The Sudan

The tasks allotted to the battalion between October, 1914, and April, 1915, while garrisoning the Sudan were of great variety. With the gunners at Khartum Fort, they constituted part of the British force then in the country, of which Colonel Gresham was commander. The detachment left at Port Sudan organised its defences, ran an armoured train, and patrolled the Red Sea in the *Enterprise*. One group, under Captain R.V. Rylands (afterwards killed on Gallipoli), guarded the railway works at Atbara. Another under Captain B. Norbury occupied the hill station of Sinkat. Important censorship work at Wadi Halfa was entrusted to Captain J.H. Thorpe, and, when he was invalided, to Lieutenant L. Dudley, who fell later in action on Gallipoli. At Khartum a half company, under Captain C. Norbury, was on arrival transformed immediately into the British Camel Corps.

For some little time after our coming the normal social and sporting life of the small British colony at Khartum was hardly ruffled by the storm raging in Europe, and we gratefully enjoyed its warmhearted hospitality. At the beginning of November war broke out between Great Britain and Turkey, and the loyalty of the Sudanese was put to the test. The Germans built upon the probability of a Jihad or Holy War, and never dreamed that the handful of young Englishmen who administered the country under the *Sirdar's* guidance could have won its loyalty against all comers.

When the *Sirdar* announced in English and Arabic the news of the Porte's entry into the War one shining Sunday morning in early November, to a large gathering of Egyptian and Sudanese officers and dignitaries at the Palace, their zealous unanimity was impressive. Hundreds of native notables contributed generously to British Red Cross funds. Sheikhs of the Red Sea Province, who had once been dervish partisans, showed me with glowing pride when at Port Sudan silver medallions with King George's likeness, given by him to them on his visit to Sinkat.

Few pages of history are more wonderful than that which records the conversion of the chaotic and down-trodden Sudan of 1898 into the peaceful and prosperous Sudan of today. Scepticism as to the uses of Empire, which too often beset the Manchester man at home before the War, was dissipated by seeing what Anglo-Egyptian sovereignty and British character and industry have achieved in a land so long tormented by slave-traders and despots. The happy black boys of Gordon College go to school with books under their arms, and play football, coached by Old Blues and cheered by enthusiastic comrades. On the 30th October (Kurban Bairam day) the Manchesters saw the *Sirdar* bestow gaily coloured robes of honour on deserving chiefs. Everywhere were signs of economic progress. The cotton-growing plantations on the Gezira Plain, the ginning factory at Wad Medani, the numerous irrigation and public health works, the research laboratories of Gordon College, the industries of Khartum North and of Atbara, all bore the distinctive hall-mark of British Imperialism.

The magic of the British name in the Sudan seemed to us to rest not only on the art of government but on the great memories of Gordon and Kitchener and the abiding influence of General Wingate's personality. The Gordon statue at Khartum is almost a shrine. The Sudan itself is Lord Kitchener's monument. During our life there we were daily witnesses of General Wingate's tact, power and example. In all Mohammedan areas of the Sudan, Great Britain is wisely defender of the faith, and Islam is wisely with Britain.

On the 19th November we were entertained at the Egyptian Army Officers' Club on the occasion of the Mohammedan New Year. On the 27th January 1915 the Prophet's birthday was celebrated with rapturous pageantry, and the *Sirdar* and Lady Wingate paid most impressive visits to the pavilions set up by the principal *sheikhs* and notables in front of the mosques at Khartum and Omdurman, while huge crowds of religious enthusiasts beat *tom-toms* and sang outside. We saw the *Sirdar* reviewing his Egyptian and Sudanese troops at Khartum, formally inspecting the schools, hospitals, barracks and prisons around Port Sudan, decorating veterans with medals, and addressing in every native dialect the political and religious leaders of the people. We found that no men appreciated the care and skill of the Red Sea Province hospital more warmly than Arabs from the then Turkish territory of Jiddah.

The whole history of the evolution of the Sudan is epitomised in the bare, sun-scorched Christian graveyard of Wadi Halfa. The sandy, high-walled enclosure is the common resting-place of four successive generations of British Empire builders: first, of soldiers who fell in the Gordon Relief Expedition; secondly, of men who died while building the railway which proved the key to Lord Kitchener's success; thirdly, of soldiers who perished in the war of 1898; lastly, of civil servants who have died while administering the country since its reconquest.

Staveacre and I touched a much earlier phase of history when we discovered and bought derelict French helmets and cuirasses of 1798 that must once have been the booty of some Mameluke. Who would wish for more romantic trophies?

The Turkish war added gravity to the battalion's responsibilities in the Sudan. The idea at the time was to treat it passively, so long as the Turks did not molest British Moslems on pilgrimage to Mecca. The Arabs were known to have little sympathy with the Ottoman Turk and his pretensions to religious authority; so Jiddah was not to be starved by non-intercourse. The Turks themselves made such a policy impossible by their raid against the Suez Canal in February, 1915, and the inception of the Dardanelles Expedition marked the final victory of the school of thought which put its faith in an Eastern offensive. Some sort of offensive, whether against Gallipoli or Alexandretta or Haifa, had become perhaps a moral necessity.

We learnt in the Sudan how Turco-German machinations were necessitating a more active policy towards the Porte. I acted as prosecutor at the public trial of a Sudanese by general court martial in the court-house of Port Sudan in the second week of December, 1914. He had risen from sergeant's rank in a Sudanese regiment to be Captain of the Egyptian Coastguard in 1907. Cashiered in 1912, he served Enver Pasha in Tripoli, became an officer of Abdul Hamid's bodyguard, and afterwards a Major of the Baghdad Gendarmerie. Long before November, 1914, he had busily plotted for a rising in Egypt and the diffusion of German propaganda all over the Sudan. Under Enver Pasha's personal direction he disguised himself in a pilgrim's robe, styled himself Suleiman Effendi, and crossed the Red Sea from Jiddah with six pilgrims.

One of these was an Howrowri Arab from Kordofan. The rest were Falatas or Takruri—i.e. pilgrims from British West Africa to Mecca—a class whose whole existence is spent on pilgrimage, brightened by

GENERAL SIR F.R. WINGATE, G.C.B., G.C.V.O., K.C.M.G., G.B.E.,
D.S.O. HONORARY COLONEL OF THE BATTALION.

spells of residence and family life at centres like Omdurman, and this man planned to pass as a pilgrim among pilgrims. The party was asked by the sheikh of the Takurna village, near Port Sudan, where they came from. They replied: "Omdurman." On the 16th November he, in beggar's clothes, sought an interview with a Bimbashi of the Egyptian Army, at Port Sudan. He told him and his adjutant that he had come on a secret mission from Enver to rouse the Sudan against the British and to ascertain native feeling at Port Sudan, Khartum, Sinja, Wad Medani, Kordofan and El Obeid.

"The Porte," he said, "knows that the English treat you badly and intends to drive them out of Egypt." The officers whom he tempted were, however, staunchly loyal. They handed him over to Colonel Wilson, Governor of the Red Sea Province. His red and blue uniform, sword and papers were discovered, but he defended himself stoutly against the charges of spying and war treason, and his interests were carefully watched by Judge Davidson, who acted as Judge Advocate. One Arabic letter found among his papers was addressed to the Ministry of War at Constantinople, and appears to have been a copy of a report sent off by him just before his arrest. It is worth quoting as a footnote to history:

I arrived at Mecca, where I met the Valy and Commandant, Wahib Bey, and gave him my information. He left Mecca for Jiddah at once for his usual work, and provided me with a boat and six civilians, who accompanied me from Jiddah to Suakin and Port Sudan on a secret mission to induce the natives to favour the presence of the Turkish government, to rise against the existing European government, and to take necessary precautions for upholding the honour of the Turkish government without anyone's knowledge. I hope when I reach Khartum, in a secret way to encourage a rising against the British troops, if possible. As for my expenses, I took from the Valy Commandant sixteen Turkish pounds and three pounds sterling for the necessary expenses of the journey by steamer and land. I have every wish for the prosperity of the Religion and for the Sultan's victory over the unbelievers.

This man in his defence denied that any Sudanese like himself would dream of plotting against the British, who had purified government, employed Sudanese in administration, and given their children schools. He was convicted and sentenced to death, but that penalty was commuted by the *Sirdar*, in consideration of a tardy confession.

One of the Falatas turned King's evidence against his other companions on the charge of war treason. Squatting on the floor of the courthouse, their rosaries interlaced with their handcuffs, they assumed the air of innocence, but were convicted and condemned to terms of imprisonment. Two were called Isa (Jesus) and one was Adam. Arab life has more than a touch of the Bible.

The whole episode brought into relief the wide ramifications of Turco-German intrigue.

Another singular case of German subtlety was that of an alleged Swiss explorer, who arrived on the 10th November at Khartum on his way from Abyssinia to undergo the Pasteur treatment at Cairo. He claimed to have had his leg bitten by a dog, and was in hot haste to reach Egypt. He satisfied our doctors as to the genuineness of his injuries and anxiety, wept when Captain Morley, most expert of surgeons, told him of the surrender of Antwerp, and was given help and hospitality. He went through the Pasteur treatment and disappeared from our ken. A few weeks later an Italian newspaper applauded the patriotism of a German reserve officer, whose zeal to serve his country had nerved him to brave the vigilance of Khartum and the too devoted attentions of the hydrophobia experts at Cairo.

At a date when all Britons of military age worth their salt were training for war, the actual work of the Manchesters in the Sudan hardly calls for description. In the personal supervision of the *Sirdar* they enjoyed a special advantage not shared by the Territorial units left in Egypt. What is of more lasting moment is the share they took in furthering the cause of peace, order and good government in the Sudan by their steady conduct and happy relations with the inhabitants. Our officers interchanged visits with the officers of an Egyptian regiment quartered at Khartum, enjoying tea, music and speeches.

With an Egyptian regiment at El Obeid we had a pleasant and symbolic exchange of colours. In the ceremonial occasioned by the Sultan's accession, a guard of honour under Major J.H. Staveacre represented the British Army in the Palace garden, and acclaimed: "*Ya-aish Hussein Pasha, Sultan Masr*" (Long live Hussein Pasha, Sultan of Egypt). The men were scrupulously careful of native sensibilities. At Port Sudan, Private J.P. Lyons, our champion boxer, who was killed on Gallipoli, was publicly thanked by the Governor, Colonel Wilson, for having saved a black policeman from some drunken sailors. The Battalion hoped it had really earned the honour paid it when the *Sirdar* accepted its honorary colonelcy.

The knowledge gained during the months in the Sudan will be an asset to such Manchester Territorials as survive, and may even exercise an influence upon local public opinion. To many, the Sudan seemed entitled to rank among the best administered countries in the world. Its civil service governs vast areas and vast numbers practically without military aid. Its selection from University graduates who best combine brains with physique is in the spirit of Cecil Rhodes. Government of blacks by whites is a commonplace; of blacks by blues, a stroke of genius.

Looking back after years of soldiering and disillusion, the first months of the War no doubt seem brighter than they really were. It is easy to forget the illnesses that sent the writer as an invalid to Luxor and Cairo, and finally to England; to ignore the heat and dust and isolation, the long glare of the African day. We think more readily of Gordon's rose-tree blooming in the Palace garden; of the long camel treks across the desert; of the wail of the yellow-ribboned Sudanese bagpipes; of our visit with Colonel Smyth, V.C., to the stony, sun-baked battle-field of Omdurman; of the lusty strains of "Tipperary" in the cool barrack rooms. It is right that this should be so. The men to whom these memories would appeal were men who enjoyed life to the full.

They played the first lacrosse ever seen in the Sudan, engaged in keen boxing competitions, rallied to football on the roughest of barrack squares, listened cheerfully to weekly concerts and the first of our long series of history and military lectures. They hunted for curios in the dusty alleys of Omdurman, enjoyed recreation in the library and billiard-room, and ran with great spirit the early numbers of the *Manchester Sentry*, first published of all active service periodicals. To this paper the *Sirdar* and Lady Wingate contributed welcome and inspiring letters, and the battalion owed its motto: *We never sleep.*

In April, 1915, the battalion left the Sudan for Cairo, where it again came in contact with the other units of the East Lancashire Territorial Division, thenceforward called the 42nd Division On the 3rd May it embarked in company with another battalion of the Manchesters on the *Ionian*, and at seven in the evening, on the 7th May, it landed at "V" Beach, Cape Helles.

CHAPTER 3

Gallipoli

The 42nd Division was soon in the midst of hard fighting, stormy weather and much privation. Casualties began early, though the first Battalion exploit under fire was happily bloodless. On the 9th May, 80 men were told off to fill water-bottles and carry them under fire over half-a-mile of broken ground to an Australian unit. They tracked cleverly across the moor, and were met by an eager Australian with the question: "Have you brought the water, cobbers?" On the 11th, the Battalion had a long, weary march to the front line. The trenches were full of water, and the gullies became almost impassable. On the 28th, Lockwood, our musketry expert, was severely wounded in the chest.

On the same day Lieutenant-Colonel Gresham was forced by ill-health to leave us. He was invalided to Malta, and thence to England. A year later he relinquished his command, without having been able to rejoin. He had served with the battalion ever since 1890. He was known to suffer from chronic illness, but he let nothing interfere with the call of duty, and his hard work overseas set a fine example to all ranks. It is, indeed, still, in 1917, difficult to think of the Battalion with any other Commanding Officer. His departure was widely regretted, and the later achievements of his men in the War are the best tribute to the many years of labour he had given to their training and organisation.

His immediate successor in command was Major Staveacre. On the night of the 28th May the battalion advanced, and B and D Companies dug themselves in under a full moon and in the face of the enemy, a platoon of C Company finishing the work on the following evening. In these operations fell Captains T. W. Savatard and R. V. Rylands, men of sterling character and capacity, and Lieut. T. F. Brown, a gallant boy, who, in the happier days of the threatened war in Ulster, had served in the West Belfast Loyalist Volunteers.

The advance of the 28th May was preliminary to the historic attack of the whole allied line from sea to sea, which had been timed for midday on the 4th June 1915. In this attack the battalion advanced as the extreme right unit of our Infantry Brigade. On the left of the Manchesters was the 29th Division; on our right was the Royal Naval Division, and on their right were the French.

During the previous night the Turks, writes an eyewitness in the *Sentry*, gave us "our first taste of bombing. They crawled down a small gully and threw eight or nine bombs on to our gun emplacement, hurting no one, but putting the gun out for twenty minutes." Meanwhile they fired the gorse in front of the 29th Division.

At eight in the morning the British guns opened the bombardment. "At eleven-twenty our whole line from the sea to the Straits got up and waved their bayonets, pretending the attack was to start." At twelve, "with wild cheers" the assault was launched. A and C Companies rushed the first Turkish trench, and captured the surviving occupants, while along a front that stretched far away to the left, similar success was won by the whole British line. While A and C Companies consolidated the trench they had won, B and D Companies passed over it, in order to take the next Turkish line. Captain (afterwards Major) C.E. Higham, always resourceful and imperturbable, was shot in the foot while crossing the trench, but Captain (afterwards Lieutenant-Colonel) Fawcus led the attack a long way forward, and held a dummy trench in the heart of the Turkish position for many hours.

Subsequently the right flank of the battalion was not only enfiladed but exposed to fire from their rear. The officers at this deadly point were Lieutenants H.D. Thewlis, W.G. Freemantle and F.C. Palmer. Palmer was badly wounded. Thewlis, a keen subaltern and expert in scientific agriculture, refused to retire, and was killed. Freemantle was of Quaker stock and, like Thewlis, a graduate of Manchester University. He was first shot through the right arm, and then through the left. He insisted on remaining with his men, though the pain was so intense that he broke his teeth while clenching them. He was then shot through the body, and died.

C Company on this right flank was in danger. Lieutenant G.C. Hans Hamilton, a prince of fighters, had organised a bombing party with Corporal Cherry, and did great work, but was now severely wounded. Leonard Dudley, an adventurous soul who had fought under Staveacre with the Cheshire Yeomanry in South Africa, was killed.

N

W   E

S

To Maidos

472

ACHI
BABA
591   545
To Kilid
Bahr

ÆGEAN

FUSILIER BLUFF
BORDER RAVINE
ESSEX RAVINE
BRUCE'S RAVINE
'Y' BEACH

BORDER
BARRICADE   KRITHIA

GEOGHEGAN'S
BLUFF

SEA

GULLY BEACH

GULLY

KRITHIA NULLAH

'X' BEACH

THE
DARDANELLES

'W'   LANCASHIRE
BEACH   LANDING

MORTO
BAY   DE TOTT'S BATTERY

C. HELLES   SEDD-EL-BAHR

To Kum Kale
(2¼ Miles)

0   1   2   3
Scale of Miles

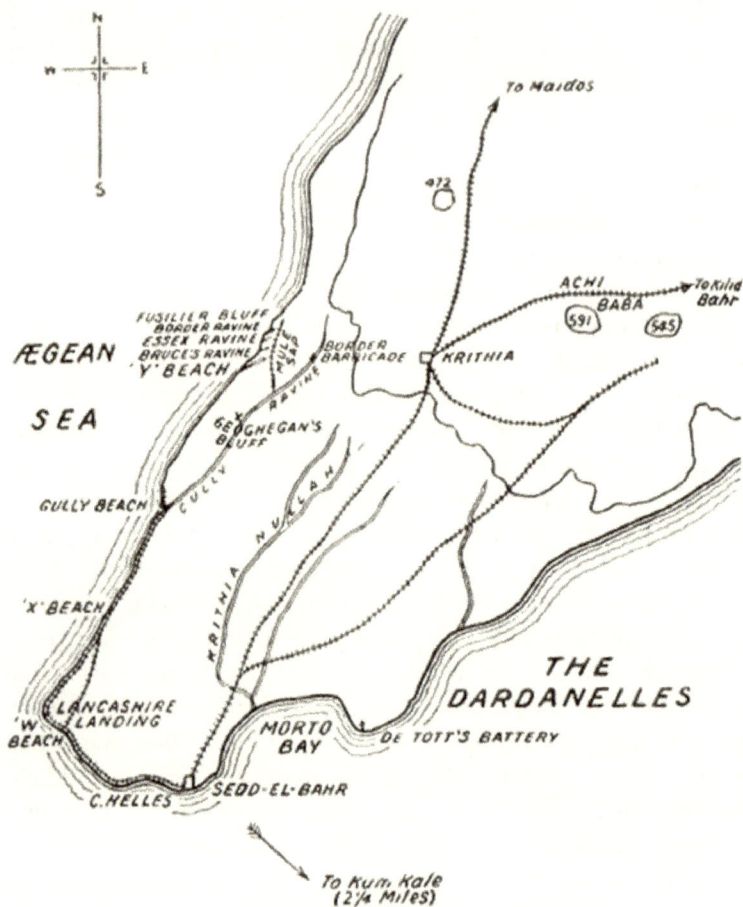

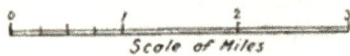

Gullies
Roads or Tracks
Contours

GALLIPOLI

Captain Cyril Norbury, who commanded the Company, had written to Major Staveacre for information, and he received this answer from Captain Creagh: "Regret to say Major Staveacre dead; also Thewlis and Freemantle. Do not know whereabouts of missing platoons. Fear most lost."

Staveacre had been shot through the back while passing ammunition to the firing line. He said to Regimental Sergeant-Major H.C. Franklin (the Acting Adjutant of our later days on Gallipoli): "Never mind me. Carry on, Sergeant-Major," and died at once.

All day long the Turks counter-attacked the Manchesters without success. Private Richardson won the D.C.M. by bombing feats, but the supply of bombs ran out early. Their use was in its infancy, and their character was primitive. C Company, among whom Sergeant M'Hugh, Corporal Basnett and Private (afterwards Lieutenant) J.W. Sutherland were conspicuous, was reinforced by some gallant bombers from another battalion of the Manchesters under Captain James, who was killed after driving the Turks from a trench, and later by some of the Lancashire Fusiliers. They held their own, and a last Turkish counter-attack, on the morning of the 5th June, was scattered by our machine guns and those of the Lancashire Fusiliers, well handled by Captains Hayes and Bedson.

Fawcus brought back about nine survivors from his advanced position after great feats of endurance, in which the Manchester units on our left had fully shared. Lieutenant T.E. Granger, who had been left behind dangerously wounded, was taken prisoner. Lieutenant Ward was killed. Lieutenant Bateman was shot through the lungs; Lieutenant G. Norbury on the scalp.

On the 4th June the Brigadier, General Noel Lee, was mortally wounded, to the intense and universal sorrow of the whole Division. He died in Malta. Lieutenant-Colonel Heys, on taking his place, was immediately killed. The retreat from the more advanced trenches to the original Turkish firing line, necessitated by enfilade fire and by the absence of reinforcements, proved far deadlier than the advance. The battle, with its preliminary operations, cost us some of our bravest sergeant-majors and sergeants—Cookson, Arnott, Marvin, Mundy, Balfe, Webster. Sergeant Lindsay lost his leg. Of them and of all the men of the 42nd Division, who gave their lives in this action, any praise is superfluous.

A broad strip of land gained securely on a wide frontage, an immense number of Turkish dead and prisoners, and a sense of great personal ascendancy, were the measure of their success, and General Sir Ian Hamilton's dispatch truly estimates its quality.

The survivors of the battalion rested for a few days on Imbros after the battle, and then returned to the Peninsula under the command of Captain P.H. Creagh. On the 16th July the command was passed to Lieutenant-Colonel A. Canning, a veteran of the Egyptian War of 1882, who had previously commanded the Leinster Regiment at Cork. We could have had no greater confidence in any possible Commanding Officer, and while he acted as Brigadier of the Manchester Territorials his influence was no less inspiring. The record of our later campaign on Gallipoli is closely associated with his name and work.

All these early scenes of the expedition to the Dardanelles I had missed. On the 17th March I had been invalided home on the Indian hospital ship, *Glenart Castle*, Alexandria to Southampton, and the only public meeting I witnessed during three years of warfare—a recruiting rally in the Manchester Hippodrome—was a poor outlet for one's activity. An offer of the command of the new 3rd line reserve unit at Southport naturally failed to quench my keenness to rejoin the Battalion, and after vexatious delays I at last sailed from Devonport for the East, on the *Simla*, on the 13th July 1915.

We reached Alexandria on the 25th, and the crowded harbour of Mudros early on the 29th. The boat was full of drafts for the 29th Division—Essex and Hampshire men, Inniskillings, Munsters, Royal and Lancashire Fusiliers, Worcesters—and rumours of the intended Suvla expedition were in the air. Our optimism was, however, chastened by the opinions of one experienced soldier on board, who insisted that we ought never to have landed at Cape Helles, but on the Gulf of Saros behind the lines of Bulair, and made straight for Constantinople with a large army, without trying to force the Dardanelles. He believed that the Germans would still take Warsaw, and thought Holland's co-operation essential to any plan of early success.

The war was still at a stage when men did not mind talking about it, and the general assumption was that it could not last long. One sailor told me a story typical of the German's ignorance of sportsmanship. A captured naval officer was courteously allowed the use of the British captain's cabin. A few moments later a crash announced that he had requited chivalry by breaking everything he could lay his hands on. Other passengers on the *Simla* were nursing sisters in dainty scarlet and grey, naval airmen who disembarked at Valetta, and the whole staff of an Australian General Hospital bound for Mudros—expert specialist officers and splendid men, with songs cheery and robust:

"When the beer's on the table, we'll be there."

Perhaps my most vivid memories, however, are of the keen young officers conducting drafts, who were so soon to fall in the great attempt at Suvla.

The fate of one of these, J.R. Lingard, then in charge of some Lancashire Fusiliers, was one of the unsolved mysteries of the Dardanelles campaign. A brave and popular officer, he was severely wounded on the 21st August. He was carried out of action and placed on a stretcher for conveyance across Suvla Beach to a hospital ship. At this point all trace of him disappeared. His fate is unknown.

In the late afternoon of the 30th July 1915 we neared Cape Helles and heard the thunder of the guns. We landed laboriously about midnight, and were led by guides to a rendezvous of the 29th Division at a point some three miles along the coast on the northern side of the Peninsula. Brilliant moonlight shone upon a sleeping French force close to the landing-place on "V" Beach. The country looked unspeakably dry and bare.

At six o'clock the following morning we were divided into details for our various units, and sleepless, unshaven and hungry, I was again guided to where the 42nd Division had its headquarters—a spot to the south of the 29th, and, roughly, in the left centre of the short line of the Allies. The narrowness and shallowness of the area of our occupation struck all observers at once. The great ridge of Achi Baba, some six hundred feet above sea-level, barring our advance upon Turkey, confronted us the very moment that we climbed to the top of the cliffs that enclosed every landing-place. We were shelled as we struck across the moorland, and then I found myself once more in East Lancashire.

A long wait at Divisional Headquarters was followed by a delightful welcome at the quartermaster's dump of the battalion, where, in blazing sunshine, I enjoyed my first food and shave on enemy soil, and abundant news of the unit. A friendly sergeant then led me up to the fire trenches some two miles forward, where the Manchesters held both sides of Krithia nullah, a ravine running up into a sloping heath, where the Turks had lain dug in for the last two months. Our way, after passing "Clapham Junction," was fringed with the graves of the fallen. I noticed Staveacre's.

It was pleasant to reach the cool burrow, which served as our Battalion Headquarters. Here I found Colonel Canning, P.H. Creagh and Fawcus sitting on the yellow, dusty ground beneath a tarpaulin. It was thrilling once again to walk among our Manchester men, now very thin and sunburnt, in shirt-sleeves and shorts, making the best of life in narrow trenches, and watching day after day the serried Turkish lines and broad, brown mass of Achi Baba. Next day (1st August), in mid-afternoon, we moved into the most advanced fire trenches, and I became O.C. of our battalion's firing line, with a small dug-out of my own in the centre of our sector. This sector was within forty or fifty yards of the Turkish position, and in the early morning, as the sun rose over Asia, we heard the *muezzin* calling the faithful to prayer.

There was a lull at this time in warfare. Casualties were few, and the periscope disclosed little beyond the vista (soon too familiar) of arid heath, broken only by patches of wild thyme, and of the intricate lace-work of sandbagged trenches stretching from the tip of Cape Helles behind us to the top of Achi Baba. But for the constant booming of the guns and the plague of flies, these first days on Gallipoli were days of peace and happiness under a quiet, blue sky. Our men were hope-ful, and a stray memorandum of mine of the 3rd August records that "P.H. Creagh bets Fawcus £1 that the Turks will be driven out of the Peninsula within a month." Our faith was great in those days.

CHAPTER 4

The August Battles at Cape Helles

In the history of the expedition to the Dardanelles, the August battles in the area of Cape Helles figure as a pinning or holding attack by the British Army, designed to occupy the enemy while the Suvla Bay landing was effected. The line of communications that linked the Achi Baba position with Maidos and Gallipoli was to be cut by our forces operating from Suvla and Anzac, and the Narrows were to be opened to our fleet by the capture of Sari-Bair. The epic of the actual Suvla effort has been nobly told in both Sir Ian Hamilton's dispatches and Mr Masefield's *Gallipoli*.

The Regimental officer at Cape Helles naturally knew very little of the strategy underlying these operations, and nothing of events at Suvla or Anzac, though Suvla was but thirteen miles and Anzac but five from Fusilier Bluff. His could only be the impressions of an eyewitness in an orbit limited to his brigade. During the whole of our Gallipoli experiences, we were only conscious of divisional organisation and personnel through the literature and correspondence of the orderly-room, or from mere glimpses on the occasion of our rare visits to the base on Gully Beach. I am glad to have once seen the commander-in-chief, Sir Ian Hamilton. He passed our Headquarters on the Western Mule Sap, walking briskly towards the trenches.

The fine appreciation of the Manchester Territorial Brigade's work on the 4th June, which he wrote in his dispatches, made his name a name always to conjure with, but to the man in the trenches, an army commander can at most be but a shining name. Consequently, the story of the fighting in August, as we saw it, must needs be silent on all vexed questions of high policy, and also on the more famous struggle to the north of Achi Baba. Its limitations are true to life.

On the 5th August we learnt that our amy was to assault the enemy's position simultaneously with the enterprise at Suvla.

Three points were emphasised in our instructions. First, the frontage and depth of the sector to be carried by each unit was carefully and personally explained to us by General the Hon. H.A. Lawrence, who was at that time our Brigadier. Secondly, we had to tell our men that the Turkish lines would have been rendered almost untenable before their advance, in consequence of the heavy bombardment, which was to precede the attack. Thirdly, we were to emphasise to the men that Turkish morale was on the wane. Prisoners, whose only words were "English good; Turkey finish," were, I fancy, responsible for this last venture in optimism.

We had every reason to anticipate that the attempt was to be a thorough onslaught, not a mere demonstration, and would probably lead to success. The discovery that the Turks had in reality been massing for an attack on our lines within a few hours of our own assault was only made afterwards.

At 2.20 p.m. on the 6th August, the British guns opened on the Turkish positions in front of the 29th Division, and at 3.50 p.m. we could see our infantry advance under a hail of musketry and machine-gun fire. Our guns lengthened range, and we saw shells fired by our warships in the Gulf of Saros bursting along the crest of Achi Baba. Through the periscope we watched the tin back-plates, worn by our men for the enlightenment of artillery observers, twinkling under the dust and smoke. Some other Manchesters were lending a hand in the battle already, and were struggling under heavy shrapnel fire to gain a footing in the trenches immediately to the north of the sector to be assaulted by the brigade on the morrow.

Then gradually the firing sank. By 4.45 p.m. there was a distinct lull. One of our Companies (C Company) under Captain G. Chadwick, was sent as reinforcements. A stream of wounded (Manchesters, Worcesters, Munsters) began to file past our lines into the winding *nullah*. We knew little as to what had happened. The sky above the shell-riddled ridge of Achi Baba was serene and purple in the glow of evening, but the fog of war was upon us.

Suddenly, at 6.40 p.m., a message came that two of our Companies were required at once to help the Worcester Regiment, who had taken part in the assault about a mile to the north of where we were. A Company (Captain A.E.F. Fawcus) and D Company (Captain H. Smedley) were ordered to comply. The men were resting for the work planned for the next day. They got ready hurriedly, and moved in fast-gathering darkness along a labyrinth of unfamiliar trenches to a position from which the Worcesters had advanced in the afternoon.

Our information was most vague. The Worcesters had gone "over the top" many hours earlier and had disappeared. They were believed to be holding trenches somewhere beyond, but they were out of touch with our line, and it was intended to reinforce them. The night was dark, and the direction to be taken after leaving our trenches could only be roughly indicated. A Company lined up first, and went over the top like one man. D Company, which was to move to the right of A, then lined up along the fire step and followed.

Our men passed into a tornado of fire, and drifted forward on a broken moor, already littered with dead and wounded. Both Companies eventually lined up in shallow depressions of ground, but there was no trench to receive them.

Meanwhile, many of our wounded had straggled back to the trench from which they started, and numbers of wounded Regulars of the 29th Division who had lain out for many hours were brought in by our men during the long night. This was the one bright touch in its story. We laid down these brave men on the narrow fire-step, and our stretcher-bearers worked nobly. Several men went out with stretchers under heavy fire, and fetched in as many survivors as they could find. One, I remember, was called Corris. At midnight the colonel and Captain P.H. Creagh, our Adjutant, left for Headquarters, where the morrow's plan of operations was being partially recast. The hours passed. At last two messengers clambered back with reports from Fawcus and Smedley. Lance-Corporal H.L. MacCartney brought the former's.

The only sensible course was for our parties to come in. I noticed that MacCartney's hand was broken and bleeding, and suggested to him that someone else should go back with my message of recall. He insisted on his ability to go, and with a companion he climbed over the parapet. A few moments later he was shot through the heart. Smedley's messenger was Lance-Corporal G.W.F. Franklin, whose services on the field won him a commission, and who played a splendid part in the subsequent annals of the battalion. He was given a like message of recall for Captain Smedley, and with it he too clambered back over the parapet and passed out into the night.

At 3.30 a.m. on the 7th August the two companies toiled homewards, having lost heavily. Davidson, a plucky Australian officer attached to us, was among the killed. He had been in charge of a working party which wandered in the darkness into the Turkish lines, and was there destroyed.

After a couple of hours' sleep, we rose to take our part in the renewed offensive. A heavy bombardment was to precede a general advance. As the front-line trenches lay within a few yards of the Turks, they were now practically cleared of men in order to avoid casualties from our own gunfire. The scheme laid down for our battalion required a north-east advance by C and B Companies out of the narrow defile known as Krithia Nullah. A gap was therefore made overnight in the barrier that had hitherto crossed the mouth of the defile and linked our fire trenches with those neighbouring. A machine gun was placed at the north-west corner of this gap under cover of the end of our fire trench.

On the south-east side of the gap, a barricade ran up a steep slope to the trenches of other Manchesters, whose assault was to be simultaneous with ours. Owing to the clearance of the fire trenches, the assaulting parties had, unfortunately, to move across the open. The *nullah* was twisted and partly covered by curving banks on either flank; so that it was hoped that our men might nevertheless avoid complete exposure. The great hope, however, was that the British guns would succeed in wrecking the redoubt that commanded the outlet of the *nullah* before the infantry moved.

We waited at the spot where the support line ran down to the *nullah* and from which C Company was to emerge, while our artillery thundered against the enemy's position. Then the hour came, and C Company, under Chadwick (bravest of the brave), moved in single file into the nullah and onward towards the gap in the front-line barricade and the Turkish redoubt beyond.

B Company, under Captain J.R. Creagh, followed in their wake.

At the same time a battalion of the Manchesters, commanded by Lieutenant-Colonel Darlington, was launched against the Turkish line on the left of the redoubt, and another, under Lieutenant-Colonel Pilkington, against the line on its right. The redoubt itself was at the apex of a broad angle of trenches.

It was at once obvious that our guns had been unable to affect the strength and resisting power of the enemy's front line. Each advancing wave of the Manchesters was swept away by machine-gun fire. A few of them gallantly reached the Turkish trenches and fell there. Long afterwards, during the last flicker of a British offensive in December, some Lowland Scots soldiers of the 52nd Division found in trenches on the west of the *nullah* the bodies of some of the Manchester men, who had also this day fought a way to their objective and perished.

We saw shrapnel bursting along the *nullah*, through which C Company was passing, and progress seemed stopped. I ran along the deserted saps that connected our support line with the front firing trench, and came to the gap. Some twenty yards ahead, a group of about thirty men were lying together in the shallow water-course, mostly dead. Another group was gathered under cover by the gap. The rest of C and B Companies were still running up to the gap from the support line through the long grass of the *nullah*, and dropping in their tracks under the constant fire of the redoubt. Chadwick and J.R. Creagh were both in the forefront of the advance, and Chadwick signalled back its hopelessness.

His subaltern, Bacon, had been the first to pass the gap, and had been killed on emerging. The whole battle in this sector was really over, and I stopped the men under cover from moving out into the open. In the late afternoon the survivors of the little group in front crawled back to safety. The dead were gathered in by the devoted stretcher-bearers under Sergeant Mort, during the evening. One party, under Corporal F. White, had alone penetrated to within a few yards of the redoubt. He held his men together through the afternoon and brought them in under cover of darkness, for which the D.C.M. was his reward. Mort had won the D.C.M. earlier in the campaign.

All through that hot afternoon the wounded Manchesters trailed back to the busy dressing-stations, pictures of suffering and patience. The attack still further reduced the numbers of the original Territorial units, already greatly diminished by casualties.

We wondered to what extent the effort at Cape Helles had eased the great task of the armies operating from Anzac and Suvla Bay. The guns used to boom all day long from the hidden north until the 22nd August, when the attempt was given up. Several weeks passed before we realised that the valiant armies there had laboured in vain, and that Sari-Bair had remained unconquered.

We were far more conscious of the limited results of the battle on the Cape Helles side of Achi Baba.

To the right of the line attacked by the Manchester Brigade and some 200 yards east of Krithia Nullah, the Lancashire Fusiliers succeeded, with great gallantry, in capturing a small plot known as the Vineyard, which the Turks in six days' hard fighting were unable to regain.

Regarded purely as a holding attack during the main enterprise

IN KHARTUM STATION.
COL. GRESHAM.   GENERAL WINGATE

IN THE TURKISH TRENCH CAPTURED ON 4TH JUNE.

from Suvla, the offensive fully achieved its purpose. It was, however, difficult to look upon it in this somewhat narrow light from the point of view of a Regiment which took part in the actual adventure.

Of the many personalities that struck one's imagination during this August battle, the majority were simply of the rank and file, whose pluck and unselfishness were incomparable. Of most I have forgotten the very names. There was a postman from Bradford, who was forty-seven years old and had thirteen children. I remember his telling me of South African experiences. He fell. Most of our men were far younger. Many were mere boys, whose days in the Camel Corps at Khartum had been their first taste of manhood. Their Company Sergeant-Major, Leigh, was mortally wounded by shrapnel while running up the *nullah*.

Of our officers, Captains Smedley and Chadwick survived to be pillars of strength during the whole campaign. About the time when I finally left the unit Captain Smedley joined the Egyptian Army as a Bimbashi, and Chadwick the Royal Flying Corps. Chadwick received a Serbian decoration.

Fawcus, who distinguished himself by his cool leadership on the night of the 6th August, left the battalion very soon afterwards to conduct a newly formed Bombing School on the Peninsula. He was the recipient of many well-earned honours, and ultimately, as a battalion commander, won wider fame in another theatre of war.

A number of the men received cards from Divisional Headquarters, expressing appreciation of their gallantry: Sergeants W. Harrison and M'Hugh; Corporal (afterwards Company Sergeant-Major) J. Joyce; Lance-Corporal (afterwards Lieutenant) G.W.F. Franklin; Lance-Corporal (afterwards Lieutenant) W.T. Thorp; Corporals Hulme and Cherry; Privates Anderson, Beckett, Bradbury, Fletcher, Hayes, Hamilton, Maher, Murphy and Walsh. Joyce was afterwards awarded the Russian Order of St George.

On the 15th August 1915 we were relieved by a Lowland Scots Brigade of the 52nd Division, and moved to what were then called the Scotch dugouts, a bivouac about two and a half miles behind the fire trenches upon the central plateau of the Peninsula. It was hot and dusty, but five minutes' walk led the weary to the cliff. We used to go down its steep side on to the coast road, full of soldiers of the Allied Armies, of carts and mules with long tassel fly protectors, and of Indian or Zionist muleteers. Across the road a lighter was moored, from which we bathed happily in a peaceful sea, with the pale blue contours

41

of Imbros and Samothrace cut clearly against the sky, and our trawlers and cruisers moving up and down on their ceaseless watch between Cape Helles and Anzac. Here and here alone was it possible to forget the brown wilderness above the cliff, and all the toil and bloodshed between ourselves and the summit of Achi Baba.

Casualties are soon forgotten in war. In the dusty and exposed dug-outs, which were now our refuge, men revived. After the recent losses, it was good to see our clever Territorials transforming what looked like dog biscuits into a palatable porridge, cooking rice and raisins, picking lice from their grey woollen shirts, reading papers (all very light and very old), grumbling, but ever cheerful. It was in the Scotch dugouts that we heard of the loss of the *Royal Edward* and of the German entry into Warsaw; but already mails and food held the first place in our minds. Man readjusts his sense of proportion as he enters a theatre of war.

On the 19th August, Colonel Canning became temporary Brigadier. I thus became Commanding Officer in his absence. The same day we left our bivouac, and after a long, hot, march, through the dusty gorge called Gully Ravine, we relieved another unit in the firing line on the northerly side of that great artery of British life and traffic.

CHAPTER 5

Trench Warfare on Gallipoli

The routine upon which the battalion entered at this stage remained almost unchanged until the evacuation. Our Headquarters, where I slept when in command of the Battalion during Colonel Canning's various short spells as acting Brigadier, were usually in some heather-covered gorge, opening upon a deep blue sea. Essex Ravine was a frequent site. The side of this ravine which faced the north-east protruded beyond the side sheltered from the Turkish fire, and was thus forbidden ground. All down the slope were spread the dismembered remains of hundreds of Turks, who must have been slaughtered in retreat by guns from our warships in the Ægean Sea. It was impossible to bury them, owing to the enemy's fire. The other side, where we slept on a rocky ledge high above the sea, was still a beautiful glen.

An hour before dawn we went round the lines, while the men "stood to." We returned for a bathe and breakfast in the open, while the destroyers used to pass to and fro between Cape Helles and the Gulf of Saros, and a pearly haze brooded over Imbros. Then back to the trenches, which were always dusty and fly-pestered, to visit men always under fire, but full of bravery and patience. Diarrhoea and dysentery were already sending many of them from the Peninsula. The trenches were often noisome.

Only in the evening, with Imbros growing fainter in the fading day and Samothrace rising huge and cloudy behind, while the red and green lights of the hospital ships off Helles shone brightly across the water, was physical vigour possible. When I acted as Second in Command, as was more usual, my nights were spent in the centre of the firing line, with excellent telephonists like Hoyle or Clavering close to me, but the nights were usually quiet, and indeed it was not until the middle of September that the Turks showed any symptoms of the offensive spirit. Our casualties were mainly caused by random shots at night, which chanced to hit our sentries as they peered into the gloom over the parapet.

After a fortnight's spell in the trenches, rest bivouacs were welcome as a change, though the name was a mere mockery. Mining and loading fatigues were incessant. I admired the humour of a Wigan sergeant, whom I heard encouraging a gang of perspiring soldiers, while carrying heavy ammunition boxes up a hillside one sweltering afternoon, with the incitement that they must "Remember Belgium."

For a Field Officer one of the most trying experiences of such breaks in the common routine was the task of presiding over field general courts-martial. Courts-martial under peace conditions are not without interest to a lawyer, but these in the field dealt wholly with grave charges, such as falling asleep while on sentry duty and other offences almost as dangerous and considerably more heinous morally. It was hard in many cases to reconcile the exigencies of war with the call of humanity, and the sense of responsibility was only partially relieved by the knowledge that a higher authority would give due weight to the extenuating circumstances that appealed so often to one's compassion.

The introduction of "suspended sentences" by the army (Suspension of Sentences) Act 1915, with a view to keep a man's rifle in the firing line, and to give an offender the chance of retrieving his liberty by subsequent devotion to duty, was probably the War's best addition to British Military Law. Nevertheless, the duty of acting as President on these occasions is found universally distasteful.

There were, however, two great charms in these short intervals in trench warfare. First, it was delightful to escape to places where you could move erect and see something besides the brown wilderness of saps and cuts. A walk to Lancashire Landing along the coast road, between great rugged cliffs on one side and the rippling sea on the other, took us past the little colony of the Greek Labour Corps, and past terraces of new stone huts and sandbag dugouts, which indicated the presence of Staff Officers. Looking seaward, we saw the hull of the sunken *Majestic*, a perpetual sign of the limitations of "sea power." We could then strike up from the beach and see the A.S.C. stores, admirably managed by Major (afterwards Lieutenant-Colonel) A. England, and pushing on to the top of the plateau, the whole area of warfare between Lancashire Landing and Achi Baba was at our feet.

Even more delightful was the long series of entertainments which we organised in the battalion, and which eventually drew large numbers from the rest of the 42nd Division. These entertainments were opened by lectures on history.

Our men became familiar with the history and conditions of all the belligerent Powers, and were kept well acquainted with the developments of the actual military situation in Europe. They enjoyed these lectures. Education has its uses, after all. Then followed concerts, which were splendidly arranged by Regimental Sergeant-Major M. Hartnett, a veteran of Ladysmith and East Africa and a pillar of the Battalion, now, alas, dead, and by Quartermaster-Sergeant Mort, himself an adept as an entertainer. These "shows" used to start about 6.45 in the evening, and the vision of our tired boys scattered in the fast fading twilight on the slope of some narrow ravine beneath the serene, starry sky of Turkey will be among our most lasting memories of Gallipoli. The sentimental song was typical of the Territorial's taste. Even now I can hear the refrain sung by Company Sergeant-Major J. W. Woods:

My heart's far away with the Colleen I adore;
Eileen alannah; Angus asthor.

At the finish, before singing the National Anthem and the no less popular anthem of the Machine Gun Section, our men always sang: "Keep the Home Fires Burning." The soldiers could have no better vesper hymn.

On the 8th September 1915 we went into a new sector of trenches on either side of what was called Border Barricade. The name was, like Border Ravine, a relic of the Border Regiment, just as Skinner's Lane, Watling Street, Essex Ravine and Inniskilling Inch recalled the activities of other units.

I can claim personal responsibility for placing Burlington Street and Greenheys Lane upon the map of Gallipoli. They are reminders of our Headquarters in Manchester.

Border Barricade barred a moorland track which led upwards to higher ground where the Turks were strongly entrenched. Below it were little graveyards of Turkish and British dead, and below them the moors contracted into the narrow defile of Gully Ravine. Here on the 15th September we lost some casualties in a mine explosion, which the Turks had carefully timed for our evening's "Stand to." Dense columns of smoke and earth shot up high into the air, and the rapidly increasing darkness of the evening added greatly to our difficulties.

Most gallant work was done in digging out buried men, a task of great danger, as the front trench was completely destroyed, and the Turks, whose trenches at this point were within ten yards of ours, were bombing heavily. Thirteen men lost their lives through the explosion. For some days afterwards this spot and an open space behind it were constantly sniped, and, as an addition to our troubles, one of our own trench mortars, fired by a neighbouring unit, landed in error in our lines, killing three men and wounding four, including Captain Smedley. Later the Turks exploded further mines in the same area when it was occupied by other units.

Our chief losses, however, were through illness. Captain P.H. Creagh, whose splendid work was rewarded by a D.S.O., left us at the end of August for good, and joined his own regiment in Mesopotamia. Before the end of September, Captain C.H. Williamson, the Brigade's excellent Signalling Officer (afterwards killed in action); Captain A.H. Tinker, at that time Machine Gun Officer, but afterwards most admirable of Company Commanders; Captains H.H. Nidd and J.R. Creagh, most careful of Company Officers; D. Norbury of the Machine Guns; Pain and Pilgrim, invaluable Somerset officers attached to us, all left the Battalion with jaundice. Burn and Bryan left it with dysentery; Morten with a poisoned hand.

There was little indeed to cheer the men in the trenches. News percolated through to us of the failure at Suvla and of the hardships endured in that enterprise. Mails from home arrived all too slowly and precariously. Death was always present. We regretted the loss of Captain H.T. Cawley on the night of the 23rd September. He had given up a soft billet as A.D.C. to a Major General in order to share the lot of his old regiment, a battalion of the Manchesters, and was killed in a mine crater near Border Barricade.

The spell in the trenches admitted of few variations. The journey to them was always burdensome. It is easy to recall the trek, on the 1st October 1915, of weary, dust-stained, overloaded men some three miles up the *nullah*, inches deep in dirty dust and under a broiling sun, to occupy narrow fire trenches, unprotected as ever by head cover, and pestilential with smells and flies. Yet once established in the trenches, life was tolerable enough.

As a field officer I was fortunate to be able to escape at times to enjoy the intense luxury of sea-bathing. Sometimes the evenings were misty, and the fog-horns of our destroyers and trawlers carried faintly across the Ægean Sea. More often the sunsets were gorgeous. The day always seemed long. Firing was frequent but targets were rare. Some men curled themselves up between the narrow red walls of the trenches, read, dozed, smoked, talked, one or two in each traverse observing in turns through the periscope across the arid belt of No Man's Land, where groups of grey-clad Turks, killed long ago, still lay bleaching and reeking under the torrid sky. Others foraged behind for fuel, which could only be found with great difficulty.

A little later dozens of fires would be crackling in the trenches, with dixies upon them full of stew or tea. Flies hovered in myriads over jam-pots. The sky was cloudless. Heat brooded over all. No one ever visited the trench except the Battalion Headquarters Staff and fatigue parties with water-bottles. Many soldiers stripped to the waist, and wore simply their sun helmets and shorts. Sickness alone drew men away. The soil was dark red, caked and crumbling. Here and there the dead were buried into the *parados*, with such inscriptions as "Sacred to the Memory of an Unknown Comrade. *R.I.P.*"

The Mule Sap connected the trenches with Headquarters. We gathered curios, Turkish and German, from among its *débris*. At Headquarters the telephone, orderly-room and dressing-station alone denoted the presence of war. They were fixed in a beautiful ravine, looking upon a smooth sea, warm in the sunlight, with Imbros ten miles across the water. The meals were of first importance, but sandbags are uncomfortable seats, and the heat was trying. Pleasant it was in the cool of the evening to go to sleep with one's Burberry as a pillow. The stars shone kindly down, as they had shone long ago upon the heroes of the Iliad on the Plains of Troy, seven miles away across the Dardanelles, upon the Crusaders and Byzantines. You were asleep in a moment, and hardly stirred until 5 a.m., when it was time for "Stand to." Daylight moved quickly across the desolate waste, and by six o'clock another day of war and waiting had dawned.

The Territorial's thoughts turn to home far more often than do those of the Regular, for to him the family has always been more important than the regiment. H.C. Franklin, who took P.H. Creagh's place as our adjutant at the end of August, and was an old Regular soldier of the Manchester Regiment, often said that the week's mail of a Territorial battalion is as large as six months' mails for a unit of the old army. He told, too, a good story, which shows the perceptiveness of Indians. He was standing near to some Indian muleteers when the Manchester Territorial Brigade disembarked on Gallipoli. He heard them say in Hindustani: "Here is another of the regiments of shopkeepers." One pointed to Captain P.H. Creagh, our adjutant and only Regular officer. He said: "But he is a soldier." Another said of Staveacre: "A fine, big man, but he also is of the shopkeepers."

The story of trench warfare during these months on Gallipoli is undramatic. A record of their little episodes is almost trivial. Yet this want of movement and initiative is true to life, and was the common lot of the three or four British Divisions then responsible for operations at Cape Helles. The campaign, in fact, came to a standstill on the failure of the great offensive in August. The objects of the Army were simply to hold the ground so hardly won in the first two months of the expedition, and to contain as large as possible a Turkish force on Gallipoli for the benefit of our Russian Allies in the Caucasus and elsewhere.

The first of these objects was attained in spite of the thinness of our line, the universal inferiority of our positions to those of the enemy, and the gradual improvement of their guns and aircraft. The *Nizam*—i.e. the Regular first-line Turkish troops—had been practically destroyed. The remainder lacked the offensive spirit after their heavy losses in August, and perhaps their hearts were not sufficiently in the struggle to welcome further sacrifice of life, with time already running in their favour. We heard of one British officer who had acted as a hostage during a short armistice at Anzac. The Turks loaded him with presents of fruit, and, pointing to their dead on the battlefield, said: "So much for your diplomatists and diplomacy!"

Our second object, also, is believed to have been gained, so far as was possible, having regard to our inadequate numbers and to the limitations of our technique of the period. Bombing used at this time to be practised by small sections in each battalion, who occupied dangerous salients called "bird-cages" in the fire trenches. Here in our Battalion, G. Ross-Bain and W.H. Barratt among the officers, S. Clough and T. Hulme among the N.C.O.'s—all valiant men—won a modest measure of fame. On one occasion Hulme picked up a live bomb thrown by the enemy and saved his comrades' lives by throwing it over the parapet with splendid self-devotion.

Our British sappers became more proficient in mining, special corps being formed from among the Wigan colliers of the Manchesters and the Lowland Scots. The guns were always active, and their co-operation with the infantry was perfected. Those who remember passing by night along the winding length of Inniskilling Inch will recall the red lamp that marked the artillery forward observation officer's post at the corner of Burlington Street, and the well-hidden gun emplacement, where Greenheys Lane ran out of the Mule Sap. The familiar street signs carried men's minds back to Manchester.

CHAPTER 6

The Strain

In the second week of October, 1915, the Army at Cape Helles was reinforced by dismounted Yeomanry from East and West Kent, Surrey and Sussex, and by some Royal Fusilier Territorial units from Malta, who were lent to the Royal Naval Division. Many West Kent officers and N.C.O.'s were for a time attached to the Battalion, and proved admirable comrades. The 42nd Division received some scanty drafts on the 23rd October. These came from the 3rd line units at Codford on Salisbury Plain, and were of excellent quality. Our draft was under Lieutenant C.S. Wood, a very able signaller.

I noted on the 21st October that of the 300 men of the Battalion then in the field, nearly 100 were on detached jobs—signallers, machine gunners and details attached to various headquarters.

The result of the shrinkage in strength was a great strain upon the survivors. *We never sleep*, the battalion's motto, was adopted grudgingly as a rule of life. The necessities of the firing line required vigilance by day and night, and the long frontages allotted to the various units of the 42nd Division entailed broken nights and laborious days for all. The men's physique became lowered. Septic sores were general; bad eyes, not infrequent; jaundice of a type indicating para-typhoid was common; amoebic dysentery very prevalent.

Loss of health meant loss of vigour. Limited to one bottle of water a day for all purposes, and perpetually a prey to flies, heat, diarrhoea and want of rest, the soldier had a trying time. Rations of a type welcome in a northern climate were unpalatable in Turkey. In July and August we were liberally supplied with vegetables and raisins, and with much-prized golden syrup for our porridge; but the latter luxury then disappeared, while for several months our only vegetables were onions, which do not appeal to every palate. Jams, even when the pots were adorned with pictures of one Sir Joseph Paxton, had very diminishing attractions.

The only strawberry jam we ever had on the Peninsula came to us in tins, from which the labels had been stripped by some kindly act of Providence. In the expedition's early days our men had been able to exchange English jams for dainties procurable by the French and Senegalese, but the monotonous and indefinable "plum and apple" of the later summer killed the trade and extinguished all foreign admiration of British jam-making. Only the flies were fascinated.

Our East Lancashire Territorials did all that was possible to relieve the strain. We had a most able medical officer in Captain J.J. Hummel, of Glasgow, who had temporarily succeeded Captain J.F. Farrow (our own veteran M.O.) in July, but indeed all the units were happy in their doctors, and *emetine* in dysentery cases was a gift of gold. Nor could a Brigade have had a more gallant and untiring padre than Captain E.T. Kerby. He and Captain Farrow both won the Military Cross. Kerby must have said the burial service over the graves of nearly a thousand Manchesters on Gallipoli.

The food difficulty we met by encouraging unofficial imports. The kindness of all at home was beyond praise. Consignments of comforts were well regulated by Major H.G. Davies, who had charge of the Manchester depot, but many came direct from innumerable friends and national and local organisations. One mother of two boys of the Battalion who had lost their lives wrote to me, while sending parcels for their surviving comrades: "I dare say that life is dreary for them, poor lads. God in His mercy has been so very merciful in that my Darlings have been spared so much. My prayers will follow you throughout, praying for the success of the whole of Our Battalion, and that you may all be spared to come safely home to the fond hearts waiting."

England need never despair while she has such mothers.

The great glory of the East Lancashire Division during the long-drawn days of October and November was, however, the temper of its men. The spiritual exaltation, that all races feel at the outbreak of war and in the hour of battle, disappears under the pressure of the daily grind. Then, in his divine good-nature, the British Tommy comes into his own. Nothing dims his cheerfulness and humour. A chorus starting with: "We are the M.G." proclaimed the jollity of our Machine Gun Section and the ingenuity of Sergeant W. Harrison.

A Machine Gun Corps of the larger type, organised under the energetic command of Captain Hayes, was a thing of the future. A long list of singers and performers—Hartnett, Mort, Addison (of ragtime celebrity), Wheelton, Holbrook, Hoyle, Clavering, Shields—adorned the programmes of our concerts. Other men like Tabbron and F.E.H. Barratt were notably cheery souls in the lines. The handful of surviving officers—Higham, Chadwick, Whitley, Douglas—with a few excellent attached officers—J. Baker and J.W. Barrett of the Somersets, and F.W. Woodward of the Sherwood Foresters—were untiring promoters of the men's well-being.

Their wants were so modest. Old magazines and football editions of Saturday evening papers, published a month or two earlier in England, sufficed for their literary appetites. Lancashire boys are not brought up to read; the *Sentry* writers were exceptional. When I once came upon a man reading the *Golden Treasury*, in Hardship Avenue, I knew he could not be a Manchester man. He was not. He came from the Isle of Man, and had joined our reserves at Southport. I found about half-a-dozen men who could enjoy *The Times* broadsheets. I am afraid *John Bull* was much more popular.

It was pleasant indeed to stroll along the narrow trenches and see how staunchly the men forgot their privations. Towards evening little parties would go, heavy-laden, into long forward saps that the engineers had thrown forward from Inniskilling Inch, to pass the night in cuttings called "T-heads," which were ultimately to be connected together and form a new trench closer to the enemy. They looked out from these lonely places in the midst of No Man's Land upon scattered heaps of corpses, and in their front upon the well-built Turkish trenches, substantially wired in and full of cleverly disguised loopholes. Two sentries were placed in each "T-head."

The man on watch was exposed to oblique fire from all directions, as both British and Turkish lines curved to right and left, while the constant sound of Turkish picks at work suggested the proximity of mines. The sap that ran back to the fire trench was very narrow, and ended in a low tunnel under our parapet. It was therefore hard to bring wounded in from the "T-head." I remember one poor fellow in A Company called Renshaw being badly wounded in the head one night, and being dragged back through the tunnel with infinite difficulty.

The Turks were quick to pick up targets. One morning at our bivouac on Geoghegan's Bluff, we noticed half-a-dozen mules stray from Gully Ravine to the moor on the summit of its southerly side, perhaps a thousand yards from the enemy's front line. We saw them shot, one by one, within a minute. As the Turks enjoyed the possession of higher ground everywhere from first to last, their power of observation was necessarily greater than ours, and no corner of Cape Helles was exempt from shell fire. It pursued us even in our bathing places.

The course of life on Gallipoli was, however, so monotonous that men became callous to all dangers. They carried on the long day's routine and the numberless little jobs included in the term "trench duties," as if nothing else mattered. Such tasks are familiar to-day to so many millions of Europeans that they need no description. Gas masks, sprinklers and gongs were ready for use in every trench, but were happily not needed.

Our men represented every Lancashire type, from the master builder to the barrister's clerk, from the wheelwright to the calico printer, from the railway carter to the commercial traveller. You would find together in one traverse Sergeant J.V.H. Hogan, a well-read ex-Socialist devotee of Union Chapel debates and old political opponent of my own, and another sergeant, whose name I cannot now recall, but who had been the petty officer of a South American liner sunk by the *Karlsruhe* in the early days of the War. Then we had famous footballers in Sergeants Pearson and Bamber. The Territorial origin of the battalion was, indeed, a never-failing source of strength. Officers and men came from the same place, enjoyed the same interests and possessed the same outlook. It was pleasant to see in the trenches, faces familiar in my own suburb of Fallowfield, and to chat with hundreds of men whose lives had touched mine in days of peace.

The worth and capacity of these men were not peculiar to our unit, but were common to the Manchester Brigade and the whole Division. One battalion contained expert miners. Another battalion, at this time commanded by Major (afterwards Lieutenant-Colonel) C.L. Worthington, had lost enormously in their valiant battles. One of their captains—R.H. Bedford—helped in our history lectures. Another battalion, under Lieutenant-Colonel MacCarthy Morrogh, with Major H.C.F. Mandley as Second in Command and Captain E. Horsfall as Adjutant, were our constant neighbours and allies. With the Lancashire Fusiliers and East Lancashires, and with the admirably run A.S.C. and R.A.M.C. we enjoyed a slighter but no less hearty friendship.

The best relief from the long strain of the trenches was a bathe in the sea, but any diversion while in rear of the firing line was exhilarating. We used to gather on the moors that lay between Geoghegan's

Bluff and Bruce's Ravine, Turkish cartridge boxes made by the Deutsche Waffen und Munitionsfabriken at Karlsruhe and labelled with inscriptions in German and Turkish, innumerable spent Turkish cartridges, abandoned Mäuser rifles, Turkish bandoliers (stamped with the English name "Warner's") and all the usual fascinating débris of battle.

On the 19th October I made a special expedition, with Captain C.E. Higham, to the southern sector of the area, where the French had held the line ever since their move from Kum Kale to the Peninsula. We walked to beautiful Morto Bay, with its graceful curve from the headland called De Tott's Battery. The ruins on this point, carried by the South Wales Borderers on the 25th April, stood out clear-cut against the bright blue of the Dardanelles and the fainter grey of the Asiatic coast beyond. We went on past French and Senegalese dugouts to Sedd-el-Bahr, a village and fort wrecked by our naval guns in the first days of the campaign. The country was open and dotted with the remains of vineyards. North of Sedd-el-Bahr was the well-tended French graveyard, more prettily kept than our own cemetery above Lancashire Landing. Here sleep many hundred soldiers, *morts sur le champs d'honneur*, their *képis* on the crosses, and their graves adorned by flowers. The Jews and Senegalese had their own separate plots.

Sedd-el-Bahr appeared to be but a collection of outer walls and broken pillars, posts and fountains, some of archaic design. On the beach below, the *River Clyde* recalled the glory of the landing of the Dublins, Hampshires and Munsters. We struggled back to our bivouac in the teeth of a dusty, warm wind, to be inoculated with *emetine* and to rest by the white coast road, while we watched our monitors riding between Cape Helles and Imbros, and landing shells in the Turkish trenches on the slopes of Achi Baba. On such an occasion Ross Bain would arrive from marketing among the Greeks on Tenedos with some greatly valued potatoes, and then all our troubles would be forgotten.

When rain came, the joy of living was hard to attain. During all our time on Gallipoli I remember but one or two occasions when we were fortunate enough to secure timber or some corrugated iron to roof our dugouts. Normally we had only our mackintosh sheets. Rain turned the thick dust to a brown morass, and the little mule carts struggling past the swampy curve of Geoghegan's Bluff could hardly clamber up the Gully Ravine. It was choked with mud.

Then the sun would come out and the flies returned in their

C Company, the British Camel Company, Khartum.

myriads to plague us. They blackened every jam-pot and clustered thickly round the mouths and eyes of sleeping soldiers. The trenches became dry and dusty. Detached legs or feet or arms of the dead would protrude from the parapet, as the soil around them fell away. Smells became all-pervading. We would seek refuge in the dug-outs, that looked out upon a crowded graveyard from the sloping incline by Border Barricade. Then would come the time for another inoculation with *emetine*, and we would join the long line of men waiting, stripped to the waist, for Captain Hummel's needle. We prayed that it might be effective, and that we should be spared the curse of dysentery and long nights of misery in and about the fly-infested latrines.

CHAPTER 7

The Limit

In the balmy days of late October it was still possible to enjoy life on Gallipoli. The ceaseless vigil of the trenches was cheered by contact with the bravest men I have known. The dirt and drudgery of rest bivouacs were assuaged by bathing, and by jolly "missing word competitions" and "sing-songs," as well as our courses of lectures and discussions on history, politics, the War, and the England to arise after the War.

Talk gravitated again and again to the tragedy of the 4th June. I have a record of one such symposium, that illuminates the infinite variety of human nature. "Franklin says that he and Staveacre could see in the far forefront of the battle Sergeant Marvin engage four Turks simultaneously with his bayonet till shot dead. But X. boggled at going over the parapet. He was told: 'You are a disgrace to the Manchester Regiment.' He replied: 'I shall never let that be said of me,' rose to climb over, and was blown to bits by a shell. Whitley carried a badly wounded man a long way under fire. Creery did splendidly." It may be added that Whitley's act was afterwards recognised by an award of the Military Cross. He became Staff Captain at Ismailia. W.F. Creery joined the Connaught Rangers and was mentioned in dispatches.

Another hero of the men's reminiscences was Captain A.H. Tinker. One night during the first month of the campaign a working party had lost itself on the moor. It was so dark that they ran great risk of straying into the enemy's lines—a fate that befell a number of our men at this period in that broken country. In spite of the proximity of the Turks, Tinker left the trenches and boldly sought the men himself, calling out loudly for them. They heard him and made their way back.

The days of initiative and enterprise had, however, passed. The wind and grit gave the strongest of us sore throats and high temperatures, and I gradually joined the crowded ranks of sick men "on light duty only." At the beginning of November we moved to the northern extremity of the Allies' line across the Peninsula, and here I saw the last phase of our warfare on Gallipoli. Sir Ian Hamilton had gone. All ideas of a renewed offensive had disappeared.

After the 24th October the Turks enjoyed direct communication with Germany, and at Cape Helles there was no sign of revived strategy or rejuvenated tactics. Our work was simply to carry on and hold out. Some of the other Divisions took steps to guard their men against the menace of a "Crimean winter" by preparing sheltered quarters. Great flights of geese used to fly in V-shaped formations high over our heads on their way from Russia to Egypt. They were augurs of our own eventual migration.

The new position of the battalion was on Fusilier Bluff, a mile to the west of the ruins of Krithia. The left ran straight down to the sea, where monitors used to shell the enemy's positions, while destroyers watched the flank, and at night played flashlights on the ravine that divided us from the next bluff, where the Turks were entrenched. This ground had been won in the brilliant British advance of the 28th June. The Turkish line was close to ours, and our men were always on the strain. Incidents were common. On the 2nd November a Turk crawled along the beach with a white flag, and surrendered. At night the Turks built up in front of their parapet, and two were shot by Sergeant Stanton. One of our men was killed and two were wounded. On the 3rd, another man was killed by a bomb, while the daily drain of sickness went on unabated. General Elliott, at this period our Brigadier, was an energetic pioneer of new methods and more vigorous tactics. He had the Mule Saps improved.

Even, however, in the secluded Headquarters at Bruce's Ravine I could not keep my health, and Hummel's art was unavailing.

The average soldier on Gallipoli broke down after a month or two. Comparatively few endured more than three months. Of our officers only Scott (the Quartermaster) and Fawcus were on the Peninsula from start to finish, though Colonel Canning, Higham and Chadwick had almost as fine a record. Few of the sick came back to Turkey.

Some, like my first batman Dinsdale, died in hospital at Alexandria or in Malta. Many went to England and passed into other units. Others rejoined later in Egypt. Somehow, in peace times we had never imagined that the battalion could be so dispersed and broken.

My departure from Gallipoli is perhaps worth a description. Would that the wounded heroes of the landing could have received a hundredth part of the same care!

I left Border Ravine at six in the evening of the 5th November 1915, with a high temperature, and feeling very ill. I walked down to the 1st Field Ambulance Dressing Station in "Y" Ravine, where Captain Fitzgerald, R.A.M.C., directed me on to the base of that Ambulance in Gully Ravine. Here my servant, Hawkins, left me, and two medical orderlies carried my traps. Alas, I left behind me a much-prized Turkish copper basin and bayonet, spoils of war, which I never saw again. We walked two miles along the rough and dusky beach, a full tide washing over our feet and throwing many dead mules high upon the pebbles. At the station I got a cup of hot milk, and spent the night on a stretcher. Next morning my case was diagnosed as one of fever and swollen glands, by Captain John Morley, R.A.M.C., most brilliant of surgeons, and at ten o'clock (cherishing a label marked "Base") I was swirled off in a motor ambulance to No. 17 Stationary Hospital above the beach known as Lancashire Landing since its glorious capture by the Lancashire Fusiliers on the 25th April.

At 4.15 in the afternoon we motored off once more and boarded a steam launch, whence we transhipped to an uncomfortable lighter. At 6.30, in the dark, we were lifted by a crane into the P. & O. hospital ship *Delta*, where 500 sick and wounded were being collected. Dinner consisted of bread and milk only for many of us, but we revelled in the luxury of bed and bath. Next morning I sat on the sunny side of the deck. The shady side, chilly in the November air, looked out upon Cape Helles, with Achi Baba rising straight behind it, and to the left upon the grey succession of landing-places, enshrined in so many English hearts.

We sailed the next morning, and thus avoided the misery of the great November blizzard on the Peninsula.

The Division remained on the Peninsula until the 29th December. Dysentery abated and the flies vanished, but gale and storm carried on the strain, and frostbite was added to the men's trials. The Turks seem to have much increased their supply of munitions, and the loss of life continued day by day. "Asiatic Annie" and other guns across the straits showed renewed activity. A mine explosion on the 4th December killed one of our men and injured eight. Two popular privates, Hancock and Lee, were killed on Christmas Day. One singular innovation was the Turkish practice of shooting steel-headed darts from their aeroplanes. Their chance of striking any man was, luckily, very small.

Nothing daunted the spirit of East Lancashire. Our men held concerts to the very last, and the football eleven survived three rounds of an Army Corps competition, losing their tie in the fourth round on a field in which shells burst repeatedly to the discomfort of the players. Captains J.F. Farrow, F. Hayes and E. Townson returned to strengthen the small band of officers, while R.J.R. Baker, who had been intercepted on his way out and sent to Suvla Bay, was released for service with us.

CHAPTER 8

Last Words On Gallipoli

The last I saw of the trenches was the tangled line on Fusilier Bluff. The last I saw of Gallipoli was the fading contour of its cliffs as we sailed in the *Delta* for Mudros and Alexandria. When we touched at Mudros we heard the first whisper of Lord Kitchener's fateful visit to the Eastern Mediterranean.

All questions relating to the initiation and conduct of the expedition are fitly left to the judgement of the Dardanelles Commission. Here have only been expressed ideas that occurred to a Regimental Officer, whose range of vision is always restricted, and whose generalisations are inevitably based on a narrow, personal experience. Yet such ideas may still have a bearing upon the history of the campaign, as the whole theatre of operations at Cape Helles was extraordinarily congested. In a tiny area, barely three miles by four, strategy had no elbow-room when once the Army was committed to the plan of operations that had been adopted. The war with the Turks on the Peninsula became purely a war of tactics. If Inkermann was "the soldier's battle," Gallipoli was the soldier's campaign.

It is easy to criticise in the light of a later standard. Gallipoli was invaded early in 1915, not in 1916 or 1917, when the whole technique of assault had been revolutionised. We landed with the methods practised in England since the Boer War, methods as out of date in France in 1917 as Wellington's methods were in 1815. On later knowledge no one can doubt that a vast concentration of gun power, infinitely equipped and munitioned, a scientific use of barrage fire, nicely adjusted to the movements of a great infantry force, itself organised to develop the fullest use of machine guns, Lewis guns, and grenades, would have broken the defences of Achi Baba.

Our Army knew none of these advantages. The artillery was inadequate and was inadequately supplied with high explosives to prepare for an attack in the style afterwards perfected on the Western Front. It was realised nowhere at this period that the *rôle* of infantry in attack is quite secondary to that of the guns. The bombardment that preceded the infantry assaults at Cape Helles in August did not last over two hours, and certainly never hit the trenches actually in front of the Manchester Territorial Brigade. The gunners could do no more than they did. The resources at their disposal were quite insufficient to atone for the army's difficulties in point of numbers and in point of ground. It would appear as if we enjoyed no real ascendancy over the enemy either in aircraft or mining.

Bombing was most unfamiliar to us on arrival. It appeals to the English sportsman greatly and came to be brilliantly practised, but it was rarely a determining element. The battalion bombers on Gallipoli were officially known as Grenadiers. Steel hats were, of course, unknown. They would have saved many lives. Visual signalling, on which pains had been lavished during training, proved of little use. The telephone, however, was a godsend, and in our battalion was admirably worked by Sergeant Stanton.

The one handicap that was above all others a constant and pervading thought in the minds of our men was the shortage in numbers. It was a common belief that more reinforcements would have carried the great advances of June and July over every obstacle. Our drafts were always too small and too few, and the want of men infinitely aggravated the exhaustion of the survivors. With but a part of its old strength, and with no supports whatever between itself and the beaches, a battalion was still expected to hold the same length of line as when it was up to strength. Some two hundred men, for instance, occupied the long stretch of trenches from Skinner's Lane corner to the eastern birdcage and its numerous forward saps, upon which men had once been employed. The task involved weeks of scanty and broken sleep, and caused our support and reserve lines to be utterly untenanted.

Fatigue work was necessary the very hour that a unit had straggled down to a bivouac from the fire trenches. So precious was man power that the doctors were forced to keep unfit men at duty until they dropped. It is impossible to imagine men more worn by sleeplessness and sickness than the jaded Manchester Territorials at the end of a fortnight in the front line. On a moving day Gully Ravine was littered with men who had fallen out of the ranks of a dozen regiments as they trudged, heavily laden, along the winding and dust-swept track.

Sir Ian Hamilton wrote of our men early in August: "The ――― Manchesters are a really good battalion. Indeed, the whole of that Brigade have proved themselves equal to veteran Regulars. The great misfortune has been that there are no drafts ready to fill them up quickly. Had they been at once filled up, as is the case in France, they would be finer than ever. As it is, I fear lest the remnants may form too narrow a basis for proper reconstruction when ultimately the drafts do make their appearance."

The drafts we received on Gallipoli were the cream of the 2nd and 3rd reserve lines, which had been organised at home under Colonels Pollitt and Hawkins. They gave up their ease and often their ranks in order to serve England better, but their numbers were small. The work of reconstruction, to which Sir Ian Hamilton looked forward, came afterwards in Egypt.

Sometimes the infantryman wondered whether, even if the essential reinforcements arrived, they would ensure victory. On this point it is difficult to judge. The home Government had committed itself to the project of an offensive on the Western Front in the autumn of 1915, in spite of the huge obstacles that confronted the Allies in that theatre of war. The tactics of the period did not even organise trench raids.

The memory that dominates all recollections of Gallipoli is that of the grandeur of the British soldier. Though he took no part in the miracle of the landings, the East Lancashire Territorial proved himself worthy of comradeship with even "the incomparable 29th Division." He ranked with the Anzac and the Lowland Scot in the great adventure. The original 1st-line of our battalion were really destroyed in Turkey with their comrades of the same Brigade, but their gallantry in the early assaults and their inflexible fortitude in the trenches-pestered by flies, enfeebled by dysentery, stinted of water, and worn out by hardships—are a lasting title to honour.

Their story, as told in the pages of the *Sentry*, was read by General Wingate a few months later "with mixed feelings of joy and sorrow-sorrow for the many good friends who have laid down their lives for their King and Country, and joy that it has fallen to the lot of the gallant Battalion, of which I have the honour to be Colonel, to have behaved so gloriously in one of the hardest and most deadly campaigns in which British troops have ever been engaged."

It is a source of pride to have known and lived with such men.

CHAPTER 9

Revival in Egypt

A large proportion of the sick and wounded invalided from Gallipoli became familiar with one or other of the Alexandria hospitals. I spent a week at Victoria College, which had become No. 17 General Hospital, with Sister Neville, whose devotion to duty the Battalion had learnt when at Khartum, as Matron. Thence I went to No. 10 Convalescent Hospital at Ibra-himieh, once the stately house of an interned German called Lindemann but now converted into a comfortable home under the care of Mr and Mrs Scott. British leniency still reserved its tempting orangery for the use of local Huns. It is the English way.

When the evacuation of Gallipoli was contemplated, every hospital was cleared as far as possible of inmates, and I was one of the many officers who in early December were turned adrift either to the hotels of Alexandria or the great waiting camps of Mustapha and Sidi Bish.

The mere narrative of a holiday period at Alexandria has no public interest. We learnt to know Levantine and Egyptian mentality better than ever. When at Khartum an Egyptian *dobey* (washerman) had amused us by soliciting Regimental custom in preference to his competitors, not on the ground that he washed clothes better or charged less, but solely, he said, because the other *dobeys* were "terribly wicked men." So at Alexandria, every pedlar was the one honest follower of his craft. Yet its population is more European than Egyptian. The shops were full of the picture post cards of Italy and France, and portraits of Venezelos were to be seen everywhere, adorned with the pale blue and white national colours of Greece. Probably Mr Lloyd George's fame enjoys even wider bounds. I have seen his likeness enshrined in wattle huts at Omdurman and Wadi Halfa.

I touched unfamiliar minor issues of the War on the two occasions when I sat as a member of the military court, which sits for the purpose of enforcing proclamations issued by the supreme British military authority in Egypt, and thus tides over the time that has to pass before the Capitulations are abolished and a regular system of uniform justice established. A day thus spent at the Carracol Attarine gives a fine insight into the blessings of British occupation.

Most of the cases that I heard turned on the adulteration and falsification of liquors. Egypt has had no licensing laws; and no effort to apply elementary principles of fair dealing to the drink trade had apparently been made until initiated under military law for the protection of the troops. Foreign wine dealers at Alexandria consequently flooded the market with spurious liquor, concocted from the weirdest raw materials. The only genuine claim they could set up for their merchandise was that it was at all events alcoholic.

Owing to the utilisation of refuse beet and potatoes, alcohol is cheap in Egypt. By blending pure alcohol to the extent of anything up to ninety per cent. of the whole concoction with any particular paste or colouring matter, it is open to wine dealers to pass off any liquid as the most popular of wines or spirits. Case after case came before the court, of beer made of alcohol and powder; wine of colouring matter, alcohol and paste; brandy of "essences"; and bitters of "Chinese elixirs." The falsifying appliances came from Europe, but the bogus labels, which described those poisons as "specially adapted for invalids and bottled in Glasgow, Scotland," or even offered 25,000 *francs* to any who could prove that so-called Greek "*Koniak*" was not "the pure juice of the grape," were amusingly Levantine. British justice is sweeping away these pitfalls for the soldier and sailor.

Egypt was at this time a centre of Anzac relaxation. To have explored the tombs of the kings with a New Zealander, paced the roof of the Cairo Citadel with Australians, and watched the colonial celebrations of Christmas in the Alexandria streets is a political education. No Englishman after the War will be ignorant of that golden New World, where all the labour is well paid, all hours of work are limited, and all shops close at noon on Saturdays. In any competition for the glory of being God's own country

Australia will be there.

We were, however, at war. As a field officer, I had the duty of attending the burial of British soldiers in the Christian cemetery at Alexandria on Christmas Eve, 1915. Since the outbreak of the War the graveyard had extended from its original site, prettily shaded by foliage, over an adjacent waste of sand and rubble, where over 2500 of our men who died of wounds or disease at this base had already at this date been laid to rest. Here sleep many Manchester Territorials. In the midst of many graves, identified only by numbers, a black cross recalls the memory of Mundy, one of our gallant Company Sergeant-Majors.

On the 30th December 1915 I left Alexandria for the Dardanelles on the *Arcadian*, Sir Ian Hamilton's old ship, once most luxurious of steam yachts but destined to be torpedoed on the 15th April 1917 in these same waters. It carried some details for the various Divisions still believed to be holding Cape Helles. We sailed in long zigzags through a rough sea to within a few hours' distance from Lemnos. We were then ordered back by wireless to Alexandria, landing there, much to our chagrin, on the 6th January 1916. Two days later Cape Helles was evacuated. It was never known whether our departure from Egypt had been a piece of bluff designed to cloak the impending move from Gallipoli, or a sheer accident arising from ignorance at Alexandria of the true intentions of the Mediterranean Expeditionary Force Head-quarters.

From the date of the *Arcadian's* return down to the end of January, the large waiting drafts at Alexandria remained in tantalising inactivity, in spite of the passage of the Gallipoli survivors southward through Alexandria. The East Lancashire details forgathered at Mustapha on the site of the famous victory of 1801, and near the pretty white ob-elisk that commemorates Sir Ralph Abercromby. The time was filled as best could be by route marches, history lectures and various com-petitions, until at last we had orders to rejoin the Division. We moved from Sidi Gaber station to Cairo, and thence by trams to Mena, where, with "forty centuries" looking down upon us, we found what was left of the Manchester Territorial Brigade, then under General Elliott's command. The Battalion numbered close on 300 men.

Our stay at Mena was short, for infinite labour was now urgently needed on the Sinai Peninsula. In the early stages of the War, the Suez Canal had been treated as itself the main obstacle to an attack on Egypt. Outlying posts like El Arish had been abandoned, and Sinai left almost bare of defences. This policy accounts for the ease with which the Turks had actually gained the Canal bank in February, 1915. It was now recognised that defensive lines should run on the Asi-atic side of the Canal in order to make it impossible for any invader to come within gunshot of the waterway. Three possible routes were open to the enemy. The northerly coast road by El Arish and Katia was the best, and enjoyed a Napoleonic tradition, but naval co-operation made its defence easy. A central track ran from El Audjo at the end of the main Palestine railway embankment to Bir Hassana, and might be used against Ismailia. A southerly approach was possible through Akaba and Nekl, and thence by the main pilgrims' road, the Darb El Haj, to Suez.

The Division was now to be employed in creating some of the new posts of defence, by which all such dreams of attack were to be dispelled. The strategy was passive, but it paved the way for the offensive undertaken in the ensuing summer.

On the bitterly cold night of the 1st February 1916 we left Mena. Before noon on the 2nd we reached Shallufa sidings. In the evening we crossed the Canal, and bivouacked in gathering darkness on a desert site known later as Shallufa Camp. The days of rest were over.

CHAPTER 10

On the Suez Canal

During February of this year the Battalion was engaged upon an inner line of works within easy walking distance of the Canal. A semicircular outpost line, which covered these works and the Brigade camp, was occupied nightly, but there was no real danger of attack. Beyond the outpost line a distant screen of posts, whose names recalled Lancashire, were in course of construction.

Life under such conditions gave no scope for ideas. The men did set tasks as fatigue work. There was no tactical training. Gangs drew a chain ferry to and fro across the Canal, while Lieutenant A.N. Kay acted as wharfmaster. Several days were given to moving camp a few hundred yards north or south within a small area. Two detached posts were held at this period. One far out among the rolling sandhills, skilfully laid out by Captain A.H. Tinker, was known for a week or two as Ardwick, and then abandoned. Another, very ably commanded by Captain C. Norbury, was the far more fascinating blockhouse known as Gurkha Post, noted for its bathing, fishing and agreeable remoteness from staff officers. It was delightful to ride out from Shallufa camp along a track called "the pilgrims' way" to so charming a spot for a swim in the Canal and pleasures impossible on the dust-swept desert. A few hundred yards to the north, a little white tower called Lonesome Post long flaunted in red paint the battalion's name and motto for the edification of passing liners. What have become of like devices that were once deep cut on the scarped cliff of Bruce's Ravine on Gallipoli?

One amusing experience of this period was to bathe in the Canal while the transports were passing with newly trained drafts for Mesopotamia or India. "Who are you?" was the invariable cry from the banks. Our war-worn men received usually the answering taunt:

"Garrison duty only! When are you going to do your bit?"

To the call: "Who are you?" from a transport, a witty diver replied: "A submarine."

The whole Canal zone from Port Said to Suez was in reality a hive of workers. A visit to the School and Headquarters of the Royal Flying Corps threw a flood of light on that brilliant service. Its observers commanded every track and camping ground of the Sinai desert.

While the Canal was being girdled by defence works the Manchester Territorial Brigade was regaining the physical vitality lost in Turkey. Apart from sandstorms, the climate was good. Sports, football, concerts, buried-treasure hunts, competitions "for the singing championship of Asia" and other sounding honours, and much bathing helped us to recover health and joy. Our numbers remained much below strength. Perhaps 130 of the original unit remained, with some 250 who had come to Turkey in drafts. To these hardly 100 were added at this period.

Such officers and men, however, as did reach us from the two reserve units at home were of the best. They lost temporary rank on re-posting, and knew that weaker vessels had succeeded to their place on English camping grounds. Those who came from another battalion had been specially fortunate in their training, and in having the inspiring influence in their midst of Captain J.H. Thorpe, but all alike were keen. Their anxiety to learn was palpable whenever we went the round of the chilly desert outposts under the starry sky.

Battalion patriotism was kindled anew by the adoption as a flash of the old Lincoln green *fleur-de-lis* of the Manchesters, a cap badge worn by us since 1889, and a relic of the conquest of Guadaloupe by the 63rd Regiment in 1759. No less inspiring was the revival of the *Sentry* on the 1st March 1917. Of its staff of fifteen when published at Khartum, nine had died on Gallipoli. Their places were filled by new enthusiasts, and one genuine poet was discovered in T.G. King.

Our one lasting loss while at Shallufa was the departure of nearly all the time-expired Territorials to England. Those under forty-one years of age were retaken later by the Government under its new powers of conscription, but the Battalion saw few of them more. These men—W. Jones, Mort, Woods, Stanton, Fielding, Lyth, Bracken, Houghton, Dermody, Parkinson, Barber—were the salt of the Regiment. During the long years when Territorial service had been irksome and unfashionable, they made it succeed. With a few old hands like Regimental Quartermaster-Sergeant Ogden, who elected to remain with the unit, they had borne the burden of the trenches manfully, and never grumbled as to their status while commissions were showered on men at home whose claims, compared with theirs, were modest.

On the 24th March 1916 the Brigade left Shallufa, and on the morning of the 25th marched into Suez New Camp to undergo training. The move was welcome, as it was imagined to lead to a departure for a more active theatre of war.

The type of training adopted at Suez derived its inspiration from the French Army, whose text-books of 1916 taught that close order drill and punctilious discipline, tempered by games and sports, were ideal means of reviving the all-important offensive spirit in units.

The four and a half weeks spent by the battalion at Suez were therefore crowded with field days and ceremonial drill. On the 21st May there was a striking review of the whole division, followed by a march past in blinding dust. Days of this type, however, even if they mean rising at four in the morning and include Brigade bathes in the warm, blue Gulf of Suez, followed by breakfast on a sun-baked shore, are the same all the world over. They are not worth discussing in writing of the fateful time which witnessed the great German attack upon Verdun and Fort Douaumont.

At all events, Suez saw the reconstruction of the Manchester Territorial units completed. The sense of vitality, without which no army can take the offensive, was fully restored. We had spirited sham fights with another battalion of the Manchesters for the possession of "Tower 16," a solitary landmark on the caravan track to Cairo, after the manner of the pre-War era. The *Sentry* blossomed as the first English paper of the country. Two thousand copies used to be sold at Suez alone. Our men competed for Colonel Canning's football cup and played a great match with the crew of the *Ben-my-Chree*, the famous seaplane carrier, sunk by gunfire, alas, some eight months later in Kastelorizo Harbour. The "Flashes" gave notable concerts.

From the 21st April I again enjoyed the command of the battalion. Colonel Canning went on leave to England, and his distinguished services were recognised soon afterwards by a C.M.G.

Towards the end of May, 1916, the division was unexpectedly ordered to move from Suez, and broken up in order to supply battalions for digging work at various spots on the eastern side of the Canal—mainly on the then most advanced screen of detached infantry posts—where the existing defence scheme had not progressed with sufficient speed. A more combative strategy was obviously contemplated, no

BACK ROW—LIEUT. T.F. BROWN, LIEUT. N.H.P. WHITLEY, LIEUT. J.H. THORPE, LIEUT. G.S. LOCKWOOD.
FRONT ROW—CAPT. R.V. RYLANDS, CAPT. H. SMEDLEY

doubt provoked by the recent action at Katia. In the late afternoon of the 25th May the battalion started on their march into the Sinai Peninsula. The transport was left at Suez under Lieutenant M. Norbury and Sergeant A.B. Wells, and with Captain A.T. Ward Jones as Brigade Transport Officer.

Among the posts thrown out into the Peninsula, none at that time was more desolate or remote than the sandy ridge called Ashton-in-Sinai, apparently in honour of Ashton-under-Lyne. It lies many miles to the east of the Little Bitter Lake. The trek to this spot by way of Kubri and Shallufa was an ordeal even for our seasoned troops in the blazing heat of an African summer. At 3 a.m. on the 27th May the battalion set out from their chilly bivouac by the Y.M.C.A. hut at Shallufa along a road made by the Egyptian Labour Corps to a site called Railhead, about ten miles off, where we rested during the broiling day. At four in the afternoon we started on the worst lap of the trek, a final two hours' ascent across the softest and heaviest sand imaginable to the high rolling dunes of Ashton.

CHAPTER 11

Sinai

The view at Ashton is superb. Looking back on Africa, we saw on the horizon the pale contour of the Gebel Ataki beyond the silvery line of the Bitter Lakes and the Canal. On its Asiatic side, the detached posts of Oldham, Railhead, and Salford, held by other battalions of the Manchesters, glittered under a torrid sky amid the great waste of desert. Facing our front, the wilderness stretched towards Palestine in endless undulation.

The sultry days spent by the battalion at Ashton were, however, spoiled by excessive heat and repeated sandstorms. Double-lined tents were only supplied after much delay, and promised wooden dining huts only approached completion by the time we left.

This arid outpost of Empire was linked to civilisation by a camel trail to Railhead. Its garrison duties were performed by some Essex Territorials, commanded by Lieutenant-Colonel Jameson, afterwards killed before Gaza. Yeomanry passed by frequently, scouting far into the waste. The Manchesters were occupied exclusively in digging trenches and in laying entanglements in the deep soft sand, "according to plan" and on a scale sufficient to daunt any invader who could have surmounted the huge physical obstacles that already barred all approach to this spot from the Wadi Muksheib and the East.

The arms of Britain have by now made these particular defences of the Canal of most trifling importance. Her foot is in Palestine. Work done at Ashton may well be gradually obliterated. Yet a few words can be said of the men who lived and laboured here in June, 1916, in a temperature rising often to 120° F. in the shade and rarely falling under 100° F. at night. No digging was practicable between 7.30 a.m. and 4.30 p.m. The men rose before four in the morning for the day's work. Progress was necessarily slow, partly owing to constant silting, partly to the common weakness of the authorities for varying the sites and types of the trenches. Materials were often wanting. Nevertheless the Manchesters won unqualified praise. Their civil life had fitted many for the task of reveting trenches with hurdles. The defences of Ashton-in-Sinai were improved in a few weeks beyond recognition.

One incident that occurred here illustrates amusingly the contrast between the outlooks of the new soldier and the old. Our Manchester Territorials were distressed to find that thousands of yards of hurdles were being lined with the best tent cloth at 1s. 4d. a yard, instead of with cheap cotton at a quarter the price. I repeated their plaint to a Regular officer of the old school, expecting sympathetic indignation. "Magnificent," was his reply. "It shows the world in what spirit England goes to war."

It was at Ashton that we first heard the news of the Jutland Battle from Colonel Fremantle, R.A.M.C., who could only give us the version spread by German wireless. A few days later we learnt of Lord Kitchener's death.

It is clear that this particular phase of soldiering has in itself no place in the annals of the Great War. Ashton is already nothing but a desert site. The tide of victorious warfare has left it high and dry. It always was high and dry. At probably no other period, however, did the personality of the Manchester Territorial show to greater advantage, as the life was one of peculiar privation. Water was carried up daily by camels from Railhead, but was most scanty, and always warm. The sand was too soft for any game to be played—too soft even to permit of trotting horses. The heat was constant and intense. The men were as cheerful and uncomplaining as ever.

To have developed such a spirit in men entirely civilian in habits and traditions was the glory of the Territorial system.

All ranks toiled together to make life in this corner of Sinai liveable. History hardly looks beyond the Army Corps at the smaller unit. Still less does she concern herself with the humble pawn in some unimportant corner of the great game. In reality, however, his lot is of moment to the race. The tone of an army is the tone of its individual men. An unhappy soldiery cannot win wars. "An army moves on its stomach," said Napoleon; and the recognition of the soldier's hunger and thirst, his desire for rest, amusement and sympathy helps, almost as much as skill and self-confidence help, to make the successful leader of men.

It was, therefore, a soldier's job to keep up the hearts of our colony at Ashton-in-Sinai. Captain C. Norbury, as acting President of Regimental Institutes, and Captain H. Smedley, as stage-manager and singer, worked on the only sound lines.

Journalism, theatrical performances, lecture courses, concerts and canteen business, as initiated and practised by the officers and men of the battalion at Ashton, were true factors towards efficiency and discipline.

After three hours' work and their breakfast, the men would gather in our recreation tent with its flaps rolled up, and listen to a lecture on some historical or military subject which bore upon the topic of the hour. They then slept and smoked and played cards or sang through the long midday heat until the time came again for digging. In the evening, on a stage cleverly made by Sergeant Taylor, the dramatic company would act some play that appealed to their emotions, or a concert party would indulge them with a medley of ragtime and sentimental songs, Addison's *Stammering Sam* alternating with Sergeant Shields' *When Irish Eyes are Smiling*. The taste of Lancashire is catholic.

On Sundays we often merged "Church and Chapel" in a common service. Davey, the Methodist *padre*, was an ex-gunner of the Royal Navy and a great athlete—attributes that enhanced his influence as preacher. "Crime," however, did not exist at Ashton-in-Sinai. Nor did temptations. The real danger was mental and physical deterioration under the depressing influence of the country and the climate, for the intense heat sapped every man's vitality. We set ourselves to combat these risks, and to give the men the food and recreation without which soldiering becomes a burden, and discipline degenerates to servitude.

Towards evening I would ride into the desert and watch from the east our men labouring on the great sand ridge in a haze of heat. On this side of Ashton there were no tracks at all. The eye could see nothing but endless sand hills, broken only by patches of dry scrub and shimmering yellow under the burning sun. If nature has changed little in the desert since Israel came out of captivity, it is easy to sympathise with their regret for the fleshpots of Egypt. So penetrating was the sun that the colour of the men's khaki breeches faded into purple.

There was, indeed, a certain charm in our remoteness from the outer world. Camping out in the wilderness had more than a touch of the desert island of boyish imagination. There was glamour in the extraordinary simplicity of a life where the higher command was but a distant name, and where men dressed themselves and spent the long, hot day as they pleased. The fret and competition of Europe were felt no more. I remember our arguing about Irish Home Rule one night till the stars paled in the eastern sky, but the episode was unique. In spite of its hardships, no manner of life was ever more calculated to banish ancient feuds, to strip human nature of envy and uncharitableness, or to mould that most perfect of all democracies—a brotherhood in arms.

On the afternoon of the 22nd June 1916 we left the wilderness under orders for Kantara. We spent several days near Shallufa sidings, and then, having obtained leave for England, I left for Suez with W.H. Barratt and W.T. Thorp, two subalterns who had made their mark while in the ranks by distinguished service in the field. Early in July we sailed from Port Tewfik to Marseilles and watched from its deck the distant camp of the Turkish prisoners from Arabia twinkling in the sunlight across the most southerly reaches of the Canal.

I need say no word more in praise of the men of our battalion, whom I saw for the last time in my eighteen years of service resting in a dusty gorge near Shallufa. Knit together by common ideals and experiences, they were, in Nelson's phrase, "a band of brothers."

We crossed France from Marseilles to Boulogne in an atmosphere of war. We had glimpses of Lyons and Paris, talked with *poilus* on leave, heard from a French officer (who professed to know) that the War would be over in March, 1917, and bought from vivacious street hawkers pretty metal souvenirs of Verdun. We saw our own wounded coming back in Red Cross trains from the first days of the great push on the Somme. Then, after exactly a year's absence, I was once more at home.

Within the ensuing month all but three of the original combatant officers still on the strength of the battalion were seconded for service elsewhere. "*The old order changeth, giving place to new.*"

A regiment in war rises like the phoenix from its own ashes and renews its immortal youth. The vicissitudes here recorded fill but a few shining chapters in what will no doubt prove a long history. They by no means necessarily contain its most distinguished pages. The close of the second year of the battalion's active service is, however, a fitting point to end this volume. It marked the stage at which the distinctively "1st line" unit, composed of officers and men enlisted and trained voluntarily in time of peace, had passed into the normal type of British Battalion of 1916—a unit born of the War, with its personnel mainly recruited and trained after its outbreak.

It is to the memory of the original volunteers of August, 1914, that this book is dedicated.

CHAPTER 12

The Territorial Idea

The experiences of a typical unit of the Territorial Force must throw light on the vexed questions that have gathered round it.

Three criticisms of the Territorial system have been made ever since its adoption in 1907. First, its establishment of 310,000 men has been regarded as totally inadequate, and before the War the country even failed to recruit numbers within sixty thousand of this modest standard. Secondly, its yearly training, which provided but a fortnight's life in camp, has been deemed so paltry as to be almost negligible. Thirdly, the Territorial and Reserve Forces Act 1907 provided a legal loophole by which the less patriotic could evade service overseas in however great an emergency. Section 13 specifically lays down that, apart from purely spontaneous offers by officers or men to serve abroad, "no part of the Territorial Force shall be carried or ordered to go out of the United Kingdom."

In reality, none of the defects which attracted these criticisms was inherent in the Territorial idea. They rather belonged to the whole military policy of the country before the War. Public opinion held that a European War was practically impossible, and that the British Army must of necessity be small in numbers and voluntary in character.

On these assumptions the limitations of the Territorial Force were simply inevitable. Having regard to the prevailing views on national defence and to the general resistance to Lord Roberts' propaganda, the Territorial scheme reduced the evils of voluntaryism to the minimum.

The difficulty as to its shortage in men was met as soon as War was declared. The Territorial Force was, in fact, capable of infinite expansion, and of being the basis of the entire New Army, had the Government so willed. Its training, again, was far better than no training at all.

Later events have proved with what speed wholly untrained British conscripts can be moulded into efficient soldiers, and that willing men can learn discipline and the use of the rifle within a very few months. Territorial training sufficed, at any rate, to enable Territorial units to relieve the Regular Army of all garrison duties abroad immediately on the outbreak of war, and in many cases themselves to take the field on active service before Christmas, 1914. Even with regard to the constitutional obstacle to using the Force overseas, fully nine-tenths of its men never dreamed of claiming immunity. The small margin, which were left for employment in home defence, mainly represented the physically unfit or boys under age.

As events turned out, two unexpected disadvantages of the system were generally experienced. In times of peace the Territorial Force had been able to influence public policy through the County Associations and the House of Commons. After embodiment, the Force itself became necessarily inarticulate under the conditions that govern all military service. Far less influential than the Regulars and far less numerous than the New Army, it went abroad early in the War, and was thus not actively in touch with Parliament, while the semi-civilian County Associations, whose personal and local knowledge might have been invaluable, ceased to have any powers over its organisation, and had no means of safeguarding its interests on questions of promotion, appointments, commands and pay.

An even more serious flaw arose from the dispersion of the Territorials all over the world from Gibraltar to Burmah in the first months of the War. An enormous volume of skilled labour was thereby lost to the country, and exemption from service, which might well have kept these men at home in the national interest, fell later to the lot of many younger and less expert workers in their stead. Moreover, a great number of men ideally fitted for commissions were killed fighting in the ranks or were allowed to serve obscurely in remote corners of the globe. Both among Territorial officers and men, a large proportion were qualified, by gifts of leadership, technical knowledge or familiarity with foreign languages, for special employment in Western Europe. There was indeed a demobilisation in this respect of a considerable proportion of the country's brain power.

Happily, the East Lancashire Territorials found an outlet for their qualities on Gallipoli.

Against all the defects that have no doubt affected the application of the Territorial idea, the historian should set its signal virtues. It is an

79

asset beyond price in soldiering to have all ranks welded together by community of feeling and opinion. Joined by ties of neighbourhood, occupation, sport and common interests, men are particularly apt to cultivate that intense patriotism of the small unit which is termed *esprit de corps*. The history of the War—like the history of all past wars—will illustrate its constant military value. It would be idiotic to reassert the old fallacy, belied by the experience of centuries, that one volunteer is worth ten pressed men.

Nevertheless the morale of a unit can only be enriched when it is recruited wholly from willing applicants familiar with its traditions and with the badges that symbolise its past, rather than from conscripts drafted from anywhere in Great Britain by the chance action of a Government department. Indeed the Territorial idea has counted for much wherever British man power has been successfully organised during the War.

Those who have believed in the Territorial Force during its struggles against popular apathy and professional distrust have been justified by its deeds in the field.

The true greatness, however, of the simple and unambitious Territorial soldiers, whose life and work are described in these pages, lies more in their spirit than in any actual achievements. All of them came from the industrial North, where the business of life is fiercely competitive, and where each man is wont to seek his own fortune without much outward consideration for his fellows. Yet in the field it would be impossible to imagine minds less touched by selfishness or less influenced by any notion of personal distinction or reward. They did their best for Britain. Honours are but gifts of the capricious gods.

Thus "to put the cause above renown" is a principle of conduct often identified with what is called the Public School spirit. Fortunately the temper which it expresses extends far beyond the governing class in England, and it animated the typical Territorial of the Great War. Like all good soldiers, he was far too inarticulate and reserved to think of putting it into words. His deeds spoke for him. *The Whitewash on the Wall* and *Hold your Hand out, Naughty Boy* are not beautiful songs, but the lads who have sung them in English lanes and Turkish gullies could have shown no greater self-devotion had their songs been as solemn as the Russian National Hymn, or as thrilling as the *Marseillaise*.

Appendix

The following is an extract from a letter on the work of the Battalion sent by General Sir F.R. Wingate, G.C.B., K.C.M.G., D.S.O., High Commissioner for Egypt, to the General-Officer-in-Chief of the Division, when the Battalion left the Sudan.

Governor-General's Office,
Khartum. 10th April 1915.

... during the few months they [the battalion] have been in the Sudan they have become thoroughly efficient soldiers in the strictest sense of the term. Route marches, night operations, field days, hard drilling in the Barrack square, digging trenches, gun and maxim drill, and last but not least, constant practice on the ranges in addition to ordinary garrison duties have transformed them into an alert body of trained soldiers capable of taking their place anywhere. You can safely rely on them to do—and do well—whatever duty they may be called upon to perform against the enemy, and I am confident that they will yield to no battalion in the division in regard either to training or fighting efficiency. Should, by any chance, the division be sent to the Near East, you will find in the battalion upwards of one hundred men fully trained in camel riding and camel management, and this knowledge may prove useful under certain conditions, but of course I have no idea where the division is to be sent and whether a knowledge of the numerous promiscuous duties required by battalions garrisoning the Sudan will find an outlet.

A sound system of Interior Economy prevails in the battalion, and the good organisation of the Regimental Institutes reflects much credit on all concerned with their management. During the time the battalion has been in my command the behaviour of all ranks has been exemplary—the men have made themselves liked by all in Khartum and are very popular with the natives.

I have the highest opinion of Colonel Gresham—he has an excellent lot of Officers, and both the Adjutant, Captain Creagh, and the Quarter-Master, Major Scott, have done particularly well. I am proud to be Honorary Colonel of such a fine Territorial Battalion.

We all are heartily sorry to bid them goodbye, and we wish them and the gallant division which you command every success and good luck wherever you may be.

Yours sincerely,

(Signed)   R. Wingate.

The Seventh Manchesters

S. J. Wilson

The Hon. A. M. Henley C.M.G. D.S.O.
Brig-Gen (Retired), late commanding
127th Infantry Brigade

Contents

Preface	87
Introduction	91
Holding up the Turk	95
Desert Life	109
For France	122
Holding the Line	126
Belgium	137
An Interlude	152
Stopping the Hun	160
Worrying the Hun	176
Hammering the Hun	192
Pursuing the Hun	210
Aftermath and Home	217
Appendix 1	220
Appendix 2	227

Preface

I first met the 7th Manchesters early in May, 1917, when they were gaining new experiences of warfare on the Western front, not far from Epehy in the north of France. They, with the rest of the 127th Infantry Brigade, and in fact the whole of the 42nd Division had already had a long war experience in Gallipoli and Egypt, but they had only recently been transferred to France. I was taking up the command of an Infantry Brigade for the first time. I did not know then what a lucky man I was, but it did not take me long to find out, and we worked together without a break from that time until the armistice.

The writer of this book passes over with considerable *sang froid* a certain operation which took place on a June night in 1917. If the 7th Manchesters, and not only the 7th, but the 5th, 6th and 8th as well will allow me to say so, I did not enjoy the same complete confidence as to the result before and during the night in question. The operation consisted of digging a complete new front line trench, a mile long, on the whole Brigade Sector, five hundred yards in advance of the existing front line, and half way across No Man's Land. June nights are short and it needed practically the whole brigade to get the job done in time. We had to find not only the diggers, but the covering troops and strong parties for carrying and wiring.

Now four battalions digging on a bare hillside within point blank range of the enemy's rifles and machine guns are not well placed to meet attack or even to avoid fire if they are caught. So everything possible had to be done to avoid raising any suspicion of what was on foot in the minds of the watchful Germans. The troops had to work at high pressure and in absolute silence. The R.E. who were to lay the tapes were the first to go forward after the covering troops; then came the wire carriers, and, as soon as the R.E. had had time to get the tapes into position, out went the diggers, who, after reaching the line,

87

had to be spaced out at working distances along the whole front. We who stayed behind spent some anxious hours. However complete the arrangements and however perfectly executed there was yet a chance that some enterprising and inquisitive German patrol might find out what was happening in time to give one of their local commanders an opportunity of hindering our work.

We had to make such arrangements as would give the appearance that we were doing nothing unusual, that we were in fact excruciatingly normal. There must be neither more noise nor less than on an ordinary night, and so the artillery and machine guns must fire their accustomed bursts into the likely places in the German lines. It was a great success. By dawn there was a, trench, continuous at least in appearance along the whole front, at intervals there were rifle and Lewis gun posts in it; and if there were places where it was preferable to pass along in the attitude of the serpent after his expulsion from the Garden of Eden and ever since;, there was nothing to show the Germans which they were. There was wire in front, and the troops got back without more casualties than averaged as a result of the ordinary nightly strafes.

Though we took on many tougher jobs later I was never again anxious as to the result.

Our great days were:—

Stopping the Germans East of Bucquoy—
                    March 23rd to 29th, 1918.
The advance West of Miraumont—
                    21st August, 1918.
The Capture of Miraumont and Pys—
                    24th August, 1918.
The Capture of Villers Au Flos—
                    2nd September, 1918.
The Battle of the Hindenburg Line—
                    27th September, 1918.
The Battle of the Belle River—
                    20th October, 1918.

In every one of these the 7th Manchesters were called upon to play a part. Whether their original role in the plan of battle had been to lead the attack or to act in support they were always in the picture before the end of the fight. I am not going to pick out this or that as their finest performances. The reader can choose for himself when he has finished the book. It is enough for me to say that, whatever task was given them, they took on cheerfully and carried through magnificently. Not only that, but they were anxious to go beyond what was demanded of them, as is well shown by the fighting at La Signy Farm which they attacked and captured on their own initiative.

I can only wish them individually the same success in peace as they won as a battalion in war. I think they will have it. For it takes first-class men to make a first-class fighting unit. Perhaps many of them will join again under the old colours. I hope so, and I congratulate in advance any commander whose good luck it may be to lead them.

A. M. Henley, Brig. Gen, (retired)

late Commanding 127th Infantry Brigade.

21st February; 1920.

Introduction

Captain Wilson's book continues the story of the 7th (1st 7th) Manchesters, which is recorded in my own book *With Manchesters in the East*, from July, 1916 until November, 1918. It is written with intimate knowledge and much understanding, and will be enjoyed by all his comrades. It was the good fortune of the Manchester Territorials (127th Brigade) to belong to the first Territorial Division (the 42nd), that ever left these islands for active service, and this active service eventually took place on three fronts. The 7th Battalion garrisoned the Sudan and fought through the Gallipoli campaign. It recruited its strength at Suez, and then helped to clear the Sinai Peninsula of the Turks. Finally it served for two and a half years in Flanders. It translated its motto, *We never sleep* into its daily life.

This volume will be a useful supplement to any general history of the War. It is based on the diary of a Regimental Officer, who won considerable distinction in the field, and whose eyes missed little of consequence. It is of even more value as evidence of what men of essentially civilian habits and traditions can achieve as soldiers. The numbers of the 7th Manchesters were never fully up to strength after April, 1915, and for many months at a time while in the East they fell to vanishing point. Yet from the day in September, 1914, when the original first-line Battalion sailed from Southampton for Port Sudan in the *Grantully Castle*, each successive draft was of the same mould.

The men came from the same neighbourhood, were of the same capacity, and had been bred with the same ideas. Their devotion was founded on a sense of duty. They were personally; utterly remote from what is called militarism, and. saw little fascination in its pomp. The survivors are now absorbed once more in the undramatic industry of Lancashire. There is nothing to indicate to an observer that they have ever left it. The last time you saw your tramway conductor may have been as a bomber in "the western birdcage" on Cape Helles; your fellow passenger may have last talked to you as your "runner," when you tramped along the duckboards from Windy Corner to Givenchy. What such men did for England will therefore illustrate for all time the potentialities of a Territorial Force.

Captain Wilson"s style of expression and cast of thought are, in my view, true to type. He is the Lancashire man of action, who affects no literary arts. These pages are bare of heroics. There is a soldierly brevity in his account of even of the bravest exploit. There is also plenty of quiet humour. The reader will search vainly for any "villain of the piece." The "Hun" is to Captain Wilson, as to the normal British officer, just a "Boche" and no more; to the rank and file he was simply "Jerry." If you want adjectives, you will have to look for them in *John Bull* or listen to speeches in the House of Commons.

For all who were in authority over him, whether Corps Commanders or Divisional Generals, Brigadiers or temporary Commanding Officers, Captain Wilson has a good word. A reader unfamiliar with soldiers' psychology might deduce that all his superior officers had been invariably models of judgment and efficiency. He would possibly be quite wrong; but it is most fitting that this book should be framed on such lines, for they are the lines which our soldiers have never failed to accept. The rough is taken with the smooth. If ever there has been incompetence men have simply blamed the system and cursed the War Office. If they happened to have been five minutes in France they might have; philosophically added *c'est la guerre*. The actual individual responsible has not been worth worrying about. Thus even with regard to this mere side issue, the author's story reflects a cardinal attribute of the national character, and therefore in its essence conveys the truth.

In my opinion, it is not, however, the whole truth. There is no reason why England in her reconstruction should forget that want of sympathy with the Territorials, which far too often marked men, to whose hands their fortunes were from time to time entrusted. This vice should be borne in mind not because the memory is bitter; but because by remembrance we may make its repetition in later wars impossible. Territorials ought never to be ousted from the command of their own units, or to be excluded from staff appointments, merely because they are not Regulars or because they fail to comply with needlessly drastic and therefore non-essential codes of discipline. Discipline is, in fact, degraded into servitude when it becomes a mere fetish.

How fallaciously it may be construed could often be seen in the tendency among powerful martinets to "drive a coach and four" through the law and procedure which regulate trials by Court Martial. The need for the "standardisation" of all infantry units in France was quite genuine; but unimaginative men in authority could make "standardisation" a burden to the spirit, and the picture of some men of this class, which is painted in A. P. Herbert's novel, *The Secret Battle*, is founded on the truth. We have all seen such cases. The grinding necessities of the Western front ended the joyous amateurism, which a Territorial unit was able to preserve through all its vicissitudes in Eastern warfare, but they did not require the prevailing banishment of individuality and of the exercise of intellect from Regimental life.

After landing in France the 42nd Division had to make a new reputation by rising from the ruck, and it is very notable that the personnel of the 7th Manchesters, as of the other units in the Division, although almost completely changed from the personnel of the Battalion when in Gallipoli and drawn from a later generation of recruits, achieved equal distinction and much greater technical efficiency. This fact points to the wonderful resourcefulness of the English people. Historically it shows how thoroughly our Army of 1917-18 was professionalised.

The later chapters of Captain Wilson's book detail very brilliant fighting by our men, which it would be idle and impertinent to praise. Such "crowded hours" are not, however, and never have been the most typical of a soldier's life. Infinitely more numerous were the hours of endurance and privation, which the 7th spent among the broken ravines of Gallipoli, among the dreary mud flats on either bank of the Yser, among the desolate craters in front of Cuinchy and Le Plantin. In their patience and fortitude amid these wastes lies their strongest title to the gratitude of Christendom.

Peace is already dimming men's memories of the War as effectually as the grass is covering the ruins of devastated France. The Manchester Territorial is back at his job. The broken home no longer feels the same first poignancy of grief. *Man goeth forth unto his work and unto his labour until the evening,* and it is a good thing for the world that he does. Nevertheless, all men and women who cherish associations with the 7th Manchesters will, I think, read and re-read Captain Wilson's work for many years to come. From amid all the hardships and miseries of soldiering which the Englishman readily forgets, the light of self-sacrifice shines upon the human race with a never fading beauty.

Herein lies the true romance of war. As the reader turns over the ensuing pages he cannot but realise something of the cumulative drudgery and hardships which these men endured for their country.

To the 7th Manchesters themselves they mean much more. The very place names of our warfare recall the memory of the comrades whom we have loved and lost, the early enthusiasms which we shall never feel again:—Khartoumn, Gallipoli, Shallufa, Suez, Ashton-in-Sinai, Coxyde, Nieuport, Aire, Béthune, Ypres, Bucquoy, Havrincourt. When we are very old, many of us will still conjure up the tune of "Keep the Home Fires Burning" on the lips of tired men beneath the stars on Geoghegan's Bluff; the thud of the shovel falling upon the sand ridges of Sinai while a blazing sun rose over Asia; the refrain of "Annie Laurie" sung by candlelight in some high roofed barn behind the lines in Belgium.

I hear them now.   Gerald B. Hurst.

CHAPTER 1.

Holding up the Turk

In September, 1914, the 7th Bn. Manchester Regiment set out for active service in the East in goodly company, for they were a part of the 42nd (East Lancashire) Division, the first territorials to leave these shores during the Great War. After many interesting days spent on garrison duty in the Sudan and Lower Egypt they journeyed to Gallipoli soon after the landing had been effected, and took a continuous part in that ill-fated campaign until the final evacuation. The beginning of 1916 thus found them back in Egypt, where they were taking part in General Maxwell's scheme for the defence of the Suez Canal. The things that befell the battalion during this long period have been admirably described in Major Hurst's book *With Manchesters in the East*, and this short history will attempt to continue the narrative from the point where it left off.

At the end of June, 1916, the 7th Manchesters made a short trip by rail along the Suez Canal, the last railway journey they were to make as a battalion for many a long day. The 42nd Division left the defence of the southern half of the Canal in the able hands of the East Anglian Territorials, and journeyed north to the Kantara region. It was not definitely known why we made this move, but there were persistent rumours that we were destined for France, where events were speeding towards a big battle. However, the 7th detrained at Kantara and there met, for the first time since Gallipoli, the 52nd (Lowland Scottish) Division. We knew very little of this coastal region of the desert. Occasional stories had floated down to us to supplement the very meagre official *communiqués* as to events there, but it was recognised as a place where opportunities of getting in touch with our invisible enemy were rather better than in the south. So it was felt that, even if we did not go to France, life would lose a certain amount of that

95

deadly monotony which we had experienced for six months.

It transpired that the 127th Brigade were to relieve detachments of the 11th Division, who, it was openly whispered, were definitely to sail for France to try their luck in the more vigorous scene of this great adventure. Most interesting to us was the discovery that we were to take over posts occupied by the 11th Manchesters, the first Kitchener battalion of our own regiment. Our astonishment and delight can be imagined when we saw that they wore the good old *Fleur de Lys* for a battalion flash on the *puggarees* of their helmets—just as we wore it, but yellow instead of green.

The battalion marched east along a good road recently made for military purposes, and eventually reached Hill 70, where the headquarters were established. Early next morning, garrisons marched out before the heat of the day to occupy a series of posts arranged in semicircular formation between two inundations about three miles apart. "B" Company took over Turk Top and No. 1 Post. Capt. Smedley, Capt. Brian Norbury, 2nd-Lt. C. B, Douglas, 2nd-Lt. Pell-Ilderton being at the former, while Capt. J. R. Creagh, 2nd-Lt. Hacker, and later 2nd-Lt. Gresty took charge of the latter. "C" Company were divided between Nos. 2 and 3 posts, with Lt. Nasmith and 2nd-Lt. S. J. Wilson at No. 2, and Lt. Nidd and Lt. Marshall at No. 3. "A" Company, who were responsible for Hill 70, was commanded by Capt. Tinker assisted by 2nd-Lt's. Kay, Woodward, Wood and Wilkinson.

The officers comprising headquarters were Lt.-Col. Canning, C.M.G., Capt. Cyril Norbury (second in command). Major Scott (Quartermaster), Capt. Farrow, M.C. (Medical Officer), Lt. H. C. Franklin, M.C, Adjutant and 2nd-Lt. Bateman (Signal Officer), while 2nd-Lt. J. Baker was in charge of the Lewis guns of the battalion. "D" Company were at Hill 40 in a reserve position under the command of Capt. Higham supported by Capt. Townson, 2nd-Lt's. Grey Burn, G. W. F. Franklin, Ross-Bain, Gresty, Morten, and R. J. K. Baker. The work of the transport was divided between Capt. Ward-Jones, and 2nd-Lt. M. Norbury.

The posts consisted of self-contained redoubts which were capable of holding out in the matter of food and water for about three days. They had been constructed at the cost of great labour by the 52nd Division, Routine was simple, our only duties being to man our posts before dawn, then improve and maintain the trenches and wire until about 7 when the sun entered his impossible stage. The same thing happened in the evening. During the night patrols were executed from one post to the next. All this carried a certain interest because we knew that the Turk might come near at any time in the shape of a flying raiding column to reach the canal. Rumours were frequent of his proximity, and when Turk Top one night frantically reported mysterious green lights, out towards the enemy, serious preparations were made for his reception.

The climax came, however, about noon one day at Hill 70 when those who were not asleep heard, with a mixed feeling of old familiarity, "s-s-s-sh-sh-S.H—flop." Most of us, after cringing in the usual manner, said, with a relieved air, "Dud." Then followed commotion. They had arrived and were shelling the post. The shimmering desert was eagerly scanned by the officers' field glasses, and all kinds of things were seen and not seen. Meanwhile someone went to look at the "Dud," and found not a shell but a large stone, still quite hot. It finally dawned upon everyone that we were bombarded from the heavens, and not by the Turk, It was a meteorite, still preserved amongst the battalion's war souvenirs, which had upset our composure.

Whilst on duty at these posts we had a visit from the Marquis of Tullibardine, now Duke of Atholl, of the Scottish Horse, who was responsible for this section of the Canal defences. Lieut.-Gen. Lawrence, afterwards Chief of Staff in France, who was in command of the northern section of the Canal defences also paid a visit, and remembered us as part of the brigade which he had commanded on Gallipoli. Important changes took place in the battalion at this time. Lt.-Col. Canning, C. M. G, relinquished the command, and returned home for duty in the Cork district. His departure was sorely regretted by all ranks, for during the twelve months he had been with the 7th, his capabilities as a commander had only been surpassed by his solicitude for the men's welfare, so that he had made his way into our hearts as a popular soldier. Major Cronshaw of the 5th Manchesters succeeded him and was soon afterwards made Lt.-Colonel. Captain Farrow, M.C., R.A.M.C., was also invalided home, after having had almost unbroken active service with the battalion since September, 1914.

About the middle of July a fairly large column of Turks began to make their way across the desert from El Arish, intending to strike once more for the possession of the Suez Canal. They moved with surprising rapidity and wonderful concealment, and some excitement was caused when a large enemy force was located by air reconnaissance, so near as Oghratina Hod, within five miles of Romani, then held by the 52nd Division. A battle seemed imminent, and this at the worst possible time in the Egyptian year. A Brigade of the 53rd Division, consisting of Royal Welsh Fusiliers and Herefords, spent a night at Hill 70 on their way to occupy a defensive line between Romani and Mahamadiyeh on the coast. There was an obvious increase in aerial activity on both sides, and camel and other traffic on the Romani road became more feverish.

On July 23rd, the 7th Lancashire Fusiliers relieved the battalion in all the posts and we marched back to Hill 40, where we found the whole brigade was concentrating. There was much to be done in equipping the men, and teaching them the correct method of carrying their belongings on "Mobile Column," for that was what we were destined to become. The equipment was worn in the usual "fighting kit" manner, with the haversack on the back and under the haversack the drill tunic, folded in four. This also served as a pad to protect the spine from the sun. Near Hill 40 there was a large patch of hard sand which the Scottish Horse, who were in the neighbourhood, had converted into a football pitch. Small wonder then that we challenged the owners to a game, and a great game it was. The Scotsmen had an unbeaten record in Egypt, which they maintained, but only after a ding-dong game which the battalion never forgot.

The next day the Brigade marched forward and made camp at Gilban, about 3½ miles N.E. of Hill 70. An indefinite stay was to be made here, and defensive precautions were taken, a ring of posts being placed all round the camp. It was soon found that the principal difficulty was that of patrolling by night from post to post. On a desert such as this there were no landmarks of any sort, and as a belt of wire such as we had been used to at Hill 70 had not been placed between the posts it was by no means easy to preserve the right direction. As we had reached a scrub-covered desert, however, this difficulty was easily overcome by making a sort of track from one post to the next by clearing away the scrub, and using this to made a clear edge to the track. The battalion was augmented about this time by drafts from home, and the following officers rejoined after having been invalided to England in 1915: Lt. Douglas Norbury, 2nd-Lt. Bryan and 2nd-Lt. L. G. Harris, while a week previous Major Allan had been posted to us from the 8th Manchesters as second in command.

In the army coming events often cast their shadow before them; and this shadow frequently takes the form of a visit by the Higher Command to the troops who are to go into action. Hence, when the

Divisional Commander, Major-General Sir W. Douglas, had the 127th Brigade paraded for him at Gilban, and when he complimented Brigadier-General Ormsby upon the fine turn out, we gathered that our long period of waiting for the Turk was over. He told us to husband our water, and these words I am sure rang through many an officer's head in the following days. The 42nd Division, he said, were expected to make a great *coup*, and many prisoners were to be taken. Two days later the preliminary rumbles of the Battle of Romani were heard, for the Turk had commenced an artillery and bombing attack upon the garrisons there.

Romani and Katia

The Turkish force, estimated at about 16,000, and much better equipped than the flying column which had made the first attempt to cross the canal in March the previous year, had been promised that they should overwhelm the "small" British garrisons before the Feast of Ramadan. They would then meet with no resistance and would enter victoriously into Egypt, a sort of promised land after their hardships across the desert. Many of them did enter Egypt and reached Cairo, but not in the way they wished. They were marched through the city as prisoners, and their presence as such undoubtedly created a profound impression upon disloyal Egyptians.

Inspired by a number of German officers, however, they fought well and vigorously in the early stages of the attack upon Romani. They had been told that once they got on the hills in the neighbourhood of the British positions they would see the Suez Canal stretched out below them, and this probably urged them on to make almost superhuman efforts. In front of Romani, in the region of the Katia oasis, mobile outposts furnished by the Australian Light Horse were driven in after hard fighting, and they fell back to other positions on the high sand hills to the south of Romani, covering the right flank of the 52nd Division. Meanwhile a frontal attack was delivered upon the redoubts occupied by the latter; and the enemy made many brave attempts to reach the summit of Katib Gannit, a high hill, in shape similar to the Matterhorn, which dominated the whole desert. He gained a footing nowhere, however, and exposed to merciless rifle and machine gun fire from the Scotsmen, suffered heavy casualties. A similar reception was afforded him by the Welshmen of 158th Brigade further north towards Mahamadiyeh,

It was apparent, however, that the enemy's intention was to force his way around the southern, side and cut the railway and water pipe near Pelusium behind Romani, and in this part of the battle the Australian and New Zealand Light Horse, who had had to discard their horses and fight as infantry, found it difficult to hold their own against repeated assaults. More terrible than the Turk was the heat and the lack of water.

Such is a rough outline of the situation when the 7th Manchesters along with the remainder of the 127th Brigade were suddenly ordered to concentrate at Pelusium. The morning of August 4th opened quietly for us, although gunfire could be heard, and bursting shrapnel could be seen in the direction of Duedar. We had settled down to ordinary routine, one company setting out for a short march, and others preparing for kit inspections and other camp duties, when suddenly, "B" Company received orders to fall in and move off, and in a short space of time they were entrained during the heat of the day for Pelusium. Before noon the whole battalion was collected On what was supposed to be a bivouac area at the new destination. But we had seen General Douglas going along the train at Gilban and he said: "Well, good luck lads, make a good bag," so we were not surprised when we found that settling down for bivouac was not to be our fate.

The 5th Manchesters had arrived with us, and the 8th were following on, while the 6th were already here, having been sent up the previous day. Our task was to go to the assistance of the Colonials and attack the Turk on the flank along with the 5th, the 6th and 8th being in support and reserve. We marched out about 4 o'clock, moving first south and then south-east. Meanwhile the battle was obviously increasing in intensity, and when we halted previous to extending, we could see the Turk shrapnel severely peppering a high ridge in front where a detachment of the Australian Light Horse, having resumed their horses, were gradually massing for a charge.

With the 5th on our right we extended into lines about 2,000 yards from what appeared to be the Turkish position on a ridge to our front. As we swept into view the enemy opened fire at long range, but very soon it was evident that they had no stomach left for a further fight. They were extremely exhausted with their exertions of the previous days, particularly of the past twenty-four hours, and the sight of lines of fresh British Infantry moving steadily toward them was more than their jaded bodies and nerves could stand. As our men climbed the enemy's ridge white flags began to appear. They were the long white sandbags carried by every Turk, and very convenient for their

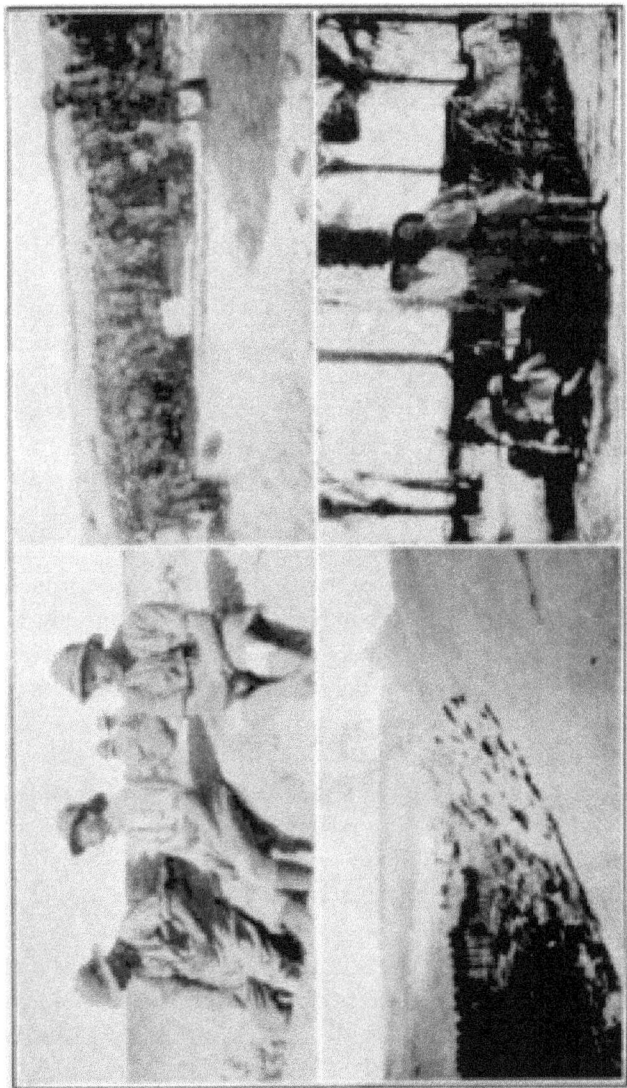

1. GROUP OF OFFICERS. N.B.—FLEUR DE LYS 3. ISSUE OF WATER—MORNING OF AUGUST 5TH, 1916
2. RIDGE OCCUPIED ON AUGUST 5TH, 1916   4. IN KATIA, AUGUST 6TH, 1916

purpose. Large bodies surrendered and they were collected and sent to the rear.

Meanwhile the Colonials had swept round the hill away to the rights and in a comparatively short space of time about six hundred Turks were seen being marched back by a few Australian troopers. The enemy's artillery had ceased fire and were obviously making attempts to escape eastwards, so with the exception of a few rifle shots from the direction of the 5th the battle in our sector was over for the day.

This was the death blow to Turkey's and Germany's hopes of ever getting within striking distance of the Suez Canal, and a vindication of Kitchener's principle that British soldiers should get out on the desert to defend the canal, and not allow the canal to defend them. But more important still, it was the beginning of that forward move so slow and weary in its early stages, which later developed into General Allenby's wonderful sweep through Palestine.

Before nightfall "C" and "D" Companies established themselves in support to the 5th Manchesters, who had now joined up with the Australians on the left, but there was very little possibility of the Turk attacking again that day, so all the troops were rested, in preparation for a strenuous attack on the morrow. Sentry groups were posted, and the battalion sat down and made a scanty meal of bread accompanied where possible with a mouthful of water. This was the first meal most men had had since breakfast. Numbers of prisoners came in during the night, each of them carrying a full water bottle. The Turk knew how to preserve a water supply, and what was of greater interest to us, he knew where to get it. It speaks well, however, for the chivalry of the British soldier that none deprived their prisoners of their water, although they were probably almost without themselves. This sporting attitude towards the enemy, the spirit of "play the game" whether fighting the clean Turk or the not so reputable German, I never failed to observe throughout the war.

Stand to at 3.30 the following morning indicated that work was still to be done, for in the half light, troops of Light Horse could be seen collecting behind a hill preparatory to a sweep forward. When they emerged in the increasing light, the enemy could be seen fleeing from a trench about 1,200 yards away. Very soon word came through that we were to go in pursuit, and while we were exercised in mind as to what we should do for water, we were greatly relieved when we were! ordered back to the ridge to fill our bottles. There the welcome sight of camels loaded with water *fantasies* met our eyes and the men eagerly assisted in the work of distribution. Three-quarters of a bottle and a *"buckshee"* drink was the ration, and this obtained, men, felt more fit for their labours. Food, however, there was none, and we had to be content with what remained of yesterday's rations. But it was felt that food was not so important if only the water would not fail.

By seven o'clock the whole Brigade were on the move, and in tropical countries in the hot season, the sun's heat is considerable at this time. After we had travelled some distance the hardship of desert marching under these conditions began to really hit us, and undoubtedly the exertions of the previous day were having their effect. Every moment the heat increased, the sand seemed to become softer and softer, and the whole ground sloped gradually upwards. Men dropped and officers had to use all the powers they possessed to get them on, but many had to be left behind to struggle along afterwards in their own time.

Meanwhile another long column of prisoners could be seen streaming away towards Romani, which we were now leaving well to our left rear. The battalion proceeded over the desert in this manner in artillery formation with platoons as units, and halting as frequently as possible. After a great physical effort we reached the base of a hill with a steep soft slope, and a sort of knife-edge ridge at the top, where an Australian outpost had been surrounded a few days before. Australian and Turkish dead still lay as evidence of the fight, and the stench from their bodies produced by the sweltering heat did not diminish the grimness of the scene.

This ridge was the battalion's position for the day, so after a short rest we scrambled to the top and surveyed the desert on the other side, lying thoroughly exhausted under the almost vertical rays of the sun, for it was now midday. The other side of the hill was exceptionally steep and dropped into a large *hod* (plantation of date palms), the first we had met on our desert travels. In this there appeared to be a well, and the temptation to go down for water was great, but how could one struggle up again? An occasional trooper visited this place but none could persuade their horses to drink, which seemed to indicate that the water was not good. Out over the desert the cavalry could still be seen pursuing the enemy, and our guns were occasionally flinging shrapnel amongst them.

Strange sights were seen. A captured convoy of Turkish camel transport was captured, and they presented a very motley appearance. They were evidently collected from the desert lands of the Turkish

Empire. They had come to the war dressed as for their more peaceful habits, so that no two men were alike. Several wore brilliantly coloured garments and head gear. Occasionally a German officer would be seen amongst the batch of weary prisoners. The navy's assistance in this fighting was marked by a monitor, miles away, standing as close to the shore as possible, although to us she appeared like a tiny toy ship. Suddenly a big flash belched forth, followed a long time afterwards by a roar, which in turn was followed by a terrific explosion over the desert to the right where the shell had arrived in the wake of the retreating Turks.

One of these shots at least had been an O.K. as we afterwards discovered, for it had destroyed a large part of a Turkish camel convoy. At four in the afternoon the battalion received orders to move on and occupy another ridge about one and a half miles in front, and "A" Company immediately set out, moving round the shoulder of our present hill. "C" Company dropped down the steep slope and waited in the *hod* for further instructions. They found there a batch of wounded Turks waiting to be carried off by the ambulance. It was with some astonishment that they heard Major Allan shouting to them from above to get back to their former position, so they struggled up the hill again with a very ill grace. However, plans had been changed and it transpired that the Lancashire Fusiliers had arrived and they were to take over our position while we went back a few yards to bivouac for the night.

It was now much cooler and men felt disposed to eat their very scanty meal. Those who had water were fortunate. Just as we were settling down for the night word came through that Katia was to be taken next day, and that we should move out at four in the morning. The enemy were believed to be holding the oasis basin fairly strongly. In our extraordinarily tired condition, brought about by strenuous exertions and lack of nourishment, we did not view the prospect with too much confidence, but hoping that a few hours' sleep might refresh us we rolled into the shallow scoops we had made in the sand, and lay down to a rather chilly night, our only extra cover being the khaki drill tunic whose weight we had roundly cursed during the day.

At 3 a.m. we prepared to move. In the dim light the eternally-blessed water camels could be seen wending their way towards our bivouac. As before there was abundance of volunteers for this vital fatigue, but most hearts drooped when it was found that the ration worked out to a pint per man! Officers and N.C.O.'s. sadly but vigorously emphasised the extreme urgency of preserving the water supply. Some resorted to drastic action and insisted that no man should drink at all without first obtaining permission of his officer, and on the day's business I am inclined to think that these officers obtained the best results. The Brigadier came to tell us we had done magnificently, but he said we should have a worse day today; water was to be had at Katia-when we got there. The men were also warned that it would probably be of little use to drop out, in fact it might be extremely dangerous, for the chances of being picked up were rather slight.

The cheery soul of the British Tommy, however, is proof against all things, and he started out on this day's trip in the same spirit with which he tackled all jobs during the war: "It has to be done, so do your best and put the best face on it." The Fleur de Lys led out the Brigade and trudged steadily through the soft sand in artillery formation. The 6th gradually got up into a position on our right, while the 5th and 8th followed in support. The march forward proceeded monotonously in the increasing heat, the men becoming more and more taciturn as the sun's power gathered.

Allowance of course had to be made for the weariness of the men and the heavy going. Then a halt was called and we waited for an hour. It appeared that the L.F.'s, who formed the left of the 42nd Divisional front, had been rather late in starting, and it was necessary to wait for them. Then the forward movement commenced again, and after some time another long halt was necessary. Our men were now in a great hollow in the sand in which there was not a breath of wind, and the sun now at the height of its fury beat down mercilessly.

There is little doubt that this lying unprotected in the heat simply sapped our energy, and everyone wished that we could have pushed on ahead. General Douglas came to cheer the men up, and announced that over 3,000 Turkish prisoners and a large quantity of material had been captured to date. For the moment, however, men had lost their grip of interest in such matters, and were chiefly concerned with their own personal affairs. They behaved splendidly and with great physical effort resisted the need to drink. Officers were grateful to one or two men in their platoons who proved a moral support to their comrades by keeping a cheerful countenance, interposing a ribald remark when things looked black, and explaining to their weakest pals the rigours of the necessity in a rougher but more intelligible manner than their leaders could have done. Such men are invaluable and are always to be found on these occasions.

Reconnoitring patrols of Australian Light Horse and Yeomanry passed through, and from remarks dropped by returning troopers it soon became apparent that little if any resistance would be met with. A detachment of Ayrshire and Inverness Horse Artillery were keeping pace with our column and occasionally they opened fire, obviously upon fleeting targets of retreating Turks. A thick wood of date palms in the distance indicated Katia, and all men gazed upon this as the Mecca in which water was to be found. Some eight hundred yards from this, however, was another *hod* which had to be traversed by the 127th Brigade, and as we were leading, it devolved upon us to make quite sure that it was not occupied. The 6th and 7th therefore extended and assumed attack formation to pass through the *hod*. This was a difficult moment and tested the fibre of men and the battalion as a whole to the utmost. The extra physical exertion and the loss of companionship which one gets in the close formation served almost as a breaking point to endurance. Perhaps the best summary of the psychology of this period is found in the words from the diary of one of the officers:—

Then it was that my energy gave out. I moved about along the line shouting at the men to preserve their dressing and cor-rect intervals. Much had to be done. We inclined first to the left and then to the right and it was very trying. Men began to drop and I could not help them now that I had lost touch with them. Then I began to lose all interest. I had become purely self-centred—if the whole platoon had collapsed I am afraid I should not have been concerned. I had almost got to such a state that if the Turks had suddenly appeared from the wood I should not have cared what the consequences were. Yet I was determined not to touch water for I recognised that that was required for the last extremity.

My head dropped and my knees would not straighten. The load on my shoulders was ten times its weight. The haversack and tunic on my back seemed to pull me down, but the greatest weight was an extra haversack which I had attached to my equipment on the left. It contained all manner of necessaries and comforts, and ties with home. I was determined not to part with it, although I confess I was almost impelled to fling it away. In other words I think I had got to the limit of my endurance, when a halt was called in the *hod*. I dropped under a palm tree with a group of men, slipped off my load, and then lay quite still for a long time. After a while I had my first drink of water for that day. We stayed there some time, and one or two of the men had found a well. But it was brackish and the men should not have touched it, for it made them worse. Several were knocked out altogether by it.

Word had come through that Katia was unoccupied by the enemy, and although it required a tremendous effort the battalion got together and proceeded to the final destination in column of route. Although not much over half a mile those last yards seemed interminable, but in course of time we were all settled in the cool shade of the *hod* and were speculating about water; a problem which seemed to be solved by the arrival of the camels. When it was found that no *fantassie* was full and many were empty it required the utmost exertion of a British soldier's good temper to prevent him from killing some of the *Gyppies* who had accompanied them, for it was obvious that they had been selling water to men who had dropped out of the column. Then we reflected that these poor devils needed it badly, so it was hard to apportion the blame. We wondered, nevertheless, why other camels had been detailed to carry on an occasion like this, flour, fresh meat (once fresh but now unfit for consumption) and candles, when they might have been better employed carrying water! Still, we were thankful to have achieved our task and although we had lost more than seventy men en route, we were proud to know that we had arrived the strongest battalion, some having left more than half their effectives on the desert.

The day's work was complete when the battalion had formed an outpost line well in front of the wood, and had dug short section trenches. Through the night desultory rifle fire could be heard in front where the mounted troops were still in touch with the retiring enemy. Next day a serious conflict took place between the cavalry and the Turkish rearguard at Oghratina, and rumours were prevalent that we had to continue the forward movement. We were not sorry, however, when it was found that we were to remain in Katia. During the succeeding days hostile aircraft were very busy, and dropped several bombs in the vicinity of the wood, the 52nd Division, who were north of us, suffering more severely than ourselves.

Those not on outpost duty took advantage of the rest and made themselves as comfortable as possible. Stakes sent up by the R.E. were used for constructing bivouacs, but perhaps the palm trees provided as much assistance as anything else. Although we had not yet learnt to use the word "camouflage" we knew its meaning, and whenever we settled down on the desert we put it into use as a protection against inquisitive aircraft. At Katia the palm trees gave us all the protection we required in this way.

CHAPTER 2

Desert Life

On August 14th the 42nd Division moved back to Romani, a further advance across the Sinai Desert being deemed inadvisable until the railway and water pipe, which stopped a few kilometres beyond Romani, had been pushed further ahead. A system of training was started, but as the men had not recovered from the fatigue of the Katia operations, and the weather was very trying, vigorous forms of exercise were given up. A number of men went to hospital with a weakening form of diarrhoea almost akin to dysentery, while the medical authorities were in a highly nervous state about cholera of which a few cases had been reported. It was presumed that this had been contracted from the Turkish prisoners and their old camping grounds.

The battalion was augmented slightly at this stage by a draft from England, while 2nd-Lt.'s. W. H. Barratt and W. Thorp returned from leave. Lt. H. C. Franklin, M.C., one-time R.S.M., went into hospital and was invalided to England, and his place as Adjutant was taken by Capt. J. R. Creagh, a position he filled admirably for more than two years. Captains C. Norbury and B. Norbury left the battalion about this time to obtain appointments in England and France and this entailed a change in Company Commanders. Captains Tinker and Higham continued to command "A" and "D" Companies, Lt. H. H. Nidd was given "B" Company, and Captain Chadwick "C" Company. 2nd-Lt. G. W. Franklin assisted the Adjutant in the Orderly Room, while 2nd-Lt. F. Grey Burn was employed as "Camel Officer;" new work brought about by the substitution of camel for wheeled transport. The bulk of the latter remained at Kantara under 2nd-Lt. M. Norbury, with Capt. Ward Jones in charge of the Brigade transport; their duties consisting chiefly in bringing rations, etc., across the canal from the main station on the E.S.R. and loading them on the trains

1. Bivouac Shelters on the Desert
2. Making the Railway over the Desert
3. At El Mazar
4. Digging a Well.

which ran over the desert. Wheeled transport could not be employed in the desert stations as roads had not been constructed.

We came to know the camel fairly well during the succeeding months, and he proved a study, perhaps more interesting than his care-taker, a member of the Egyptian Camel Corps' distinctive in his long blue *garrabea*. When a company was on duty at a distant outpost the time for the arrival of the ration camels was also the signal for the ra-tion fatigue to fall in. Then the string of animals would leisurely wend their way through the gaps in the barb wire, their noses held high in an aristocratic leer, each led with a head rope by a blue smocked *Gyppie*. The Q.M.S. would appear: "'*Tala Henna, Walad. Barrac Henna*'" and so forth. A wonderful flow of British-Arabic, grinningly compre-hended by the natives, always produces the desired result.

The camel gets down in a series of bumps and not without cau-tious glances at his head, the men unfasten the complication of ropes and commence the work of unloading. Somebody shouts: "Mail up!" and this brings out a number of interested faces from the entrances to "bivvies." After the rations have been sorted out, word quickly goes round, "Six to a loaf again, and no fresh meat today," so everyone looks gloomily ahead to the prospect of swallowing quantities of bully beef and biscuits. Other camels have carried up trench and wiring mate-rials, and when all are off-loaded they get up wearily and solemnly depart leaving the outpost to its solitary existence. If there is only one officer he feels his solitude very much, for in spite of the camaraderie with the men and particularly the senior N.C.O's. there is a feeling of restraint due to the requirements of military discipline, and he misses the value of perfectly free intercourse.[1]

It soon became apparent that an advance across the desert in the direction of El Arish was contemplated, and that the speed of such an advance would depend upon the rate at which the railway and water pipe line could be constructed. The function of the troops was to protect it from raiders so that work could proceed in comfort, a duty shared by the mounted troops and the 52nd and 42nd Divisions. In September, therefore, the 7th Manchesters left Romani for garrison duty at Negiliat, about twenty kilos. further east. About this time Capt. Chadwick, who along with Lt.-Col. Cronshaw, had been decorated with the Serbian Order of the White Eagle in long delayed recogni-tion of their magnificent work in Gallipoli, left the battalion to join the R.F.C. in England and France. Capt. Townson succeeded him in

1. Quoted from an Officer's Diary.

the command of "C" Company.

As the health of the desert troops was not good after their long strain under the tropical sun, a system of rest and holiday cure, suggested by the medical authorities, was begun. Batches of men and officers were sent off to Alexandria and encamped at Sidi Bishr, just outside the town for a week, during which time they were free to do more or less as they pleased, a concession highly relished by everyone. The sight of civilisation alone was in itself almost a cure, but the change of the surroundings, the lack of military duties, the sea bathing, and the enjoyment of everything that dear old "Alex." could offer worked wonders. Further, the hot season was drawing to a close and men began to feel more normal, so that by the end of October the troops were as fit as they had ever been in their lives. The 127th Brigade were withdrawn to Romani whilst this work of recuperation was in progress, and the beginning of November saw us back again at Negiliat.

Meanwhile, the mounted troops, closely supported by the infantry, kept constant touch with the Turk. When the railhead reached the outpost line it was necessary to move the enemy by force and to this end engagements were fought at Bir el Abd, and at El Mazar, both of which resulted in the Turk withdrawing upon El Arish. His aircraft was always busy, but the bombing was not often effective. Even the natives in the E.L.C. (Egyptian Labour Corps) began to grow accustomed to these raids and steadily resisted their impulse to dash back along the line when a *taube* was sighted.

The return from hospital of 2nd-Lt. Jimmy Baker and of 2nd-Lt. Joe Chatterton at this time was greeted with pleasure by the battalion, and all were interested in the arrival of the new Padre, the Rev. E. C. Hoskyns. It was not long, however, before he had made himself thoroughly well-known to every man who wore the Fleur de Lys, and his cheery face was eagerly welcomed in every "bivvy." During unbroken service with us until July, 1918, he maintained a proud record of spontaneous popularity with all ranks, and especially with his brother officers.

On the night of November 3rd the eastern climate displayed a side to its character not often revealed. During the previous twenty-four hours we had witnessed extraordinary flashes of lightning, and this was followed by a distinct coldness and a few showers of rain in the afternoon, a new experience which caused much amusement amongst the men. In the evening, however, matters ripened, and after a joyous display of heavenly pyrotechnics and thunder all round the blackening, heavy sky, we were subjected to a violent downpour, accompanied by lurid lightning flashes. Tremendous hailstones came down, smashing through the few remaining flimsy blanket shelters that were still standing, so that we were left in our nakedness to bear the full fury of the storm. We felt that God's spectacular display on the mountains for Elijah's benefit had been at least emulated, but it was the still, small voice that was best appreciated again, when it remarked that it was a good job the cooks had just finished making "gunfire" or we should never have had a dixie of hot tea to cheer us up in our discomfort. Although the men had to stand all night on sentry in the outposts in their wet things they took it very good-humouredly.

A fortnight later the battalion moved forward again a few kilometres and constructed new outpost positions at Khirba, covering a cavalry post some distance to the south. This was necessitated by the fact that the Turk was still holding Nekhl in the heart of the Sinai, from whence a raiding party could easily strike north to cut our communications, for the railway Was now well beyond Bir el Abd. When not actually on the outpost line we did a good deal of training, and a range having been constructed, some useful field firing was accomplished. An exciting football competition resulted in "C" Company defeating the Sergeants' team and carrying off the battalion championship.

A more elaborate forward move commenced about this time, the railway having reached El Mazar, and when a Brigade of the 53rd Division arrived to relieve us, we began to gird up our loins and prepare for a stiff march. We knew, however, that endurance would not be tested as in the "Katia Stunt" for the weather was so much more favourable. On the morning of December 3rd, having reduced our stores to mobile column dimensions, we loaded up the long suffering, but grousing camels, and marched forth to the cheery strains of a drum and fife band, kindly provided by the 10th Middlesex. We plugged steadily on through the soft sand and finally camped for the night inside the outpost line in front of Bir el Abd.

Next day the march continued and we reached Salmana. We enjoyed nothing better than this new activity, and possibly the most delightful part of it was the construction of temporary shelters at the end of the day's work. Perhaps the most trying part was the provision of the usual protection for a column such as we were, that is the advance, rear, and flank guards, for this often entailed covering a greater distance and enjoying less frequent halts. The day following provided a new interest. We proceeded through a region of *sabkhets*, which are large flat stretches of hard ground, the remains of dried up lagoons, for by this time we were marching almost along the coast. These *sabkhets* were a very welcome change from the difficult soft desert sand. Tillul was our destination and we settled down amongst Argyll and Sutherland Highlanders of the 52nd Division, who had arrived a few days previously. Next morning they played us out of the camp with their bagpipes and we had a good stiff march to El Mazar, and there we fell in with elements of the other two Brigades. After two days' rest we marched out again and occupied a position just inside the defensive line, which was then being held by the 6th and 8th.

The battalion remained a few days in this district, and when not actually in the outpost line and digging trenches, we were taken out in front, a company at a time, to act as a protection to the E.L.C. who were engaged upon railway construction. Whilst on this work we got our first glimpse of El Arish, the goal to be gained after this heavy striving across the desert. The Turks were supposed to be holding a strong position between ourselves and the town, and the idea seemed to be to push the railway as far as possible, and then eject the enemy so that work could proceed.

Our men were thoroughly impressed with the wonderful rapidity with which these "*Gyppies*" accomplished their task. They were divided up into gangs, each in charge of another native who had been raised to the dignity of two stripes and a stick. The stick he used freely on the men who failed to keep up his standard of work. Using their curious adze-like shovels they pulled the sand into baskets and ran away with it to where it was required, and whilst they toiled a simple but noisy refrain was sung to the leadership of the "Ganger." The whole spectacle presented a seething mass of rapidly-moving, blue smocked, brown figures, busily working on the bright yellow sand. The result of four hours of this sort of thing would produce about 500 yards of good level track including shallow cuttings and embankments. Then the train would arrive with more sleepers and rails and these would be carefully but quickly laid in position.

Another job we had to do in this neighbourhood was digging wells. When "C" Company went off for a couple of days to do this they discovered what a formidable business it was. It was necessary to go down to a depth of about twenty feet, and as the well was sited in very soft sand the task can be imagined. A huge hole, about forty feet square had to be made to allow for the slope of the sand, and the

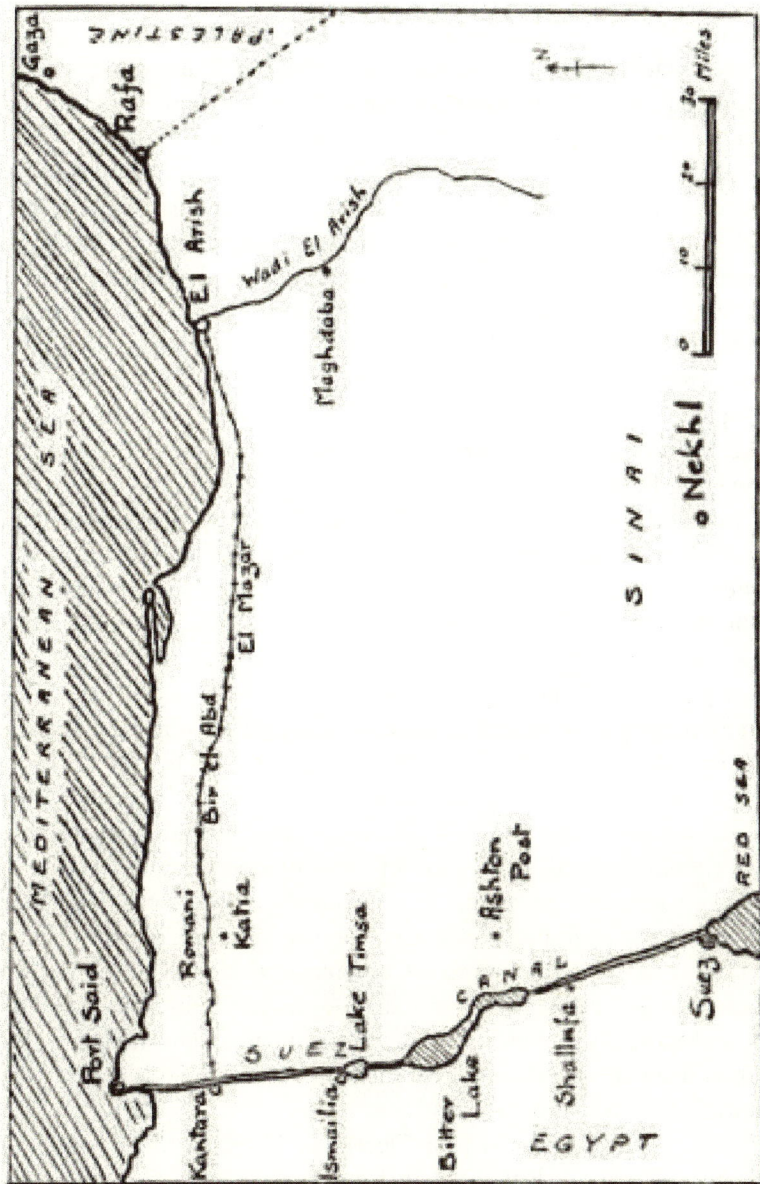

THE SINAI
DESERT

deeper we went, the higher grew the mountains of sand all round the hole, so that the men had to be arranged on tiers above one another. In this way a shovel full of sand from the bottom travelled up through various pairs of hands before it was finally thrown clear. This tedious business continued until water was struck, and then a corrugated iron frame was sunk at the bottom, and the tall sides of the well built upon it. After this all the sand that had been so laboriously chucked out, was heaved back again. A pump was fixed by the R.E. and troughs made along side, to be filled as often as the well could furnish sufficient water (in this case twice a day) for the use of camels or horses.

At El Maadan an important railhead was being constructed for the storage of water, which was kept in large and small canvas tanks. We took a great personal interest in those tanks with our thoughts resting securely on Katia. Matters were gradually developing towards an engagement of some magnitude, and it was now known that the general scheme was for the mounted troops to make a detour in order to turn the enemy's left flank, whilst the 42nd and 52nd Divisions would make an advance parallel to the coast. That is to say in effect the infantry would deliver a frontal attack upon the Turkish troops covering El Arish.

It had been further decided that the 127th Brigade together with the 5th East Lancashires would execute the first shock of the 42nd's effort, so we had a feeling that once again the Fleur de Lys would be "in the limelight." During the evening of December 29th there was a rapid and wonderful concentration of troops of all arms in the hollow ground near the railhead. The two infantry Divisions were there in force, whilst the Australian L.H., and N.Z.M.R., together with the Yeomanry were simply waiting for dusk to move off to their appointed stations. Behind all this preparation there was a curious feeling that there was no enemy to fight at all, and betting ran high as to whether we should find any Turks near El Arish or not. It was suspected in high quarters that the enemy had got quietly away a few hours before. However, we slept peacefully until 3 a.m. and then Company Commanders were summoned to a Conference with the C.O. to receive orders to get ready at once to march—backwards not forwards! The Anzacs carefully reconnoitring in the night had finally entered El Arish, and saw no one there except the native villagers. So "the stunt was a wash-out," the bird had flown.

The 42nd marched back on December 21st to El Mazar, and faint rumours began to drift about that day that we were to leave Egypt.

General Douglas commiserated with us for not having had the pleasure of a good scrap! "But," he said, "never mind lads, you will get more than you want very soon." Now, what did that mean? Profound speculation as to the probabilities can easily be imagined. France, Salonica, trouble in India, Mesopotamia and even an advance into Palestine (scouted as absurd by most people) were freely discussed. The main consideration just at present, however, was that the Christmas of 1916 was going to be spent under much pleasanter conditions than the previous one on Gallipoli, and concurrent with rumours about fighting there were more substantial rumours about turkeys, plum puddings and beer.

I am glad to say all three materialised, and these together with Christmas Carols by the divisional band contrived to produce a Yuletide feeling. In fact everyone had as good a time as could possibly have been expected in the desert. Luckily the parcels from home, including comforts from various institutions, etc., also arrived in time. El Mazar was our abode for more than three weeks, and we heartily wished a cleaner piece of ground could have been selected to live upon. In past days the Turk had been stationed here in force, and he, not being of a sanitary disposition, had bequeathed to us a store of body lice of new and large dimensions. I don't think the fighting strength of the 7th, including all live stock, had ever been so large in its history.

A delousing apparatus made from an old engine and truck was sent up on the railway to cope with the problem, and perhaps it had some little effect—in helping the young ones to grow quicker. Most men were agreed that there was nothing to equal the double thumb action for certain results. Another scourge here, probably also due to the filthy sand, was the alarming development of septic sores. These unpleasant things did not require a wound or scratch to start them, but they broke out themselves as a small blister on any part of the body. In the case of a good many men it took the form of impetigo, an extremely uncomfortable sore rash on the face, and both officers and men appeared day after day on parade with appallingly unshaven sore chins, and bandages visible on arms or knees, etc.

During our stay here the news continued to be good. On Christmas Eve the mounted troops, not satisfied with the Turkish escape from El Arish, suddenly pounced upon Maghdaba, about twelve miles further south, up the Wadi, and after a short fierce fight destroyed the garrison, only a few making their way out of Africa. A more brilliant affair, however, was the lightning raid upon Rafa, on the border between Sinai and Palestine, and about thirty miles beyond El Arish, the starting point of the raid. In a few hours a large mounted column, consisting chiefly of Anzacs had covered this distance and had taken the Turk completely by surprise. The enemy put up a stern fight, however, and after his reinforcements had been destroyed on the road from Gaza he gave in. The prisoners from these engagements continued to have the desired effect upon the dissaffected natives in Cairo on their arrival there.

Less was heard about our leaving Egypt after the New Year, and rumours received a mortal wound when the Division turned its face to the east once more and marched up, a Brigade at a time, to El Arish. The 7th accomplished this march in three easy stages, the first day taking us to Maadan, and the next to Bitia. A few days' stay here helped us to appreciate its natural advantages, and as far as the desert went, it almost had pretensions to beauty. There were glorious palm groves, bright clean sand to live in, hard flat stretches for football (greatly appreciated), and a roaring sea close at hand on a wonderful beach for bathing. If El Arish were in Belgium, Bitia would be "El Arish Bains." The return of British power to this corner of the earth was epitomised one day in the sight of a Bedouin caravan pursuing its peaceful purpose. The old sheik stalked proudly in front, while his family and goods were disposed on various camels, and a small flock of pretty black goats pattered along behind in charge of a sturdy brown lad. Surely they at least had witnessed the Turkish retirement with satisfaction.

El Arish and After

On January 22nd, 1917, the 7th Manchesters reached their "farthest east" in the final stage of the march to El Arish. Most of the day's labours had to be accomplished in a blinding sandstorm, which fortunately had subsided when we arrived at our destination. As we reached El Arish one had a curious feeling that the canal zone was being left well behind, and as far as mileage was concerned it certainly was, since the Suez was one hundred miles away. Nevertheless, up to now one had felt that really we were on canal defence, and however far we went out there had been little change in the country so that one hardly seemed to progress. Now, all that had been left behind, and we were amongst new scenes.

This growing impression was completed on our arrival. We pitched camp on a hill north-west of the town and about six hundred yards from it, so that we had a perfect view of the place, which resembled a picture out of the Bible, and was not quite like anything seen in Egypt. It was obvious we were in a new country—in fact we were knocking at the gates of Palestine, but no one amongst us knew that an entry was to be made into that country. The affair at Rafa, for instance, had only been a raid, and the Turks had once more strengthened the place. British territory had been cleared of the enemy and it was felt that a system of frontier defence would be constructed, and small garrisons left to maintain the boundary.

Eight months had passed since the battalion left the vicinity of peaceful civilisation, so to meet it again, crude though it was amidst the mud huts of El Arish, filled our men with extreme curiosity. The town was placed out of bounds because of the fear of cholera, small pox, etc., but there was much of interest to be seen. Groves of fig trees surrounded the place on the edge of the *wadi*, and it was a matter for speculation as to where they obtained their sustenance for it was apparently just bare desert. Vines and date palms were also grown, and I presume these, with fishing, constitute the main source of life to the inhabitants. The natives, incidentally, had a most pleasing appearance, and their older men reminded one forcibly of the patriarchs. They had a strikingly manly and independent carriage, quite different from the lack of respectability of the lower class Egyptian. There is probably a good deal of Arab blood in them, which may account for the fearless manner with which they look the foreigner straight in the face.

We were not surprised when definite orders arrived to prepare ourselves for a return to the canal. The transport started first for they were to trek the distance, while the personnel were to have the pleasure of riding on a train. The men accepted this statement rather warily for such a thing had seldom been known during their experience with the battalion. On January 30th all the animals in the Division assembled near our camp preparatory to commencing the trek when the aircraft alarm was sounded. This was immediately followed by eight bombs in quick succession. One of these unfortunately dropped amidst our transport column killing two favourite riders, "Bighead" and "Jester" and destroying two or three mules. Fortunately only one man was injured, and more luckily still, no bombs dropped in the camp, although they were near enough to be unpleasant.

The day's excitement was later heightened by a camel going "*macknoon*" in the middle of the camp. Attacking his native keeper he broke loose and our men had to "run for it." By an ingenious manipulation of ropes round his legs, and a well-aimed blow behind his ear from a tent mallet flung by one of the men, he was subdued and brought to earth, but not before he had destroyed a "bivvy" and some tents. Even this did not complete the incidents of the day, for evening found us clinging with might and main to tent poles, tent curtains, "bivvy" shelters, etc., while a furious sand storm did its utmost to fling them down.

The next day something of a sensation was caused by a sudden order to furnish one officer and two N.C.O.'s. per company as advance party to journey at once to Port Said, there to embark on February 2nd for an unknown destination. Two days later the battalion entrained in "*trucks de luxe*," and after a nine hours' extremely lumpy journey we reached Kantara. There was a feeling that having helped to escort the railway to its present destination we had really earned that ride. On the journey down we met elements of the 53rd Division marching up to take our places at El Arish, and we shouted greetings and expressions of goodwill to them. At Kantara a draft from England with 2nd-Lt. G. Norbury in command joined the battalion. A pleasing feature about this draft was that it was largely composed of old members of the original 7th who had been wounded or invalided from Gallipoli, such men as C.S.M. Lyth, Sergeant McHugh, Q.M.S's. Andrews and Houghton, being amongst its numbers.

The 42nd Division crossed the Suez Canal for the last time on February 5th, twelve months to the day after the 7th Manchesters had crossed over to the east side at Shallufa for the first time. The first days march ended at El Ferdan, very much to the relief of everyone. We had been, all the way, on a good hard road—a new experience after the life on the desert—and this brought into play muscles of the leg, not used on the soft sand. Everyone suffered badly from aching shins and thighs and very sore feet, so that next day, when the trek was completed to Ismailia on hot, dusty roads many men fell out, and we were a weary crew on arrival at Moascar Camp.

Our three weeks' stay here was occupied chiefly in preparing for our new scene of activities, now definitely known to be France. Eastern kit was handed in—helmets, shorts and drill tunics—and the battalion seemed to have been exchanged for a new one dressed in khaki serge and caps. With our helmets we lost our flashes, or at least the characteristic Fleur de Lys, but they were replaced by a divisional flash to be worn on the upper arm of the sleeve of the jacket. This was a diamond in shape, each Brigade having its own colour, the Manchesters being orange yellow, with the number of the battalion indicated

on it by a red figure. Being close to Lake Timsa, we frequently indulged in bathing parades under ideal conditions, for after all Ismailia
is really one of the beauty spots of Egypt. Complimentary farewell
parades were held, one on the occasion of the visit of General Dobell,
and the other a march past the C.-in-C, Sir Archibald Murray, down
the Quai Mehemet Ali in the town.

Altogether the 7th enjoyed themselves during these days and made
the most of the end of their long sojourn in the East. We were seasoned troops and were well conversant with the customs of the country. A few pangs of regret at leaving these things behind can easily
be understood, although an important consideration, and one that
weighed heavily with the men, was the possibility of getting leave
from France, a thing unknown in this place. Hence it was with mixed
feelings that the battalion boarded the train at Ismailia on the evening
of March 1st for a rapid journey to Alexandria. No time was lost here
for we detrained on the quay side and embarked at once.

CHAPTER 3

For France

Wearers of the *Fleur de Lys* gazed their last upon one of the countries of their toils from the deck of the ship *Kalyan* as they steamed out of Alexandria harbour on March 3rd, 1917. There were many present who had accompanied the battalion on their venture from this same harbour nearly two years before, to try their fortunes upon ill-starred Gallipoli, and I have no doubt they wondered what these new experiences would bring them. One thing is certain, however, and that is no one imagined we should be compelled to continue our wanderings for full two more years before the last journey home could be made. And yet, so it was.

The *Fleur de Lys,* for the first time since it had been adopted by the Manchester Regiment, was borne to the soil of France, the country that gave it birth, and whose kings wore it proudly for hundreds of years, by Englishmen who had pledged themselves to fight in and for that fair land. "Fair Land!" I hear someone scornfully mutter. However much we were destined in the days to come, when wallowing to our waists amidst the soil and water of France, to think very much the reverse, it would be impossible to forget the glory of our Southern entrance to this sad country.

The battalion made the trip across the Mediterranean in good company, for the ship was shared by ourselves and the 8th Manchesters (the Gallant Ardwicks) commanded by Lt.-Col. Morrough. We had an opportunity of renewing our acquaintance with Malta, so vivid in its intense colouring, whilst our escort of torpedo boats was changed. Perhaps the following extract from an officer's diary will suffice to epitomise whatever incident there was in the journey:—

. . . It was more or less boisterous all the way, and on occasion decidedly so—a vastly different voyage from my journey out. The much-vaunted German submarine 'blockade' was not conspicuous, for we neither saw nor heard of a submarine. Undoubtedly, of course, one is conscious of the menace, and a good deal of what might be enjoyment of the sea is spoiled by this horror. One thinks not of the sea as inspiration of sublime thoughts and all things the poets tell us of, but as a receptacle for submarines . . . and for us if we are hit. It was decidedly disconcerting to contemplate a dip during the heavy weather. There would be little chance of being picked up I should imagine.

Still, we were able to appreciate the colours of Malta, the grand snow-capped mountains of Corsica and the neighbouring islands, while the entrance to Marseilles is a sight I shall never forget. For colour and form I think it is perfect. In a sense Plymouth resembles it, but as a cat the tiger. Here the rocks run down in their limy whiteness sheer to the sea, with *chateaux* and churches on impossible peaks, backed by tremendous stern giants. Why will they not allow us on shore to get a closer view?. . . Just above my head the men are concluding a concert with the 'King,' the '*Marseillaise*' (I wonder do they appreciate that here it was first sung in its grandeur under Rouget de Lisle), and then with what should be our national song, 'Rule Britannia.' Well might they sing that with zest after the voyage we have concluded today.

After standing out in the harbour at Marseilles for 24 hours, we first set foot in France on March 10th. No time was wasted at Marseilles, and we were soon entrained for a long journey northward. In the first hours before dark we were able to enjoy the magnificent scenery of the coast region near Marseilles. At Orange we halted for a meal at midnight. Next day was a glorious journey up the Rhône Valley, passing through Lyons, Chalons-sur-Saone and Dijon. Wherever the train stopped crowds of enthusiastic French people collected to greet us and the news of the fall of Bagdad made us doubly important to them, for not only were we British but they knew we had come from somewhere in the East.

The following morning we arrived at the environs of Paris, and after a stay at Juvissy continued our journey past Versailles and on through Amiens to our destination at Pont Remy, a few miles from Abbeville. It was pitch dark and raining. Imagine the shock to troops straight from Egypt, where they had left a beautiful dry climate, when they jumped out of the carriages into four inches of squelching mud. Then we were told we had to march six or seven miles through the cold rain to our billeting area at Merelissart. However, we were amongst new surroundings and new modes of doing things, and conditions were vastly different from those we had just left, so the sooner we became accustomed to them the better.

Despite the midnight hour everyone found subject for fun in the French barns and *shippons* which were to be our temporary homes. Lt. Hodge and Lt. Taylor who had worked hard allotting the billets for us joined the battalion here. Lt. Sievewright had rejoined us at Alexandria on the boat, he having been invalided to England from Gallipoli. Lt. G. Harris left to take charge of a Divisional Bombing School, and ended his service with the battalion, although later he became the Brigade Intelligence Officer, when we saw a good deal of him again.

After three days the battalion moved back to Liercourt and there the work of refitting commenced. We had much to learn about organisation and methods of warfare as practised in France, and vigorous training was commenced at once.

Major-General Sir W. Douglas left the division, and his successor, Major-General Mitford, lost no time in getting us ready for the line. Just at this time, and whilst Col. Cronshaw and other officers and N.C.O's. were up in the line for instruction, the German retirement on the Somme and the Ancre to the Hindenburg line took place. As soon as brigades were fitted out they lost no time in moving forward into the war zone, commencing with the Lancs. Fusiliers. At the end of March the 127th brigade entrained for Chuignes and from there the 7th marched forward to Dompierre, which had been the scene of such heavy fighting by the French in 1916.

We thus got our first impressions of the devastated area of France, and I am sure there was not a mind in the battalion into which these impressions did not sink deep. The misery of it was by no means diminished when we arrived at our destination, for accommodation had to be found amidst impossible ruins and in the scattered half-destroyed dug-outs amongst the trenches which criss-crossed the village. All this had to be done in pouring rain. When at last we settled down it was found that our new homes were also shared by huge rats who capered about in a most homely manner.

Dompierre was our abode for a few days whilst the battalion made daily excursions through the mud in the direction of Villers Carbonel to execute road making fatigues. Major Scott concluded his long period of active service with the battalion about this time, being invalided to England. His place at the Q.M. Stores was later filled by Lt. Rose of the R.W.F's. After this period we moved into Peronne, and were installed in more comfortable dwellings, for although the town had been badly knocked about, it was possible to find more or less good cover for troops. The great boon here was the plentiful supply of timber from the destroyed houses, and every group of men had its roaring fire. The battalion and indeed the brigade was still on fatigue, repairing roads, railways, bridges, etc. Meanwhile the division had made its debut in France, the 125th and 126th Brigades having taken over part of the line during the pursuit of the Hun.

The 7th suffered their first casualty in the new theatre of war at Peronne in a rather unfortunate manner. Whilst on a fatigue of salving telephone wire on the battle-swept ground of Biaches, just outside the town, Pte. Gibson of "C" company was accidentally killed by a bomb, whose explosive mechanism he had unwittingly set in action when pulling up the wire.

CHAPTER 4

Holding the Line

EPEHY

On April 27th, our period of fatigues ended, the 7th Manchesters marched out of Peronne in the full panoply of war, not gaudy, but serviceable for modern requirements and not lacking the element of weight, with the certain knowledge that their next deeds would be accomplished "in the presence of the enemy." The enemy of 1917 and after was not so elusive as the Turk of the Sinai, so there was no possibility of marching on and on and never feeling his force! That night was spent at Villers Faucon, and next day preparations were completed for relieving the 4th East Lancs. in the front line trenches east of Epehy. An advance party of an officer and a few N.C.O.'s. per company had been sent forward to learn dispositions and other information about the line, and the thousand and one minute details about rations, tools, Lewis guns, water, guides, intervals between platoons and sections, etc., etc., had all been dealt with when we got on the move once more in the early evening.

Everyone expected to take over trenches such as we had in Gallipoli or had read about, but we were rather staggered to find that the battalion front was not vastly different from the outpost positions we had made on the desert. This is explained by the fact that the front was just in process of solidifying from the liquid state as a result of the German recent retirement to a safe position. The enemy therefore looked calmly down upon us from his elaborate Hindenburg system of trenches beyond Vendhuile whilst we expanded our isolated outposts into organised continuous lines. He himself, however, was also busy digging a sort of outpost work in advance of the main line of defence, for he had held up any further British advance principally from a bulwark of land mass called the Knoll on the western side of the canal, while his main line was really on the eastern side.

Because of the disjointed condition of the front there was always a danger, when going from one company to another, of men wandering into the Boche lines. This unfortunately did occur one night to a couple of men of the 7th who had to make their way with L. G. ammunition from the Quarry to the Diamond (a forward isolated redoubt) for they struck a wrong direction and walked into a hail of enemy bullets. One was killed and the other wounded. Pte. (afterwards L.-Cpl.) Summers and Pte. Johns distinguished themselves on this occasion, for, realising what had happened, they volunteered to go out and recover the men. After being away for more than two hours, constantly sniped by an obviously-startled enemy they found them and were able to bring back the wounded man. Unfortunately this deed was not recognised by the higher authorities or they would have been the first to have won distinction for the battalion in France.

Little Priel Farm came in for a good deal of hatred by the Boche, and the variations in its contour was a daily source of interest to the troops in the vicinity. The battalion observers in the innocence of their hearts and the zeal born of the new opportunities to put their training into practice, selected the corner of the garden for an O.P. and just as things were growing interesting in the field of view of the telescope, the Hun instituted a "certain liveliness" of a different sort. Repetitions of this sort of thing convinced the observers that no useful purpose could be served by staying there, so they left—fortunately without mishap—and they were eager to inform the I.O. that their new position was infinitely superior to Little Priel Farm! It was in this vicinity that Pte. Wilbraham was killed by a shell. This news saddened the whole battalion, for he was our champion lightweight boxer, and we had been entertained many a time on the desert by his clever exhibitions.

There was naturally a good deal of digging to be done in this sector, and although relieved eventually in the front positions by the 5th, the battalion found itself up in the line each night making continuous trenches. It was in connection with this work that we lost our brigadier, General Ormsby. On the night of May 1st, he, with a number of R.E. officers, was examining the position near Catelet Copse when the Boche suddenly started a short hurricane bombardment. The trench he was in was only waist deep, and soldier and leader to the end he disdained to take full advantage of the scanty shelter, preferring to set an example of calmness and steadiness under fire to his men. A piece of shell struck him in the head and he died almost immediately. This was a great blow to the brigade, just at the commencement of their adventure in the new warfare.

It was sadly remarkable, too, that he himself was the first officer casualty in his brigade. A few days later, during which time Lt.-Col. Darlington of the 5th assumed command, the new brigadier arrived— General Henley, D.S.O.—and we were fortunate to keep him as our Commander until the end of the war. The brilliant record of the 127th Brigade in France is testimony to his qualities as a leader, and it was not very long before every man and officer in the Manchesters was proud of him. General Ormsby always remained, however, as a tender memory to those who had served under him.

Villers Faucon, which had been the rear H.Q. and transport lines was invaded by battalion H.Q. and two companies when the battalion moved back into reserve, but we did not stay long here, because the 126th brigade required assistance in the completion of their trench system in front of Templeux, and to do this we had to move into the quarries in that district. The other two companies carried out similar work in the vicinity of Lempire and Ronssoy. There was very little of interest during the succeeding days after which the brigade moved out to Roisel prior to accompanying the division to the Havrincourt sector of the front.

Havrincourt

At the end of May the battalion marched out with the remainder of the brigade from Roisel and in one day reached their destination behind the Havrincourt Wood sector. We there remained for a short period in the region of Ytres and Fins. Little time was lost in the necessary preliminaries and we relieved a battalion of the Duke of Cornwall's L.I. of the 21st Division in support in the wood. "D" company were early unfortunate and suffered a number of casualties from heavy shelling on the shallow trenches which they manned near the western edge of the Wood. The enemy had noted the continued movement in this vicinity, and suddenly decided to pay attention to it in the usual manner. This spot was always remembered afterwards as "Where 'D' Company were shelled."

Conditions at Havrincourt were rather different from those at Epehy, although the same characteristics due to recent consolidation still prevailed. It was more interesting, however, and in many senses more "livable," a word of deep meaning on the Western front! In the British lines—the canal, the slag-heap (or more correctly slag-heaps) and the wood dominated all other landmarks. The canal, a portion of the Canal du Nord, was in course of construction at the outbreak of war, and its deep, well-laid bed is one of the engineering wonders of this part of France. At Havrincourt it first runs west to east and then sharply bends to the north towards Moeuvres past Hermies. The left of the 42nd divisional front rested on the bend, after running over a huge chalk and limestone slag-heap which stands at the corner. Going southwards the line roughly skirted the eastern edge of the wood which lies upon a slope facing the east.

Before their retirement, the Germans had cut down all trees on this forward slope, some said in order to make use of the timber, others for tactical reasons, so as to leave us exposed to view. I should say both reasons weighed heavily with them, but principally the latter, for it was noticeable that the woods in their own lines had not been so denuded. Havrincourt village lay behind the enemy's front line on a ridge that dominated our own positions. Further beyond were Flesquieres, Marcoing, Premy Chapel and Ribecourt, where the main line of resistance of the Hindenburg system could be plainly seen, while further over to the left on the highest ground was Bourlon Wood, which was to become so famous in the history of the British army.

Every day the battalion observers watched parties of Germans, large and small, working on these rear trenches apparently quite unconcerned about the fact that they could be plainly seen. Periodically our air service issued aeroplane photographs showing the extraordinary development of these trenches, their elaborate construction, the concrete dug-outs, and solid rows of heavy barbed wire, until it almost came to be recognised that an assault upon them would only be attempted by the maddest of leaders, and the prospect of having to take part in it took one's breath away.

The chief job of the battalion was to guard by day, and get command of by night, the large extent of No Man's Land which varied from 400 to about 1,200 yards across. The day work was easy, but at night it was fraught with quite interesting possibilities. The Boche was not very inimical here, and seemed anxious to lull us into a feeling of peace and security so that, I suppose, he could get safely on with his digging, for he had still a good deal to do. His outbursts of shelling, therefore, although at times disagreeable, gave one the impression that its chief purpose was to remind us of his constant presence. At times, especially in the evening, it seemed to afford him amusement to dust our lines indiscriminately with gas shells.

Our gunners, however, were not so lenient and they frequently made excellent use of their good ration of ammunition, so that we were able to make daily notes of the changes in the scenery, particularly in Havrincourt village. Considerable interest was aroused one morning, soon after our arrival, by the sudden disappearance of Havrincourt Chateau in a cloud of red brick dust and smoke. This was always a mystery and a frequent source of controversy. Did the Boche blow it up, and if so, why? Or did it go off as a result of our shelling, and again, if so, why? Some said they saw stretcher-bearers moving about amidst the debris afterwards, which rather indicated the second theory.

We enjoyed the advantages of a continuous front line here, but naturally a good deal of time had to be spent in perfecting the system, both in digging and wiring. The brigade was given an opportunity of leaving its mark on the war-geography of France, two copses in No Man's Land being dubbed "Wigan Copse" and "Dean Copse" by the 5th, while we were responsible for "Manchester Trench" and "Cheetham Hill," "Henley Lane" serving to keep green the memory of the brigadier. Two great chalk craters showed up in front, "Etna" and "Vesuvius" respectively, and one of the jobs of the patrol commanders by night was to find out if the former was occupied by the Hun. We very soon found that it was, and that he appeared to use this and the two copses as starting points for his patrols.

Thus, when our parties went out at night, the possibility of an encounter in No Man's Land was never remote, and indeed there were a few clashes of this sort. It was all a great education for the battalion, for such work as this had not often come our way in the Gallipoli days, and there had been no opportunity of practising it since. It was considered advisable to get as many officers and men as possible out on patrol at some time or other, for there was a noticeable difference in a man's morale, and in his attitude towards trench life, once he had returned from such an adventure.

He was conscious of having in a way asserted his manhood—more than his pal who had not been out—and the dim uncertainty of what there might be in front of our wire had gone. He knew now what was there—nothing. He was acquainted with the ground in such a way that if the enemy did wish to attack he knew exactly where he could get him with Lewis gun, rifle or bombs. A spirit of confidence was thus engendered in the whole battalion, as was eventually shown when a few ventured out on patrol in broad daylight, and obtained some very useful results.

Realistic gas drill was indulged in occasionally at night because the enemy had an irritating habit of putting over a few rounds of gas, either shell or T.M., at irregular intervals. He caught out a few of the East Lancs. by this trick, which naturally produced a state of "wind" in the division so that everyone was more than ever "gas alert." After a few nights of gas alarm, in the middle of one of which the transport officer had to commandeer a fatigue party (in gas helmets) to extricate a full water-cart from a shell-hole, most of us became "fed up." Another night someone imagined he felt the pineapple smell of the type of gas the Hun then used, and the alarm was passed along the front trench. One of the officers on duty was determined to make sure this time, and stopped the passing of the message. He made his way along the trench where the men by this time had assumed their gas helmets, until he came to one stolid, oldish man who was on sentry, staring truculently out in front without his gas protection on. "Jones," said the officer, "can you smell pineapples?"

"What, sir," he grunted, "I could if I had a tin of 'em under my nose!"

One night, while we were in support to the 5th, one of their officers, in charge of a patrol sent out to investigate the ground around "Wigan Copse," got into the Copse and discovered a Boche post there. The startled enemy had apparently made off. The next night the 7th took over the front line at an unfortunate moment, for the Hun had decided that "Wigan Copse" must be "retaken" at all costs, and they began the business with a barrage all over the place but particularly on our front line, just as we were beginning the relief. It was decidedly unpleasant, and we had no idea what it was about until we heard the brutes cheering as they rushed into the empty copse. From a report which we captured later we found that this was another addition to their long list of "victories," and I have no doubt that a few iron crosses were doled out to commemorate the occasion.

After three and a half weeks' continuous duty in and around Havrincourt Wood the battalion moved out for a week's rest to Ruyaulcourt in brigade reserve. It was a pleasant diversion and we made the most of the glorious weather with football matches and very successful sports, the latter largely taking the form of comic dress contests.

The affair of "Wigan Copse," and the constant patrolling activity exercised by ourselves and the 5th in that direction had induced a lively interest in this spot, until finally it was decided to raid it, and the 7th were selected to do the job. As this was the first effort of this nature attempted in the division there was naturally a good deal of anxiety as to the result. The 8th were to co-operate with a diversion on "Dean Copse," and if possible, of course, they also were to obtain prisoners. "C" Company (Capt. Townson's) were honoured by the C.O. in having to supply the raiding party of 40 men, and 2nd-Lt. Hodge was put in charge. His qualities as a leader, and his expert knowledge in bayonet fighting left him undisputed as the officer most fitted for the business. He took his men off to Ruyaulcourt, when we had gone into the line again, and there trained them vigorously "over the tapes" for the task in hand. Each time he took them "over" they were inspired to a fiercer zest for the blood of Boche, so that when they returned to the Slag Heap on the night of July 2nd every man was primed up like a fighting cock.

Careful reconnaissance during the preceding nights, and long scrutiny by day through telescopes and field glasses left no doubt as to the weak spot in the Hun armour. He had placed low wire in front of the copse but had no protection on the flanks. A track leading from the front line showed how his men moved up to occupy this outpost position and also the probable route taken by patrols. As it also seemed evident that the copse was held at night only, the plan of the raid was obviously to give the enemy ample time to settle down in the outpost, and then dispose the raiding party so as to strike in on an exposed flank.

The western side was selected, because there was little or no danger from the canal, and it left the 8th a free hand to deal with "Dean Copse." At the appointed time our men filed quietly along and got into position across the track without any alarm being raised. Lewis guns were posted at one or two points to cut off retreating Huns. At 1.8 a.m. exactly, our guns opened fire, not upon the copse of course, but upon the enemy main lines. A remarkably good and accurate barrage was put down on the German front line, which formed a crescent within which lay the two copses, especially on known M.G. positions; while, by request, the Australian heavy guns from the next divisional sector northwards joined in with crumps on strong points behind the front line. Simultaneously the raiding party leaped up and rushed into the copse like howling *dervishes*.

Some hours of a deathly, eerie silence, the nerve-racking quality

132

of which is only known to those who have experienced it, and made all the more impressive by the fact that it occurred on a front which is not usually quiet, was followed by a sudden din and an unexplained mad charge of the hated English. It must have put the fear of God into the Germans of "Wigan Copse," for they made no effort to resist and tried to "run for it." In fact one poor devil—a youngster—who had been lying out in the grass on sentry (but must have been doing his work rather badly) got up and ran with our men. Hodge noticing his unusual headgear, seized him by the scruff of the neck and flung him bodily, rifle and everything, back to his men. No one wanted him at the moment, for the "fun" in the copse had to be encountered yet, and he went from hand to hand until one of the covering parties took him in charge.

Two more prisoners were secured on the edge of the copse. Several other Germans who offered resistance were bayonetted while Hodge shot one or two with his revolver. Then it was discovered that the Hun had not left himself so badly protected as we had thought. Interlaced among the branches and shrubs at about five feet from the ground were strands of barbed wire which caused a few nasty cuts and scratches on the faces of some of our men. It was found to be impossible to go through the copse because of this, but Hodge had good reason to be satisfied with the night's work. He had secured his toll of prisoners as ordered, without sustaining a single casualty, and had inflicted other casualties on the enemy, for his men had emptied rifles and Lewis guns at the few flying Boche and into the copse, so he gave the word to withdraw. The men had crawled out at the beginning like fighting cocks, but they came back like roaring lions. They were naturally in a great state of excitement, because it was their first venture of this sort, and it had been crowned, after a glorious five minutes' rough and tumble, with unqualified success.

2nd-Lt. Hodge was decorated with the Military Cross for this feat—the first M.C. in the division in France—and this was really the beginning of a brilliant career for him as a soldier. He was eventually transferred as a Company Commander to the 5th East Lancs. with whom he obtained the D.S.O. From there he progressed to Major with the L.F.'s, and finally finished the war as Commanding Officer of the 8th Manchesters, leading back the cadre of that battalion to Ardwick Green in March, 1919. He is unreservedly one of the officers whom the Fleur de Lys are proud to claim.

Sgt. McHugh and Ptes. McLean and Braithwaite received Military

Medals on this occasion, and they also were glad to know that they opened the long list of decorations that the battalion was to obtain in France.

I have spent some little time on this "Wigan Copse" raid because it is an important event in the history of the battalion. The 7th Manchesters never looked back after that show, and they held up their heads in the proud consciousness that they had attempted a good thing and had achieved it. It gave them confidence—for there was a reputation to live up to, and all felt that they could not possibly fail once a job was begun. And so it was. Nothing the battalion ever touched in future went wrong, and there has been no incident in the war which the 7th need look back upon with remorse or regret.

Another important event in our life at Havrincourt was the digging of a new front line about 500 yards in advance of the old one along almost the whole of the divisional front. The 5th, being the collier battalion, achieved their part of the business on the Slag Heap, while the 7th and 6th worked on their right. The first night was a great success, there was not a whisper of protest from the Boche, and we had cut through an almost continuous line, adequately protected by concertina barbed wire, and particularly strengthened at various points where posts had to be held during the next day.

The enemy must have rubbed his eyes rather vigorously next morning when he saw what had been accomplished during one night. However, he soon began to register on the new trench, and unfortunately an isolated tree (Cauliflower Tree) helped him in this work. We were not surprised therefore to have our labours frequently interrupted on the next night's digging by violent displays of wrath accompanied by pyrotechnics. One of these was particularly spectacular, eliciting from a digger the remark: "Wouldn't Jennison be damned jealous if he was here now!"

Rumours increased about going out for Divisional rest, until elements of the 58th (2nd line London Territorial) division began to appear and make reconnaissances of the front, from which we augured good. One of their C.O.'s on being told that we had arrived in France in March, was quite delighted, and said he had been searching the British Army for troops who had come out after they did. They arrived a month before us—but from England! Nothing pleased Col. Cronshaw better, and he carefully led him through the exploits of the 42nd from the day they sailed from England in September, 1914. The London C.O. left the dugout with a more or less chastened countenance, and I presume he still continued his search.

July 8th was our last day at Havrincourt, and although we were glad at the time for the promise of a respite from trench duties, we have since frequently looked back on those sunny days with great pleasure, for by comparison it was a "bon front," and picturesque withal, which can hardly be said about any other sector we learned to know. The light railway was utilised again to take the battalion to Ytres, and after a night there we marched first to Barastre, and then to Achiet le Petit, beyond Bapaume.

ACHIET

The 127th Brigade resided under canvas about the battered village of Achiet le Petit on patches of ground not too incommoded by shell holes. The war had passed comparatively lightly over this portion of France, but a short walk westward took one to the battle-scarred fields of the fierce Somme fighting, and this was useful to us for we could pay visits to these districts to learn something of modes of battle in those days.

One day, the Brigadier took a number of officers to Thiepval and recorded his own personal experiences of the fighting around there. On another occasion a brigade scheme took place on the famous Gommecourt trenches. We little guessed in those days that we should actually be fighting for our lives in those same trenches in less than twelve months. It seemed as though the tide of war had rolled over this ground for ever, and that the very earth would cry out if it were to hear again the shrieking and tearing of shells that came to wound it.

Intensive training was the order of the day, and realising that we had still much to learn the work was seriously taken up. The men came from Lancashire, the division had been sorely tested by fire in Gallipoli, and by endurance in the Sinai, so that hard work under able leadership was all that was required to uphold the flag of achievement which had yet received no stain. As the days wore on, and we had almost forgotten our trench activities at Havrincourt, rumours began to float once more about an early move, and this move was to be connected with a big stunt coming off soon "up north." At any rate no one disputed the suggestion that our next contact with the enemy would probably be of a more serious nature than the last.

Let it not be supposed, however, that these rather sordid thoughts occupied our minds completely whilst we remained at Achiet. Officers and men took full advantage of the period of rest, and the weather fortunately was exactly suited to enjoyable life under canvas. The thing of the moment only concerned us, and this was more often than not an important football match with another battalion, a game of cricket, a sports day, a visit to the divisional concert troupe—"Th' Lads"—who gave some very good shows about this time. Boxing was a great thing, and Pte. Finch, who was, poor chap, killed and buried in this spot the following March, knocked out all comers in the divisional heavyweight. Some of these events took place in a huge crater, which had been transformed into a sort of Roman amphitheatre, produced by the blowing up of a large and deep German heavy ammunition dump. In the divisional sports also, the officers proved that they were at least the most able-bodied in the 42nd by winning the Tug-o'-War cup.

On the whole, we look back to the weeks at Achiet as a period of solid training, plenty of "Spit and Polish," but "lots of fun." On the 1st of August we got word of the big offensive at Ypres amidst all that disastrous rain, and we expected to move up there any day. It was not until three weeks later, however, that we did move, and then it was known definitely that we were for Flanders. The battalion marched down to Aveluy, near Albert, on an enervatingly hot day and remained one night in huts there. The next night they entrained and proceeded to Poperinghe in Belgium, and so added another country to the list of those they visited during the war.

CHAPTER 5

Belgium

YPRES

Ypres! That wonderful place, the sound of whose name makes the heart of the Englishman at home glow with pride, but makes the soldier, friend or foe, shudder at the mere recollection. It was the scene of much stern work, and if Belgium has been dubbed the Cockpit of Europe, surely the "Salient" was the cockpit of cockpits. More men lie buried in that small patch of ground than one cares to think about, and when instances of the unreasonableness and veritable folly of war are cited from other fronts, they can always be equalled by experiences at Ypres.

In many respects, however, the 7th were lucky in this sector, for we did not actually go over the top during our stay. Other units of the division carried out what would be termed minor operations (which are anything but minor operations to the people concerned), but the 7th escaped any such work. So far as we were concerned it was a continuation of line-holding, but under vastly new conditions. It would be useful, perhaps, to indicate the nature of these conditions.

As all the world knows the third battle of Ypres commenced on the 31st July, 1917, preceded by a terrific concentrated bombardment of the Hun positions lasting about ten days. The effect of this bombardment was to obliterate all signs of life on that part of the earth, with the exception of a few horrible, naked, and shattered trees. Nothing green was visible anywhere. In fact the land looked as though it had been a very choppy earth-brown sea suddenly frozen to stillness. Everywhere was shell-holes, shell-holes, shell-holes—large and small. Only by careful searching could one ascertain where enemy trenches had been. Dotted about over this terrain were the Hun "pill-boxes," concrete shelters in which the enemy had made their last machine gun fight. Whereas at one time they had been skilfully concealed from view, they were now standing stark above the ground which had been torn away from them. Some of the pill-boxes, indeed, had been smashed in by direct hits from the heavies, so deadly had been our gun fire during those ten days.

The opening of the British offensive had brought bad luck with regard to weather. The men had gone over in a terrific downpour of rain, so that all the advantage lay with the defences. The tanks had struggled wonderfully with the appalling conditions, but the ground was against them, and most of them were "ditched" before they were knocked out. A few, however, had got well ahead, until they were out of action, and it hardly required field glasses to be able to distinguish them within the enemy's lines, now functioning, by the cruelty of fate, as German pill-boxes and sniper-posts. Such was the salient in the early days of September when the 42nd went up to take over the "line."

It was ascertained that we were to relieve the 15th division, a most excellent division consisting chiefly of highlanders of the New Armies. They had fought over this ground in the first days of the offensive, and after a short rest had come back again to help to hold the positions taken and to initiate "minor" operations. They were situated astride the Potijze Road, due east of Ypres, and that is where the advance parties from each battalion of the division found them. The first impression was: "What a contrast with Havrincourt!" It was the exact antithesis in every respect. This was a country where the desire to kill and destroy had developed to an unimaginable intensity. Nothing of use was to be left by either side, and every yard of ground almost was searched by the gunners to carry out their cruel game.

As evidence of the meaning and determination of the business the 18-pounders were packed axle to axle amongst the mud and shell holes, ready to bark forth their loud defiance to the Hun. The 4.5 howitzers were visible in batches at various places. Further back, but still closely packed were the 6-inch howitzers, the 60-pounders, and the heavier calibre guns. The huge, ever popular 15-inch and large naval guns lay beyond Ypres, and were not for the eyes of the ordinary infantryman, but evidences of their sound work would be found when the advance continued. It required very little imagination to picture the German guns similarly placed and in similar numbers, for this offensive had alarmed the enemy, for did it not threaten the existence of their submarine bases in Belgium, to say nothing of their hold upon Lille?

His defence was careful, however, as we found to our cost, and, however much the papers at home kept up the morale of England by sneers at the "pill-box," the soldier on the spot regarded it with extreme caution and respect. After all they were the only things that stood the test of this bashing method of fighting and their very existence, when everything else was destroyed, was ample proof of the fact. Tacticians from the highest general to the platoon sergeant tried hard to discover the most effective and least costly manner of "dealing with a pill-box," and the highest in the land eagerly snatched at ideas from the man out of the line if they bore the scent of feasibility about them.

One never knew if it was in pursuit of the solution of these tactical problems that the higher command persisted during those sad August and early September days in their policy of "minor" operations. Certainly no part of the salient was ever at rest. Local attacks were launched here, there and everywhere, but comparatively few succeeded, or if they did it was merely a temporary success. While our advance parties were in the line the Black Watch and the Gordons of the 15th division, executed a night attack on "Gallipoli" and Hill 35, a job which had been previously attempted, and very little advance was made. Those who had reached the foremost position were immediately expelled or captured, or killed where they stood, by the Boche counter attack next morning. Losses were very heavy.

The 42nd took over the right portion of this front near the Frezenburg Ridge, and the 61st division the left. Incidentally, the latter again attempted Hill 35 but with equal success. The 125th brigade was given one of these unfortunate tasks, with the 6th Manchesters in support. They were to take the Iberian, Borry and Beck Farms, now no longer farms, but strong pill-boxes well defended by a system of outworks. They carried out the job and suffered heavy casualties, so heavy indeed that they could not withstand the inevitable Hun counter attack which came in the evening and was delivered by fresh storm troops brought up for this purpose from the rear. After they had attained their objective they realised the peculiarity of the strength of the German defensive system. They were subjected to heavy cross machine gun fire from the enemy positions which had not been attacked. It was evident that unless these latter were taken also they could not hold on. In other words, the policy of local attacks was suicidal and was, in fact, playing into the German scheme of defence.

While these things were taking place the 7th had moved from behind Poperinghe to Toronto Camp near Brandhoek, where it enjoyed its full share of the evening's excitement from Hun bombing planes. On September 7th, the battalion went by train to Ypres as far as the Asylum, and from there filed cautiously by platoons through the town, past the ever famous Cloth Hall, whose scraggy skeleton could be only dimly discerned in the darkness, and through the Menin Gate. A short distance along the Menin Road, and then we turned off and eventually got on "J" track—the interminable length of duck boards that carried generals, privates, rations, ammunition, runners, artillery observers, and all the other various persons and impedimenta of war, through the maze of shell holes up to the forward positions.

There were a number of these tracks all leading out like arteries from the bases of organisation to the front line. They were labelled at intervals with small boards bearing the distinctive letter or number of the track painted in white luminous paint so that they were equally legible by day or by night. These were the only guides in this desolate waste, and woe betide the man who in the night came across a spot where shelling had obliterated a good portion of the track, for it was a difficult job to pick it up again, and frequently a nerve-racking experience.

With the exception of a few bursts of 4.2's at intervals none of which came uncomfortably close, the battalion were fortunate in having a peaceful passage that night, and the relief of the 7th Lancs. Fus. proceeded without incident. We were in support in old German positions just in front of Cambridge Road, headquarters being established in the shafts of a dugout which had filled with water. Oh—how we longed for the comfort of Havrincourt! But we never allowed this thought to cause depression, for it was all in the game and other men had had much worse things to do.

I think the dominant note of our stay in this sector was shelling. It was an ever present serious factor, and a most disturbing one. Men were killed and maimed "for doing nothing" so to speak. They were merely on the spot, and there was nowhere else to go. Tactical reasons demanded that they should be there, should scratch a little cover and remain, and there they cheerfully remained—and waited. Officers moved about and tried to get their men interested in their surroundings, in their comfort, in their protection, and in the rigging up of a defensive battle if necessary. The men understood and worked with a will, and laughter and song rang out over the torn earth. But every man knew that in a place like this almost anything might happen; however, the worst would never happen to *him*—the other fellow perhaps, but not him. That, I imagine, was one of the secrets of sticking it.

Undoubtedly the Boche was putting up a fight for this bit of ground, and his guns never ceased, only in the grey hours of dawn was there any semblance of peace along the front, and then one felt that he had just temporarily put a hand over the mouth of the guns in a straining attitude of watching and listening for a movement on our part. A sudden withdrawal of that hand and they would all bark forth together in a terrible chorus. It was a strain for all, and faces began to show the lines of wearing mentality. Our persons lost their spruceness too. There was mud clinging to us, we were unshaven, equipment hung rather loosely, but our rifles and ammunition were still as ever, and Lewis guns would be found in good condition.

After two nights the battalion occupied the front positions, relieving the 5th Manchesters, and headquarters were established in a good sound pill-box at Wilde Wood. Another attack was being planned upon Borry and Beck, to be carried out by the 5th, with ourselves in support. Meanwhile our job was to dig new trenches out in front as jumping off places for the attack. They were successfully completed, but when the enemy saw them he paid his usual attention to them and as a result 2nd-Lt. Chatterton (C Coy.) was badly wounded, and eventually lost a leg. He was an extremely popular figure both with officers and men being known to everyone as "Joe," and his absence was keenly felt, for he had gone out originally with the battalion in 1914.

Luckily the plan of attack was abandoned, and apart from a feeling of personal relief everyone felt that a wise thing had been done. There was little hope of the enterprise proving any more successful than that of the L.F's., especially as similar attempts had just been made left and right of us and had failed miserably. It was clear that the only way to ease the situation was to carry out a big attack on a wide front. Evidences of the imminence of such an attack showed themselves very soon, for advance parties from the 9th division came up to learn the front, and they intimated that they had a "big job on."

One night one of our patrols out in No Man's Land, heard not far from them, feeble calls for help. Making their way across the shell holes towards the sound they found a man with a smashed leg and absolutely exhausted. He was brought in and proved to be an Inniskilling Fusilier who had taken part in an attack some four or five weeks previously! He stated that he had kept up his strength by eating the food and iron rations and drinking the water which he had found upon the dead men around him. It seemed incredible that such a thing could have happened, but on making inquiries concerning his division, the number of which I have forgotten, it proved to be perfectly true. Surely this case presents physiological and psychical problems worthy of consideration.

We were relieved again by the 5th and went back to our old support position. After two days the L.F.'s. came up again to relieve the brigade, but the bulk of our battalion continued to go up in the evening to dig in a corps cable which was being laid as far forward as possible. By the time we completed the last of our journeys to the east of Ypres, we were a battalion chastened in body and spirit. Many big gaps had been made in the ranks, and it was when we settled down to the more comfortable and peaceful existence that these gaps were keenly felt.

A most noticeable absentee was R.S.M. Hartnett. He had been badly hit by a piece of shell at Bill Cottage, and later died in hospital at Rouen. Hartnett's work with the 7th Manchesters has nothing but good to show. He had been a sergeant instructor with the battalion in pre-war days, being sent to us by the 1st Manchesters, and had gone out in 1914 to the Soudan. He stayed on through Gallipoli, and became R.S.M. when Franklin was made adjutant. A keen, regular, disciplinarian and the scourge of feeble N.C.O.'s., he was an untiring worker in entertainments. His song in Gallipoli—"*Oh, Achi, Achi Baba*," to the tune of the "Absent Minded Beggar" will never be forgotten, while some of the sketches that he wrote and had performed were masterpieces of good humour. C.S.M. Clough, of "D" company, was appointed as his successor and although the post of R.S.M. is a difficult one to fill, he did some excellent work, particularly in the line.

Toronto Camp sheltered us again for a night or two after which we moved nearer to Poperinghe. It was evident by now that we were to leave Ypres altogether, and no one exhibited any regrets, but there was a peculiar feeling that the division was rather under a cloud, and apart from a natural partisanship in the matter, everyone was indignant at the unfortunate opportunities which had been afforded us to make our reputation in this country. All were emphatic that had we been given a sporting chance in a general attack, there would have been nothing wanting in the final result. However, there was a violent spring clean through the division. The G.O.C. left us, as well as a number of the staff. In accordance with an army scheme to move round commanding officers, Lt.-Col. Cronshaw was exchanged for the C.O. of the 8th Worcesters—Lt.-Col. Carr, D.S.O.—and bade a sad farewell to the 7th on September 20th. The men sent a good many regrets after him, for he had done sound work, and had had a big hand in the creation of the fair name of the *Fleur de Lys*. We were pleased later to see his name in the honours list for a D.S.O. in recognition of his work with the 7th Manchesters.

On that day the battalion marched to Winizeele and there we were joined by the new C.O. A sort of kinship sprang up when it was discovered that he had been wounded at the landing on Gallipoli with the Worcesters of the famous 29th Division.

NIEUPORT

It was now apparent that our destination was north, one more step in the direction of Blighty, towards which we had constantly moved since leaving El Arish. But it was as near as we ever should get until the final crossing. We were to join that small, isolated batch of the British Army which had taken over the coastal sector from the French with such high hopes in the middle of the year. Ever since the first furious German onslaught in 1914, when the *Kaiser* had come in person to see his myrmidons seize the coast road to the Channel Ports, and when they met the wonderful defence of the Belgian and French troops culminating in the flooding of the Yser lowlands, the Nieuport sector had settled down to a quiet front.

The intention was for the British Fourth Army, under General Rawlinson to steal quietly in, and on an appointed day to startle our friend the enemy by a quick turning movement along the coast, which, worked in conjunction with the Ypres offensive would free Ostend and Zeebrugge. A far-reaching conception, but unfortunately doomed from the first by its over-importance. The Hun had found out. Someone had told him there were British soldiers on the coast, so he stampeded—not in the way we should have liked but in a disastrous manner for ourselves. It had been part of the scheme to preserve the secrecy of this movement by not bringing up the guns when the infantry came, for there is nothing like gun positions for "giving the game away." So soon as the German knew, however, that the British had arrived, up came his guns very quickly, for he was well aware that they had not come for a rest, especially in view of other activity near Ypres.

The 1st division had taken over the Coastal sector with the 32nd division in front of Nieuport on their right. On the coast the line ran through the sandhills on the east side of the Yser, while on the right of this the ground was very low lying and was largely flooded from the five canals which converge near the town. In July the Huns smashed down all the bridges over the river with shell fire and then attacked in overwhelming numbers, with the result that amongst the sand dunes, being unsupported either by artillery or infantry, the battalions on the east of the river were completely blotted out. Very little progress, however, was made against the 32nd Division, and their line remained more or less intact. It was impossible to retake the lost ground, for the wide river mouth had now to be crossed. This incident altered the whole face of the situation, for a general advance over the inundated sector alone was out of the question, and the scheme was given up. A number of guns was brought up to form an effective background to the infantry and that was as far as matters developed.

When the 42nd arrived they found, by a curious chance, the 66th division in charge of the coast sector. This division was composed of the 2nd line battalions of our own units, so there was a tremendous amount of interest in each other displayed by both sides. Friends met friends, and opportunities for these meetings were further afforded by the fact that most units relieved their own 2nd line battalions.

The 7th, after a novel experience of being carried up to the coast on motor 'buses from Winizeele, were "debussed" at Coxyde, where they billeted themselves comfortably in the deserted houses. The Boche had paid this place some attention prior to his attack in July, and had not really left it alone, so that the civilians had made a rather hurried departure. A few had elected to remain, and were to be seen walking furtively about the streets with that curious strained look that the war-driven peasantry of France and Belgium always wore. Here we met the 2nd battalion of the Manchesters, and were glad of the opportunity to make their acquaintance.

A 7th officer, then Capt. L. Taylor, was amongst them and it may be mentioned here that later in the war he added lustre to the Fleur de Lys by winning, with the 2nd Manchesters, the Military Cross with two bars, which decorations he fortunately lived to carry home after the conflict. Whilst here the 2/7th being anxious to prove their mettle, challenged us to a game of football, from which we carried off the honours by a comfortable margin. Needless to say, this match excited considerable enthusiasm.

After a couple of days we took over the brigade support position, where we were charmed to find ourselves living in huts amongst the sandhills behind Oost Dunkerque Bains. There was a fly in the ointment, however, for the enemy knew about this camp, and being in possession of a couple of high velocity 5.9 guns for which this place was a suitable target, he pooped them off at us occasionally in the evening time. The night before we came, indeed, a shell dropped upon a hut occupied by 2/6th Manchester officers, killing four of them. Although we were worried this way, there being little feeling of security under a thin wooden or canvas roof, we fortunately sustained no casualties. On October 2nd we took over the front line from the 5th, and were now in the unique position of being the left battalion of the whole Western Front.

It was an extraordinary place to fight in—like having a real war at Blackpool amongst the houses along the front. Nestling in the corner made by the mouth of the Yser and the coast, is the seaside resort ostensibly belonging to the town of Nieuport, for it is called Nieuport Bains. The war had arrived here suddenly, apparently, for an engine and trucks still stood in the station, much battered now of course, while every cellar was filled with most expensive furniture which the people in their rapid flight had been unable to remove. All the houses had been of the new and large type, particularly those overlooking the promenade, but they were now skeletons of their former glory, and to see property of this kind in such a state only served to bring home still more forcibly the cruel destruction of modern war.

The French had made this front, and with typical French ingenuity they had connected all the cellars of the houses and so constructed a perfectly safe communication trench to the front line. This C.T. was continued backwards as a sort of tunnel along the beach, but it was really a camouflaged trench, just covered with a layer of sand. Flash lamps were thus greatly in demand on this sector. As well as watching the Hun on land we were expected also to keep a look out to sea for submarines and any other vicious craft, and the two posts allotted this duty were armed with wonderful pom-pom guns that no one had the courage to experiment with. Still "the man behind the gun" had a comfortable feeling of importance so long as there was nothing to shoot at. In that eventuality one trembles to think what might have

NIEUPORT, AND COAST SECTOR.

been the effect upon himself and the remainder of the crew.

Patrolling was also a queer business. In warmer weather it was accomplished in bathing costume and tin hat, with revolver between the teeth or behind the ear, but cold nights discouraged these efforts, and we sneaked about on our side of the river wondering what we could do. We were now at the seaside and there was the usual crop of mad holiday projects. One of these was to experiment with a new gas to be projected into the Boche front trench across the river. Then Lt. Morten was to pilot a boat over, hop into the said trench, and return in possession of a "*gassee*" from whom the results would be studied. Morten went down the line with a sturdy crew of A.B.'s. from "D" company to practise rowing, but luckily that was as far as the scheme progressed. Then we had our sea-serpent.

An odd sentry or so had sworn to having seen a boat on successive nights knocking about the river. A careful look-out was instituted, but no one in authority caught a glimpse of this "mystery ship." After six days of this sort of thing we were surprised to find ourselves relieved by the 20th D.L.I. of the 41st Division. They had just arrived from Ypres and the 42nd were to take over the sector on the right. The 127th Brigade, however, went out into reserve at La Panne and there we had a splendid time.

It was about this time that the new divisional commander arrived—Maj.-Gen. Solly-Flood, D.S.O., who was destined to raise the fair name of the 42nd to rank with the proudest of the British Army. He had been for a time the director of training at G.H.Q., and this fact filled us with awe but none the less with pleasure, for every sensible soldier knows that success in the field is the product of good training. We expected strafe upon strafe whilst out of the line, but it was a joy to find that the new commander knew that the best results are obtained by instructing everyone down to the meanest soldier in his job rather than by bullying. What could the Manchesters better wish for then, than to have Generals Henley and Solly-Flood? It was indeed a lucky chance that had brought us under his command. The 7th were also able to welcome an old friend in Major Hurst who suddenly rejoined the battalion from England about this period.

La Panne had not altogether lost its characteristics as a pleasure resort, for it was the place where the tired officers of the Belgian Army came for a rest cure. King Albert and the Queen frequently stayed at their residence here in their usual quiet, simple way. The Belgians told you with pride how their monarch could at any time be seen walking by himself about the streets of the town or along the country roads like any other officer in the army. A story was told how a couple of young, dashing French flying officers met the Queen on the beach one day but, not recognising her, started a conversation. She, seeing the possibility of a good joke, invited them to her home, and they gleefully accepted. Picture their consternation when they were presented to the King! Altogether we spent an extremely pleasant fortnight in this place, and it was by way of a study in contrasts that October 20th found us installed in the Redan on the opposite side of the river from Nieuport.

This town is a sister in misfortune to Ypres, but the destruction was even more complete because it was almost in the front line, and shells of all calibres dropped in it well-nigh continuously day and night. Peace-time bridges, of course, had been obliterated, but soldiers had built others to connect up the front line defence, which was east of the river, with the rear. Who will ever forget Putney Bridge? Lancashire men who knew nothing of its parent in London, had now perforce to take a lively personal interest in this wobbly structure. There were two others but they were not so famous as this because they were not so frequently used. Many things can be camouflaged to deceive aircraft, but I think a bridge over a river would tax the most ingenious in this art, hence, although hidden from direct observation from the enemy lines, the Hun had the exact position of these bridges, and, what was more disconcerting, he also had the exact range.

So he "dusted" them at irregular intervals with various calibres, and trips across resembled the noble game of running the gauntlet. This portion of night reliefs was naturally particularly exciting. The late Lt.-Col. Marshall, V.C., when second in command to the 6th L.F.'s., provided an amusing story for the division one day when a couple of officers failed to salute him in the middle of Putney Bridge, he walking calmly across, and they—obviously hurrying. He pulled them up and strafed them duly, then, to force his point, he stood on the bridge and caused them to pass him two or three times in a dignified manner and salute him correctly. Luckily the Boche did not interfere in this little humorous interlude.

The Redan was a large triangular redoubt, with the base resting on the river and having an artificial moat through the middle and on its other two sides. It had been built many years ago to defend Nieuport and in this war had played its part. The enemy had paid a good deal of attention to it with heavy shells so it was considerably knocked about.

Most of the concreted dugouts, however, were still intact, and they served to house a good portion of the 7th in their support position. Headquarters inhabited the ever famous Indiarubber House. This resembled an innocent barn in appearance, and the Hun had hit it hard many many times, but his shells had only bounced harmlessly off the solid concealed concrete—hence its name. The French, in the quiet days, had "done themselves well" here, and we thanked them for the excellent supply of electric light which they had handed over.

It was when we took over the front line, however, that the real meaning of the Nieuport sector was revealed. The ground was torn and devastated like the Salient, but here the destruction and misery was increased by floods, ever present in a greater or less degree. It had been impossible to dig in the low ground, so the defences consisted of breastworks which had been very much battered since the enemy had established his superiority here in guns. Over this area the Boche had uninterrupted observation from the ruins of Lombaertzyde, which lay on slightly higher ground just within his lines. It was thus practically impossible to move about by day, for the sight of khaki brought down a hurricane of whizz bangs, special batteries being apparently told off for sniping of this nature.

Further, as we lay in a very sharp salient just here our men could be plainly seen behind the breastworks by the enemy on their right rear, and these people indulged in long range machine gun sniping. Since our purpose was a "peaceful" one in this sector, we could see no value in inviting the enemy to indulge in artillery and M.G. target practice on us, so we lay "doggo" during the day. Everything had to be done at night, and runners to the companies found this their busiest time, wading thigh-deep through stretches of water, and picking their way amongst innumerable shell holes in search of Company Headquarters. This front also lent itself to heavy trench-mortar work by the Hun, and "minnies" were constantly stealing over with evil intent to batter down our flimsy breastworks.

Battalion H.Q. and the signallers will probably not easily forget the morning when they found themselves the objective in this kind of work. One shot dropped plumb on the H.Q. concrete shelter, half removing the roof and scattering the contents of the orderly room in a disrespectful manner, whilst the next one pushed in the signaller's dug-out, wounding L.-Cpl. Wild. It was the *sang-froid* of A/R.S.M. Clough on this occasion, coupled with his sound work generally in the line, which earned for him the Belgian *Croix de Guerre*.

Although the casualties were nothing like so numerous, still our men agreed that for general conditions they preferred the Ypres sector to this, and it certainly was a most depressing spot. One of the great troubles was the number of canals, which, owing to the destruction of the dams and locks, etc., were now affected by the tides, causing them to overflow and flood our defensive works. This was another source of glee to the Hun, and he played a most amusing game—to himself—of allowing us to build up a dam and then promptly knocking it down with 5.9's and 8's.

One night, a new officer to the 7th, 2nd-Lt. J. H. Milne, was in charge of a working party on one of these jobs when they were suddenly subjected to heavy shelling. The dam was smashed and Milne found his party broken up on each side of the canal. Realising that one or two of the men on the opposite side of the canal to himself had been hit, he, along with Sgt. Heath and Pte. Titchener, scrambled across, although the shelling had not ceased, and looked after them, getting them to places of safety. Milne received recognition for this, while Sgt. Heath and Pte. Titchener were awarded Military Medals.

On the night of November 1st a most unfortunate incident occurred. We were out in support again and were to relieve the 5th the following night in the front line, the usual advance parties having been sent up. Lt. Sievewright had gone up for "B" company, and whilst there some scheme had been suddenly formed to go out a short distance to examine new wire that had been put up. The party had ventured out beyond the wire, however, and were suddenly assailed with a hurricane of bombs from what appeared to be an enemy patrol or covering party. Sievewright and two officers of the 5th were killed and two other ranks wounded. It was an exceedingly unfortunate event for it was quite an impromptu venture and it would appear that the usual patrol precautions had not been considered so seriously as they would ordinarily have been.

This was a strange front, however, and extraordinary things happened, our brigade not being the only one to suffer from mishaps, for on another night the commanding officer of the 8th L.F.'s, whilst visiting his outposts wandered into a Boche post and was never seen again, while the late Lt.-Col. Marshall, V.C. (previously mentioned) did the same thing, but after a short scrap with a Hun he managed to get away.

We had the 2nd Matrosen (Naval) division in front of us, and they were really an enterprising lot. Undoubtedly our pressure upon

Paschendaele was making the German nervy on this sector, and he was under an obligation to keep alive and display a vigorous activity. Further, his morale was considerably heightened by the Teutonic success in Italy which his wireless sets were busy blazoning forth to all the world. This will account, therefore, for the sudden arrival of an enemy patrol outside one of our isolated posts one night. They flung in bombs over the scanty wire, inflicting casualties, and then rapidly departed. This was a sting which had to be avenged, and while the 5th were in they took first toll by meeting a Hun patrol in No Man's Land, and after fighting it out returned triumphant with two prisoners, who proved to be Bavarians, thus giving a valuable identification. When we took over, our chance came very soon for a patrol was met on the same game as before.

The result was discomfiture of the enemy and the capture of a wounded petty officer of the Matrosens. From these two events we could approximately deduce the enemy divisional boundary. The next night, determined to assert our superiority over the Boche, another of our patrols from "A" company, journeyed forth, got through his wire, located a post, and then filled it with bombs.

After seventeen days of amphibious soldiering in front of Nieuport we were relieved by the 125th Brigade, and went back for a welcome rest to huts near Coxyde. Rumours drifted around about accompanying the 41st Division to Italy, but they did not materialise. Bitterly cold weather suddenly arrived, however, which made us aware of the flimsiness of the French huts in which we dwelt.

CHAPTER 6

An Interlude

The 42nd Division added to its list of new experiences when it was relieved at Nieuport, by a division of French troops. We afterwards heard that they had demonstrated their capacity for common sense in warfare by evacuating all the horrible ground in front of the Redan, which we had clung to with characteristic British bull-dog tenacity.

Lt.-Col. Carr, D.S.O., having proceeded on leave, Major Allan commanded the battalion during the succeeding days. It was found later, however, that the C.O. would not return, having been placed on the sick list at home. The division was destined for Bethune and it was a very pleasant five days' march that took us to that area. On the first day, Nov. 16th, passing through Leffinckoucke, near Dunkirk, we reached Teteghem, while the next day took us to Esquelbec, just outside Wormhoudt. The following two days required only short distances to the Hazebrouck district, but the fifth day was longer, and, marching past the divisional commander in Aire, we arrived at Mazinghem, a small village just off the main Lillers road.

The battalion spent a few days here, and a really happy time it was. The villagers had not become blasé to British soldiers, and they gave our men a hearty welcome in their billets. It was with no small pride that the curé, with whom the padre and myself were lucky enough to be billeted, informed us that General Pètain had at one time spent many happy days in his house, for his uncle had been the curé here. Whilst in this village we received the news of the wonderful Cambrai attack by General Byng, and we had a curious feeling that he had no right to do that without asking the 42nd to help him, for we naturally possessed a fatherly interest in Havrincourt and all its works. The first flush of news gave us no details, and we were perplexed to know what had happened to "Jerry's Wire" which we knew was formidable enough. Then the stories of tanks upon tanks drifted through, and we began to understand it.

It was here that Lt.-Col. Bromfield, of the Leicestershire Regt. first saw the 7th and assumed command. He was due for leave, however, and had just emerged from a trying time at Paschendaele, so Major Allan was soon left in charge once more. We did not remain long at Mazinghem for our duty was to relieve the 25th division in the line at Givenchy, before La Bassee. As everyone knows, this was one of the sectors of the original British line so that everything connected with it was essentially English. Since the fighting at Festubert in 1915 comparative peace had reigned along this front and we were content to allow it to remain so after our noisy experiences at Ypres and Nieuport.

Givenchy was once a mining village situated on a spur of the Aubers Ridge, which, running west to east, looks down upon the flat ground, stretching uninterruptedly northwards through Festubert, Neuve Chapelle and Laventie towards Armentieres. Someone had facetiously suggested in the trench diary (a beautifully bound document that had been handed down from battalion to battalion from early days) that "Givenchy Church be kept in a state of repair for the Huns to register on," and therein lies an important fact. Had the church tower been standing, and one could have got into it, a glorious view of a large part of Northern France would have been obtained. Looking eastwards one saw La Bassee half concealed by thick woods while to the northeast were the outskirts of Lille. Southwards and south-west were the mining villages of the Lens district with their huge conical fosses. In other words, Givenchy was an important tactical point and the fiercest efforts of the Boche in 1914 had failed to move British troops from it, although at the end of the fighting it lay in a very sharp salient, which was only straightened out after Festubert in 1915.

Since those days typical old-fashioned trench warfare had prevailed. There were wonderful ramifications of trenches, front line, duplicate firing line, support trenches, reserve trenches, and numerous communication saps, all built on the old style with numerous sandbags. On the flat ground to the north it had been impossible to dig down for defence, and both sides had built up earthworks on the somewhat marshy ground, so that sandbags were again the most noticeable feature. Running behind the breastworks in this portion was a convenient trench-tramway—for rations, ammunition, etc. To the south of Givenchy were the famous La Bassee Canal and the brickstacks.

When mankind started to fight each other under the earth, as well as on it and above it, No Man's Land in front of Givenchy began to be really churned up. Huge craters had been blown up by both sides in such numbers that they formed the most distinctive feature of this part of the line. The whole of the ground across the ridge between the lines presented the appearance of a model of the Alps on a rather large scale. These craters had to be carefully represented on all trench maps, and they bore distinctive names such as Warlington Crater and Red Dragon Crater. Both sides had pushed forward saps as far as possible through this difficult ground both for observation and sniping purposes. Great mine shafts extended under No Man's Land, and the curious could go down these and listen to the Huns knocking about and digging above.

The great advantage of the quiet nature of this front was the possibility of daylight reliefs, so it was in the afternoon of November 27th that the 7th dribbled across "Westminster Bridge" over the canal, and took over the support positions evacuated by the 1st battalion Wiltshire Regt. in the vicinity of "Windy Corner." We were astonished to find cottages and rows of houses, very little damaged, within 600 yards of the front line, and we reposed comfortably on wire beds inside them instead of in holes in the ground. In fact, across the canal, just behind Harley Street, and at an equal distance from the front, there still lived a Frenchman with his wife and kiddie, who dispensed eggs and chips to hungry Tommies! Surely this must be a "*bon front.*" I am afraid things looked vastly different after the Hun attempt to smash through the 55th division here in the following April. It was with the probability of this attack in view that the 42nd division began to stiffen the defences, and as well as holding the line we interested ourselves in digging, concreting and wiring.

G.H.Q. were convinced that Germany would in the Spring make a supreme effort to break up the Western Front before the American Army became an effective force in the field. The offensive spirit was to be kept in our pockets for a short time, and we were to turn our attention to the defensive idea. They had also decided that a system of "defended localities," skilfully sited and constructed, would be the most effective method of breaking up the attacking hordes. That is, the British front would consist of a series of posts, each self-contained, but mutually supporting, that would act like a huge breakwater to the Hun waves. In accordance with this general idea, the line near La Bassee was reconstructed, and a good deal of hard work was put in during those winter weeks. Later, when we heard how well the 55th division had stopped the enemy in the localities that we had done so much to perfect, we felt a good deal of pride and satisfaction that they had proved a success, and complimentary messages were exchanged between Maj.-Gen. Solly-Flood and Maj.-Gen. Jeudwine, commanding the 55th division. A combination of the work and fighting qualities of Lancashire men had been too much for the Hun.

It must not be imagined that it was all a bed of roses on this front, for the enemy had his unpleasant moments, particularly at night. There was a steady flow of irritating casualties, and when Corporal O'Connell and Pte. Bowie of the regimental police were killed at headquarters one night, we felt that old familiar faces might not be so permanent amongst us as might be supposed. The cruel disruption of war was ever present. Still we had the satisfaction of knowing that the Boche received as much and more than he gave. The battalion snipers occasionally registered hits, and in this type of warfare there was plenty "of good sport" to be had owing to the short distance across No Man's Land and the large gaps in the sides of the enemy trenches. Our gunners also indulged in sniping with good results, and it was exciting to watch the rapidity of the sequence of two or three grey figures jumping out of a trench and the bang, bang, bang of an 18 pounder shell or two in their close vicinity. But our excitement must have been as naught compared with that of the aforesaid grey figures!

The reliefs in this "model sector" came round like clock-work. A battalion did four days in the front line, four days in support, four days in the line, and then four days in brigade reserve. After thirty-two days of this the brigade went out for sixteen days in divisional reserve. It was all so beautiful and soothing that it seemed as though the problem of perpetual motion had been solved and the war had come for an eternity. The enemy did the same thing, and we knew when he did it. He left us alone on relief days and we returned the compliment. Thus on December 9th we effected a peaceful passage into brigade reserve at Gorre Chateau. In a noisy sector this chateau and all the village in the vicinity would have been reduced to ruins, but here the civilians had not been interrupted in their daily work, and the chateau itself was a wonderful billet for troops, accommodating the whole battalion comfortably. In fact, nearly twelve months later orderly room received bills for the use of the electric light in the officers' mess!

Whilst here Major Allan was sent to hospital, from which he was eventually invalided to England, and did not return to the battalion again. He had had a long, useful career with the 127th brigade since the middle of 1915. Family affairs had caused the regretted departure of Lt. G. W. Franklin, and his place at the head of the transport was taken by Lt. Wilkinson, after a brief period of duty by Lt. C. R. Thorpe. Col. Bromfield returned from leave just after we went into the line again at Givenchy after the four days' rest. This spell in the line was marked principally by cold, frosty weather and most of the battalion figured in the trenches in wonderful fur coats popularly known as leather jerkins.

The Manchester brigade were fortunate again in being out in divisional reserve for 'Xmas. Excellent fare was provided for the 7th in the shape of turkeys, pork, 'Xmas pudding, extra vegetables, barrels of beer and extra rum rations, so that hilarity was the order of the day. There being a good deal of snow about at this time tactical exercises frequently took the form of intercompany snow-ball fights. To have Major Hurst with us during this period previous to his departure on Courts-martial work could not have been more opportune, for he had ever been most energetic on the social side of the battalion.

With reminiscences of his impromptu concerts and lectures on Gallipoli and in Egypt we knew we should not look in vain for something from him. His was the master-mind behind this Yule-tide festivity, while a delightfully funny sketch written by him in which Gwendoline de Vere of Greenheys Lane figured prominently, gave the officers and sergeants of the 7th an opportunity of displaying their dramatic skill. The inhabitants of Bethune, where most of the brigade were in billets at this time, will not easily forget the efforts of the 127th brigade to make the most of its 'Xmas rest. The Boche made unpleasant contributions to the proceedings by way of long range shelling by day and bombing by night, but although the 8th and the civilians suffered somewhat by these displays, the 7th escaped practically unhurt.

In the opening days of the New Year we returned to the line in the Brickstacks sector south of the canal, and the heavy snow and frost having been succeeded by a sudden thaw accompanied by rain, the condition of the trenches in the low ground can be better imagined than described. Leather jerkins were quickly supplemented by "boots, gum, thigh," and the British soldier came to assume the appearance of a Yarmouth fisherman. Runners, etc., arriving at company H.Q., would first demand from the harbour master permission to navigate their course through the troubled waters, while facetious notices indicated times when pleasure boats could be taken out. This amphibious warfare was extremely unpleasant, and it further delayed the work on the new defensive positions.

Captain Jimmy Baker and Lt. Jack Morten, whilst on a midnight prowl in No Man's Land almost met with disaster, and the performance came to an undignified close after they had extricated one another from deep muddy water to make their way back to dock minus gum boots. We knew that the Huns must be in a similar predicament, for their ground was equally low, and we could only laugh when on one occasion dawn revealed one or two of them jumping about in the open in attempts to dry their clothes and to restore life to their numbed bodies. It hardly seemed the game to fire upon them.

Kindness to a German is often misplaced, as we found when his "travelling Circus" of heavy trench mortars arrived. Having unobtrusively got these weapons into concentrated positions near his support line he suddenly loosed them all off one afternoon at an extremely annoying and rapid rate of fire, peppering all the trenches that we had spent such time in getting into habitable condition. It was a nerveracking experience while it lasted but the 7th stuck to their posts ready to meet any Hun attack should it develop. What the enemy had really intended was never quite understood, but a small party of Boche got across No Man's Land that night. One of "B" company's posts saw them, however, and attacked them.

One German got into our trench and Pte. Saunderson chased him but failed to get him. Jerry, in his hurried departure, left behind him his cap and one or two other articles and these, together with a collection of battered trenches and a few slight casualties, were the only souvenirs we got out of this "stunt," with the exception of the M.M. awarded to Pte. Saunderson, for his plucky conduct. The divisional commander was in the battalion area at the time, and he afterwards sent us a congratulatory message on the steadiness of the men, a compliment of which we were justly proud.

On January 22nd we moved out to Le Preol into brigade reserve. The 7th were particularly fortunate in coming out of the line at this time, for we did not go in again before the whole division was relieved. After our allotted period at Le Preol it was the brigade's turn for divisional reserve, and this was accompanied by another move back to Hingette, near Locon. One of our functions in this position was to back up the Portuguese if they should be attacked, for they lay on the left of the 42nd. This entailed a careful reconnaissance of all the ground behind their positions, and the siting and construction of defended localities in that area. So the battalion found itself digging and wiring once more in new soil.

The 55th Division, having recovered from the severe handling they had received in the enemy reply to "Cambrai," eventually took over the line, and on February 12th the 7th marched back to Burbure, near Lillers. The end of the 42nd's tour of duty in this sector had been marked the previous night by a highly successful raid by the 9th Manchesters which had taken the Boche completely by surprise, and had furnished quite a number of prisoners and machine guns. The warning rumblings of the German offensive storm now steadily increased to a marked degree. His guns were growing in number, range and activity, and what had once been peaceful back areas were steadily becoming more uncomfortable. This was displayed all along the front, so that it was impossible to deduce from that fact alone where his blow would fall. There was a good deal of suspicion, however, about the Portuguese front, and the duties of the 42nd, as 1st Army reserve, were clear if the attack took place there.

Eventually the division, without having to move again, became G.H.Q. reserve, which meant that we were liable to be sent to any part of the British line when Germany commenced to strike. With the aid of motor buses, parties of officers and men made reconnaissances of the defended localities behind the Loos and Hulluch sector, so that by now we were more or less conversant with the larger part of the 1st Army front. The divisional commander lectured officers and N.C.O's. of all brigades concerning the work of defence, and it was about this time that he instituted the divisional motto:—*Go one better*—which was taken up and acted upon with such popular enthusiasm by everyone connected with the 42nd. In fact, if a coat of arms of the East Lancashire Division had been designed in 1918, the following three features would have stood out clearly:—

During the month of February the drain upon the manpower of the British Empire caused by the war made itself apparent. It was found to be impossible to maintain in the field four battalions per brigade, and a reduction to three was ordered. Then took place the solution of a most confusing Chinese puzzle. Some battalions were broken up, and the fragments sent to others either in the same division or in other divisions, while in the case of many units, particularly territorials, there was a transfer of a sort of *cadre* which was amplified to full strength in its new division. The 42nd Division lost the 6th L.F.'s., the 4th East Lancashires and the 9th Manchesters, and the 8th Manchesters were transferred to the 126th brigade, which was now composed of 5th East Lancs., the 8th and 10th Manchesters, while the 127th brigade was left with the 5th, 6th and 7th Manchesters.

A whole company of seven officers and 200 men of the 2/10th Manchesters from the 66th Division came to wear the *Fleur de Lys,* and we were glad to welcome them as comrades. In the heavy fighting that followed they proved themselves to be good stuff of the regular Oldham type, while they themselves forgot their natural initial heart burnings and grew proud of the Cap badge and flashes that they had adopted.

Our period of rest was divided between Burbure and Busnes, and in both places the *mesdemoiselles* and the *estaminets* were a source of real delight to the men of the 7th. As might be expected, some good, solid training was achieved, and this was interspersed by most enjoyable football competitions and cross-country running. In fact, the middle of March found the division extremely fit.

CHAPTER 7

Stopping the Hun

"Good God! What is the matter with the Boche tonight?" Such were our ejaculations on the night of March 21st at Busnes. The coming of darkness had brought with it the long-drawn out, familiar "A-zoom, a-zoom—CRASH—CRASH—CRASH," of enemy planes but in closer proximity than ever before. Previously they had confined their attentions to Bethune each night, but on this particular evening Lillers was the objective, and plane after plane came over maintaining an almost continuous bombardment throughout the night. An ammunition train standing in the station, was hit, and the terrific explosions that followed at irregular intervals accompanied by huge fires added to the evening's excitements. Next day, wires from G.H.Q. enlightened us. The German offensive opened on the morning of March 21st, the fifth and third armies being engaged. The front line defence had been overwhelmed, but we were led to suppose that the enemy was being held up amongst the defended localities.

We afterwards learnt that intensive bombing of back areas and particularly of railheads and junctions had taken place that night in the whole of the British area. One of the objects of this was to impede the movements of reserve divisions, and when it is known that detailed instructions had been issued for the entrainment of the 42nd at Lillers in case we should be required at some distance, such a policy as this is easily understood. But the German had reckoned without the London omnibus driver, who before the war had served another kind of "General." Arrangements were rapidly completed in twenty-four hours, so that on the morning of March 23rd the whole division, in battle order, found a huge fleet of buses ready to convey them to-"Somewhere in France."

The French villagers smiled confidently at us as we journeyed northwards in the direction of the Portuguese front, but they did not know, poor souls, that this was the only way the large convoy could "about turn," nor did they know, although perhaps they guessed, that the Portuguese front would collapse the following month and they would be fleeing for their lives before the blonde beast. We eventually turned our faces south and rode the whole of that day without stopping over the dusty roads of France. The Hun had been extraordinarily lucky in weather, there having been hardly a drop of rain for more than three weeks, so that the ground was perfectly dry for his operations.

Nightfall found us still travelling, and the day of 24th March had almost broken before we "debussed" to find ourselves in the devastated area of the Somme lands, near the village of Ayette. There was no rest to be had. Uncertainty as to the situation in front and also as to the future possibilities necessitated an immediate adoption of tactical positions, and the 127th Brigade took up a defensive line, on an outpost principle, to cover the ground between Ablainzevelle and Courcelles. Until this had been achieved no man was able to turn his thoughts to sleep, in fact the sun had been up some hours before this was possible. The day produced a complexity of events in the handling of which Col. Bromfield proved himself to be at once human and masterful. In the first place, a "battle surplus" had to be decided upon.

This was a small group of officers and men, selected as far as possible from each rank and from each type of specialists, who remained behind the line whilst the battalion was in action. In the event of the battalion being obliterated by casualties, they would form the nucleus of a new unit. Choice generally fell upon those who were considered due for a rest from the line. When the necessary officers and men had been abstracted the Company Commanders were Capt. Tinker, "A," Capt. Nidd, "B," 2nd-Lt. Harland, "C," and Capt. J. Baker, "D." Headquarters comprised the C.O., Capt. J. R. Creagh, Adjutant; Lt. C. S. Wood, Signals; and Lt. S. J. Wilson, I.O.; while Capt. Philp, the M.O., and Padre Hoskyns were in confident control of aid post arrangements.

We had now become a part of the third army, and as such we were destined to remain until the conclusion of the war. General Byng was not a stranger to the 42nd, for it was as a part of his corps on Gallipoli that they made their first fight against the Turk. As the reports have it, "the situation was obscure" on this portion of the third army front. As far as we were concerned the 40th Division had experienced a very severe handling but were still fighting gamely. They had recaptured Mory twice and were now expected to be in possession of the greater part of the village, while the Guards on their left were only yielding ground inch by inch. What had happened to the right of this was not very clear. The orders of the 127th Brigade were to go up and relieve some fragments of the 40th Division in Mory on the night of the 24th, and when darkness fell we set out with this object in view, but such plain, straightforward work as that was not to be achieved in these queer days. Events moved quickly and a change in the situation was an hourly occurrence; it therefore devolved upon unit commanders, and as far as possible commanders of higher formations to act with initiative and resource.

The head of the brigade column had reached Gommecourt when word was received that the enemy was attacking again, and there were vague reports that Behagnies had either been captured or was being hard pressed. It was considered inadvisable to continue the journey to Mory, and more important to hold up this possible enveloping movement. We were therefore deflected to the right, and then those things were done which we used to practise on the desert, but never expected to put into use in France. We moved across the open in artillery formation by battalions and finally deployed into a defensive position. Meanwhile the guns were hammering away at S.O.S. speed from their hastily improvised positions either on or near the roads.

The difficulty of all this work was not diminished by the darkness, and it was with some astonishment that we found the 125th brigade coming through our lines diagonally. One or two stragglers from other divisions came in and told stories of heavy enemy attacks, but a gunner major rode back from the front on a white horse, and said the situation was not so bad as these men's reports had intimated. Still, there seemed to be a good deal of confusion, and the 7th were somewhat bewildered, not knowing quite what to expect next. Meanwhile they longed hard for daylight in order to get their whereabouts and some idea of the lie of the land.

As daylight approached on the 25th it was obvious, from the increasing proximity of rifle fire on our left, that Mory had fallen and the line was falling back steadily. Quiet seemed to reign now, however, in the direction of Behagnies. We later discovered that the L.F.'s. had received orders to push on and cover the Behagnies-Sapignies Road, and this they had successfully achieved in the night. At the same time the 126th Brigade was in touch with the enemy in front of Ervillers,

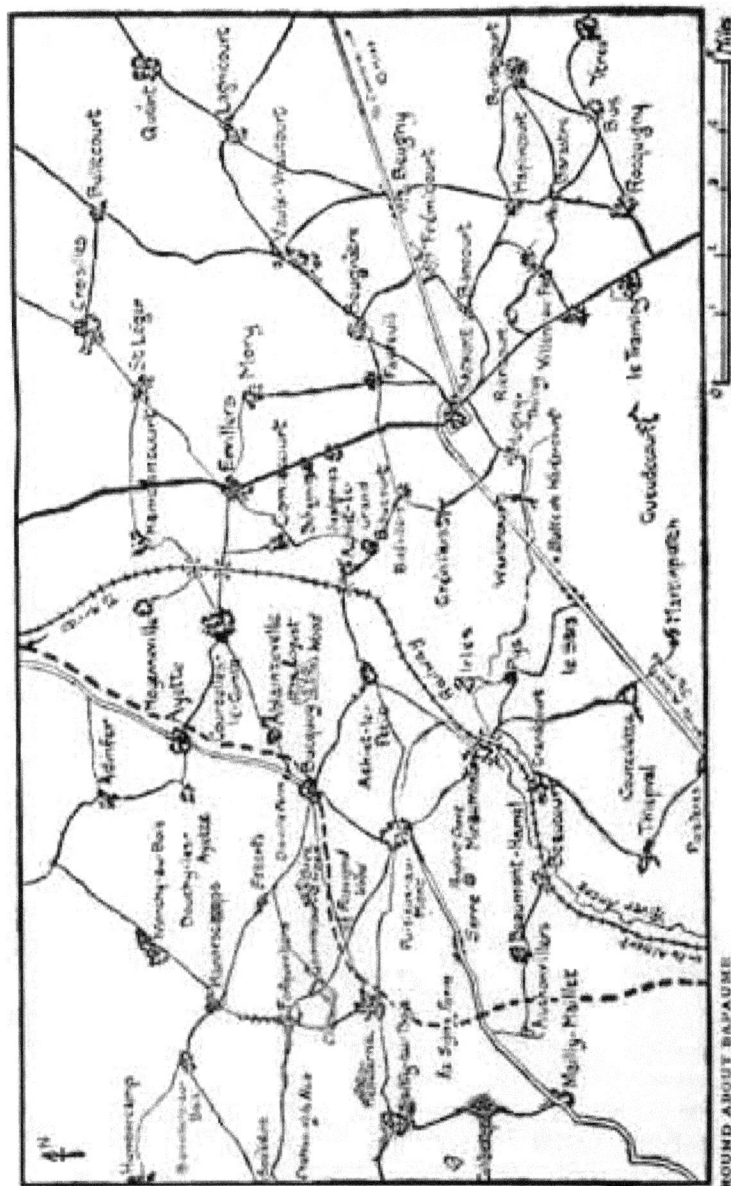

ROUND ABOUT BAPAUME

so that on the morning of the 25th all three brigades were in the front line and were rigging up an impromptu battle with the Hun. The enemy soon made his intentions clear and he commenced a vigorous assault. What troops still remained of the 40th and other divisions, when they found that the 42nd were in position, gradually dribbled through in search of a long-delayed and well-earned rest.

They had been fighting without respite since the morning of the 21st. The 6th Manchesters were now on the right of the division in the vicinity of Bihucourt, but they were uncertain as to the state of affairs on their right. As a matter of fact, although we were not aware of it at the time, Bapaume had been taken and a large gap had been left in the line south of our right flank, through which the Huns were pouring in victorious mass. The New Zealand division and one brigade of Australians, with the 62nd Division on their left were hurried forward, and after very severe fighting stopped the enemy rush about Hebuterne, some miles westward of the position we held on March 25th.

Meanwhile we were in blissful ignorance of our hazardous position and the Manchesters were preserving strict guard over an exposed right flank. The 6th came in for a good deal of heavy fighting in the vicinity of Bihucourt, but they held the village all day. The headquarters of the 7th was in an old shallow dugout close to the light railway that had been constructed from Achiet-le-Grand to run eastwards in the direction of Bullecourt. This railway wound its way through a sort of valley to the north of which lies Gommecourt and to the north-east Mory. Due east on higher ground are Behagnies and Sapignies where the L.F.'s. were making such a fine stand. This high ground continues southwards towards Bihucourt and Bapaume, and it was along this ridge that most of the day's fighting took place.

During the previous night the 7th had been spread out fanwise in out-posts covering the shallow valley, and it was not long after daylight before the enemy began to drop shells indiscriminately about this ground. "C" and "D" companies were ordered forward to assist the 5th and "A" and "B" were left in support. Tanks came up and they courageously crawled out over the ridge and did some very sound work before being knocked out by guns which had been brought up to unwonted proximity. It was whilst crawling out to rescue a wounded man of the crew of a tank that Sergeant Heath, M.M., was mortally wounded. The 127th brigade could not be driven from their positions and they dug themselves in, in small section posts, confidently awaiting nightfall and the next day's fight. The attacks died down and when darkness came, digging parties went up to assist in the work of consolidation. Events as described above, however, had decided otherwise, for about 10 p.m. a divisional staff officer arrived with orders to fall back to a line of defence between Logeast Wood and Courcelles.

Casualties had been fairly heavy in this day's work. Capt. J. Baker and 2nd.-Lt. B. Taylor had gone down wounded, while Col. Bromfield, Capt. Creagh and the M.O. had all been slightly wounded by a shell which knocked in the entrance to the headquarter's dugout. They remained at duty, although the C.O. suffered considerably from an internal bruise in the stomach which made it impossible for him to walk without assistance. The arrangements for clearing the wounded became confused when Gommecourt was evacuated, for there the Advanced Dressing Station had been established. Then it was that the Padre displayed his vigour, courage and resource. He commandeered a hut close to Achiet and had a large number of wounded from various battalions collected there. Eventually he was able to get an ambulance which carried many of them back to the Casualty Clearing Station, but this process suddenly stopped.

All sorts of conveyances were then seized and men were gradually carried back. When the order to withdraw became known matters were critical, but the Padre continued his labours. Difficulties were not diminished when the Hun commenced to drop 5.9's near this spot. Hoskyns was slightly wounded, but he was bound up and carried on his self-appointed task until sometime after the last of the brigade had gone by, leaving him with no one in front but the Hun. Not until the last man had been carried safely off did he leave this place, and then he collected various stragglers and marched them up as a platoon to join their own units! This, and his continuous plucky and considerate work in tending bodily as well as spiritual needs during the next few days obtained for him a well-earned M.C.

The night of the 25th-26th was even more strenuous than the previous one. About 11.30 p.m. the withdrawal commenced, and was very skilfully carried out, so skilfully, in fact, that the German battle outposts could be heard firing intermittently for hours after our troops had retired. After steady plugging, man-handling everything, we reached a system of admirably prepared trenches north of Logeast Wood. The pioneer battalion 7th Northumberland Fusiliers, who had come to the division in February, had been working upon them all day, and, excellently sited as they were, they inspired everyone with a great feeling of confidence. Men took a lively interest in their posts, and after a considerable amount of organisation sentries were mounted and the battalion settled down for a rest until the enemy should arrive. It was now 3 a.m. At this hour it so happened that the division had received another urgent order to fall back still further. Staff officers made their way on foot through the congested roads behind the front and searched dimly for the various brigades, a most uncertain task in view of the rapidity of events. We were found eventually and the brigade major aroused us from slumber to transmit the news.

Once again the 7th rose up, shouldered their burdens, and strode backwards. "What are we going back for? What does it all mean? We held up Jerry yesterday—why retire?" It all seemed very unsatisfactory and we were very tired. Food had naturally been scanty and only obtained in snatches, but much energy was being consumed. It was a disappointed battalion that straggled wearily through Logeast Wood. We were only just in time, however, for advance parties of the enemy were already entering the east side of the Wood as we emerged from the south-west side. Here we found some explanation of things. Col. Wedgewood, of the 6th, reported bodies of the enemy moving forward to strike in on our southern flank, and this news had the effect of an electric shock amongst us.

Col. Bromfield at once ordered positions to be taken up to face the enemy who were advancing from the south and south-east. "A" and "D" companies moved out quickly to seize the high ground and one or two Lewis guns opened fire at the bodies of grey figures in the distance. Meanwhile, however, the brigadier had decided to cover the Bucquoy-Ablainzevelle road, and so touch up with the 62nd division, who had some hours previously occupied a position from Hebuterne to Bucquoy, and were at that moment resisting violent efforts on the part of the Hun to turn our right flank. It was, therefore, in the latter village where we met the gallant Yorkshiremen of the 2nd line West Riding Territorials. Gen. Henley personally assisted in getting the platoons of "B" and "C" companies into position, and then "A" and "D" companies were ordered to withdraw to their line.

When the withdrawal had been completed the 7th were on the right of the division, with the flank resting on the edge of Bucquoy village. The road from Bucquoy to Ayette, which was almost south to north, is an important one and is marked by a row of trees on each side. As one walks from Bucquoy along this road, another road branching off to the right from the edge of the village is seen leading down to Ablainzevelle. The road junction marks the highest portion of ground in the vicinity, and there is a long sweep eastwards towards Logeast Wood and Achiet-le-Petit. It was when we noticed the latter place that the whole irony of the situation broke upon us. Eight months ago we had been enjoying a blissful period of rest on this self-same spot, and such features as we now gazed upon had merely been used for the purpose of containing a supposed enemy in the working out of a tactical exercise—a sham fight. Now—the enemy could not be more real or more alive. He was here with the sole intent of destroying us by any possible method if we would not vacate our position. What happened?

The 7th was assured that this was at last the spot where resistance would be offered. There were no trenches, and the men lay out in the open on the sloping ground east and south of the Ablainzevelle road, with intent to dig in as soon as possible. "C" company were on the right, and they were rather fortunate in being on the site of an old camp, because in these days of modern war it is necessary to dig a hole in a tent even, as a safe-guard against bombing. "C" company then disposed themselves amongst these circular holes, and later found them useful protection when the heavy shelling commenced. "B" company, in the centre, were totally exposed, while "A" company on the left, in touch with the 6th, were almost as bad, although two platoons were able to make use of the sunk road. "D" company were behind in support and could occupy portions of an old Boche trench running east and west.

Headquarters lay out in the Ayette road at first until an old Boche dugout, not completed, was found farther up the road, and then they got into it. Platoons had barely been allotted their areas when clumps of Huns began to appear on the ridge we had just vacated. They proved to be teams of light machine gunners, and without preliminaries in the matter of searching for cover, they promptly opened fire, and soon there was a perfect hail of grazing bullets swishing over the battalion area. German officers calmly walked about directing operations and the whole scene resembled a "stunt on the pictures" rather than modern war. They had made a mistake, though, and if they were seeking dramatic effect it was only short lived.

Our men were delighted at the perfect target they presented on the skyline, and rat-tat-tatted merrily in reply to the Hun swish. By this time also "D" company of the Machine Gun battalion had taken up a position and they also joined in the conversation. The enemy then considered the advisability of concealment, and he disappeared from view. Small parties of his infantry meanwhile had dribbled forward, considerably helped by old systems of trenches which extended down into the low ground. Our men were ready, however, and met them with a heavy fusillade whenever they showed themselves.

Between Logeast Wood and Ablainzevelle was a camp of Nisson huts, which had been protected against bombing, in the usual manner, by thick walls of earth round each hut. The enemy was now making the fullest possible use of these, for they afforded him most excellent protection. Luckily they were on a piece of ground fully exposed to us, and we were able to get some idea as to his movements in that direction. It was soon evident that they were to be utilised as a stepping stone to a further advance. First, light M.G's. and snipers were brought up, and these dribbled out of the huts into Ablainzevelle, where they established themselves to the discomfort of our men, for they were well on our left flank and could take some of our position in enfilade. The battalion suffered a number of casualties from this cause.

Unfortunately also, our guns had not got a clear conception of the state of affairs, and one battery fairly peppered the H.Q. road with shrapnel, inflicting about a dozen casualties, while others covered our own forward positions with the same kind of shell, and so added to the list. I am convinced that there is nothing more demoralising to a soldier in defence than to come under the fire of his own guns, so, to say the least, these moments were very trying. The difficulty of communicating with the rear caused a further delay in the correction of this serious blunder, and our men had to maintain a grip on their positions whilst subjected to fire from both sides, for by this time the enemy had got his guns up, impudently close to the front line, evidently with a view to a further advance, and was using them to advantage. Some of them could be distinctly seen on the outskirts of Logeast Wood, and it was obvious that most of the others responsible for our discomfort were in the Wood itself.

Further away the roads from Grevillers, Bapaume, Loupart Wood, etc., could be seen choked with masses of advancing Germans. If only we had had a few 60-pounders, what perfect execution we should have accomplished. There were batteries of guns, companies of infantry, columns of transport, staff-cars, and all the impedimenta of a moving army. I expect the heart of every Hun of them swelled with the pride of achievement. They were marching to the last victory that was going to obliterate the hated English and end the war. They were

168

not yet aware that just here there was a row of troops, from right to left, New Zealanders, Australians, Yorkshiremen, Lancashiremen, and Guards, who did not intend to concede another yard of ground.

How we longed for the heavy guns during the days that followed, but they could not, of course, come into action until the infantry line had been stabilised. Weeks later we heard stories of the doings on those roads behind the lines, and perhaps we should not judge too harshly, for traffic control was difficult and there was obviously an excessive demand upon transport. Add to this the disturbing lack of news and the peculiar shape of the front, for whereas we were facing east, the 62nd Division with the exception of one battalion in Bucquoy were facing south, and some explanation may be found for the slight degree of confusion.

The divisional artillery, 18-pounders and 4.5 howitzers, remained faithful to the infantry, and the 42nd gunners never showed up to prouder advantage than they did during those stern days. It was not they who had fired upon us. They were too close to us to make any mistake in that way, for during the heaviest fighting they had their guns within 1,600 yards of the front line, and where cover was unobtainable either for gun or man. Needless to say they suffered very heavily both in personnel and material, for the enemy aircraft soon found them, and they were hammered and gassed mercilessly. Their forward observation officers maintained a liaison with the H.Q. of the infantry battalions, and in addition to courageous work in searching for targets and correcting gun fire they showed the greatest consideration for our needs.

Although the 7th occupied a commanding position it was singularly bare and exposed so that cover was difficult to find. During the first few hours "D" company of the M.G.'s. had all their guns but one put out of action, and almost all their officers and men became casualties. They had pluckily worked their weapons in the hastily sited positions until knocked out—not before, however, they had carried out savage execution amongst the more venturesome Huns, and they certainly had the effect of making the remainder hesitate. The nature of the ground made it difficult also for the battalion observers to work, for it was evident the enemy F.O.O.'s. were specially searching for such people, and the moment they fixed up a telescope down came a hurricane of shelling, the close proximity of the Boche guns making their fire extremely accurate and deadly.

The result was that after the first day's fighting, of the observers only two, Cpl. Maguire and Pte. Wilmer, remained. Not to be daunted by the fate of their comrades they clung to their task, and when shelled out of one spot immediately found another. They kept the enemy under close watch and strung together most valuable chains of evidence as to their movements, gallant work for which both received the M.M.

The signallers also suffered heavily. Wires were difficult to keep in repair but the linesmen continued to go out during the heaviest shelling, while others maintained a system of lamp signalling to the brigade behind a pile of ammunition boxes until a 5.9 dropped plumb amongst them with dire results. Other signallers at once found a new spot and kept communication going. But these were searching days for everyone, when physical endurance and mental stamina were stretched to their furthest limit. As the day wore on, the guns that we had seen in the distance gradually came into action against us until shells were raining down continuously on all parts of our line.

Obviously, the enemy infantry had given up the hope of further progress, for our men were like terriers, keenly watching for the slightest sign of a Hun helmet, and the artillery were left to do their worst upon us. Just before dusk the M.O., Capt. Philp, was killed by a shell whilst bending over a wounded man on a stretcher. No cover could be found for an aid-post, and it had to be established in the open at a convenient spot on the ground. In fact, the only dug-out in the area was that occupied by H.Q., and it was shared by Col. Wedgwood of the 6th, so that two battalion H.Q. were confined in a spot no more than seven feet square, while the entrance faced the enemy in an exposed part of the road.

Darkness had brought quiet at last, but no rest. Rations had come up and they had to be distributed. Similarly with ammunition and water. Also the enemy might attempt a night assault, for it was not to be expected that he would be satisfied with this very pronounced re-entrant in his line. The 6th, whose line ran close to the edge of Ablainzevelle, sent a patrol into the village. The small parties of Boche fled at their approach and left two M.G.'s in their hands. Our patrols searched all the low ground in front but could not find the enemy.

Next morning, March 27th, about 9 o'clock, the battle re-opened with redoubled vigour. Fresh enemy troops had been brought up and they made a determined attempt to push forward. A terrific bouncing barrage came down upon our positions, but the men stood up to it, in spite of the heavy casualties, and opened fire upon the groups of Boche who attempted to get across the open. The main infantry assault took place near Ablainzevelle, and here the 6th had the work of repelling them, but after some hand to hand fighting the enemy fell back and confined his energies to sniping and M.G. work. Meanwhile, the landscape was steadily changing its appearance in the 7th sector. What had once been good roads and respectable fields were shell-pitted and strewn with debris, a pile of S.A.A. boxes that had been left behind had been hit and in the fire that resulted there was a disturbing display of fireworks from the exploding cartridges. The trees were losing their accustomed beauty, many having been smashed down completely. But picture the trepidation of the aid-post detachment, now in charge of Capt. Greville, for they lay close to a huge dump of shells that was liable to be hit at any moment. During the quieter days Bucquoy had evidently been an ammunition park, and as not much of the stuff had been removed, it was an exciting spot to fight in.

All day this steady pounding continued, and when the enemy infantry definitely gave up their efforts to get near our line they supplemented the shelling by an unceasing hail of traversing M.G. fire. Yet, through this the runners and stretcher bearers performed their appointed tasks, and there was no period when perfect touch was not maintained between the C.O. and any part of the front line and also back to brigade H.Q., nor were there cases of wounded men being left unduly exposed after they had been hit.

The constant stream of runners, etc., of both battalions converging on the H.Q. dugout, exposed to observation as it was, soon made the truth of the matter plain to the enemy, and he began to pay attention to it with 5.9's. An anxious moment came when he hit the entrance and buried a number of men standing in the improvised steps. All were extricated, however, and those who were wounded carried away. The entrance was cleared, steps constructed again, and the work carried on as usual. "D" company lost its commander again, for Lieut. Morten was hit, and this left Lieut. Gresty in charge.

Evening again brought a welcome respite, and it was decided to minimise casualties by reducing the garrisons of the front trenches, for by now a sort of trench had been made and a little wire had been put out in front the previous night. One platoon per company was taken out and sent back, where they were placed under the command of Col. Blatherwick of the 5th, who remained in brigade support. Daylight of March 28th brought a resumption of the enemy effort at least to straighten his line and masses of Huns could be seen gradually collecting in the Nisson huts. In the previous days the 18-pounders had kept this spot under fire, but Col. Bromfield decided to call for howitzer assistance to smash down the earth walls round the huts, a plan which met with great success. Our shells dropped plumb amongst them, and Huns could be seen dashing about in all directions in search of more effective cover. Our shrapnel barrage had been considerably improved also, and the moment the enemy left their positions it promptly came down and drove them to earth again.

The 7th were worn out, and the men were losing their spruce appearance, but rifles and L.G.'s. were kept clean, and amidst the terrific shelling of that day they asked for nothing better than that Jerry would try to come across to give them an opportunity for revenge. The enemy's guns had increased in number, chiefly the heavy variety, and it was now his obvious intention to blow us off the ridge. The heavy pounding never ceased. Many gallant deeds were performed by runners, stretcher-bearers and ammunition-carrying-platoons through this inferno. Lieut. Bagshaw was awarded the M.C. for his work in leading ammunition fatigues, but the supreme decoration of all—the seal of death—came to a large number of the *Fleur-de-lys*. Amongst the officers—Capt. Tinker, Lieut. Walter Thorp and Lieut. Ludlam were killed outright, while Lieuts. Woods and McLaine were mortally wounded.

After a final effort in the late afternoon to advance against our positions in a line of small sections, which was met with the usual devastating fire, the enemy gave it up and occupied the remaining hours of daylight with fierce shelling. Our heavy artillery had at last returned and got to work and their shelling began to have effect, for it was noticeable that the Boche shells were now arriving from a greater distance than formerly. The 6th had an exciting episode that day. A party of courageous Germans, led by an officer, had pushed forward and were throwing bombs amongst them. Lieut. Mall decided this must be stopped, and he led one platoon over in a short sharp charge.

Fifteen Huns were bayonetted, and Mall returned triumphantly with the officer and one man as prisoners. They proved to be Jaegers, and although the officer told us nothing the man was very voluble. It was some comfort to find that of one fresh battalion that had entered Ablainzevelle, about forty only remained. A couple of packets of Woodbines were found in the pockets of the officer—loot from the canteen at Achiet-le-Grand. The soldier told us that this form of German enterprise was reserved for the officers.

This day, March 28th, marked the end of the heavy fighting. The German thrust had been checked, and the effort to reach the Coast had failed. A glance at the map will show that, had the advance continued here the Arras position would have been seriously threatened, and the Germans would have been well on their way to Abbeville and the Channel Ports. That night the 7th were overjoyed to hear that they were to be relieved. The L.F.'s. took over the brigade sector, but the relief had been ordered so suddenly that there was no time for reconnaissance, with the result that it was almost dawn before the last platoon of the battalion had struggled over the crest line to the old system of trenches 1,500 yards further back in dead ground. Heavy rain, during the evening had converted these neglected trenches into veritable ditches of mud.

A few cubby holes had been constructed by the previous occupants, and filled with mud though they were, our men dropped into them and fell fast asleep. It was the first undisturbed sleep they had had for nearly a week, a period which had seemed more like a month. During the afternoon the battalion received orders to furnish a billeting party which had to proceed to Gommecourt. Billeting—this was indeed bliss. They received a rude shock on arrival however to find that the word was a misnomer. We were to relieve the 15th Hampshires of the 41st Division, who had just been hurried back from Italy. They occupied trenches on the edge of Gommecourt village in support to the front line, which was only about 400 yards away.

The astonishment of the battalion on arrival about 3 a.m., on March 30th, when they found the nature of their new headquarters, can be easily imagined. They were indeed "fed up"—back to the old game, mucking about in a muddy trench, keeping a keen look-out when on sentry (for owing to a gap in the front line a portion of our position virtually was front line), and still shell dodging. We were also becoming rather disreputable for the weather had broken, and mud became the ruling element. In this manner, Easter Sunday was spent. But there were cheering rumours about going back for recuperation, and these kept our spirits up.

April 1st—All Fools Day—we might have known. The brigade went back to the old spot and thus settled all rumours for the present. Our work was not yet done. The 7th went to the support trenches they had recently vacated, but the 41st divisional R.E.'s. had been busy upon them during our absence, and a few habitable bivvies had been made. The 5th and 6th were further back behind Essarts. The Hun had converted Essarts into a perfect hell, and at irregular intervals he subjected it to tremendous bombardments with his largest guns, particularly during the night. Our transport knew something about this, for their road passed through the village when bringing up rations at night. In this connection Lieut. Wilkinson distinguished himself by the courageous manner in which he got his column through during the most anxious moments. His job at this time was not an enviable one, but we could always rely upon his arrival each evening, very seldom late, with his store of rations, water, rum and bundle of letters.

After three days in reserve the brigade took over the front line, in practically the same position as before, but there had been a readjustment of divisional boundaries, so that we were now on the left, while the 125th Brigade were on the right, and their line ran in front of Bucquoy. The 7th were in support at first, so we only moved about 400 yards to trenches vacated by the 8th Manchesters.

At dawn on April 5th the Hun commenced to send over thousands of gas shells in the direction of Essarts. It was a dull, misty morning—perfect conditions for this form of devilry—and we could hear the brutes whistling and whining over our heads for more than three hours. The intention was, of course, to silence our guns, and the object of this was to make an attack upon Bucquoy all the easier. He came over at the L.F's. and there was heavy fighting all the morning, but he did not progress much. The 8th L.F's. suffered severely, losing all their officers, including Lt.-Col. Davies (previously of the 6th Manchesters), who was killed. The enemy's intention had been to take the village and push on with a view to straightening the line, but he only captured the eastern portion of the village, and that only after very heavy losses. Similar progress had previously been made against the division on the right, and this made the L.F. situation impossible.

We afterwards learnt that a large number of gas casualties had gone down from the Essarts district. In their solicitude during the bitterest days the division had called upon the battle surplus of each unit, and had made a composite battalion of them to act in reserve amongst the trenches N.E. of Gommecourt. These people, as well as the gunners, came in for the gas shelling, and it was very disappointing to hear of our own men, like C.S.M. Shields, Sgt. Tabbron, etc., who had been left behind as battle surplus, going down gassed. Fortunately, most of them rejoined the battalion later. During this day's fighting some L.F's. were staggered to find an old French woman in a cellar in Bucquoy, and they had the utmost difficulty in persuading her to leave her "home." That was her abode and she was prepared to live in it whatever the conditions.

The next few days resulted in a complete victory for mud. Rain continued, and work as we would the conditions could not be conquered. Men stood in it, and when they could, slept in it. To move about meant wading through it, in places up to the thighs, and this was steadily wearing out the last flicker of humanity and grit in our men. Casualties were also increasing. Lieut. Bateman was wounded in Essarts whilst on his way back to the battalion from a Course, and in "B" company 2nd-Lt. Woodworth was hit.

Eventually we relieved the 5th in the front line near Ablainzevelle, where we found the trenches in an even worse condition, if that were possible. Real joy possessed our souls, although it is doubtful whether at the time we were capable of appreciating it, when the news was definite that the division was to go right out for a rest. On the night of April 7th, the 2nd 7th West Ridings (62nd Division) came up and relieved us, and the Fleur de Lys set their faces joyfully to the west and marched off in good spirits, although with exhausted bodies, conscious of having done their duty in stopping the mad rush of the Huns.

CHAPTER 8

Worrying the Hun

Never since the weary entry into Katia did the 7th Manchesters present such a sorry appearance as they did when they straggled into Soustre in the grey hours of April 8th. It was an effort to drag one leg in front of another, and our feet were sodden and painful. Almost every particle of clothing and equipment was smothered with red, clayey mud, and thin, tired faces were covered with a many days' growth of beard. Here we struggled into a row of lorries and were carried off to Vauchelles to be housed in huts vacated by some army school. After a good meal and a sleep we were roused in the middle of the afternoon to be told that another move had to be accomplished. With imprecations on the staff and all its works we fell in and marched off to Louvencourt to occupy billets, and were at last assured that we had settled for a rest.

The next few days we spent in recuperation and cleaning up. The rapidity with which the men recovered their smart appearance was one of the striking features of the war, and indicated the wonderful desire for fitness that the Britisher had acquired in his soldiering days. Col Bromfield, however, had not been able to withstand the strain, and to the regret of everyone departed to hospital with pleurisy, a circumstance made all the more depressing when we learnt that his return was highly improbable. A more popular C.O. never commanded the 7th, and we were always proud of his high opinion of us. In his dealings with all ranks, from the second in command to the lowest private, he had ever proved himself a perfect gentleman, while his control of matters during the most anxious times inspired an unswerving confidence. As a gallant leader and commander his name stands high in the records of the battalion.

It was by no means certain that the enemy would not open out with another onslaught on this front, for he was making desperate efforts to reach Amiens further south, and a break through here would make his task much easier. With the assistance of Chinese labour lines of trenches had been dug, and they were speedily wired in by batches of Royal Engineers and Labour Corps. The first system to be defended if the front line collapsed was called the Purple Line.

Behind that was the Red Line, while further back still was the Brown Line, protecting Doullens. It was here during these troubled days that the historic meeting took place between Sir Douglas Haig and Marshal Foch, when the latter took over supreme command. As well as regaining lost energy the 42nd Division had to be responsible for a portion of the Red Line in the event of a break through, so at various times parties of officers and N.C.O's. made trips to it for reconnaisance purposes, and schemes were evolved for the possible disposition of companies and the siting of L.G. posts, etc., under the leadership of Major Higham, now commanding the battalion.

After a week at Louvencourt we moved up into the line again, the division relieving the 37th Division in the Hebuterne and Rossignol Wood sector. No one was sorry to get into a fresh part of the line. We felt that we did not wish to see the Bucquoy-Ablainzevelle road again! For some time now the 42nd had been one of the divisions of the IV. Corps, commanded by Lt.-Gen. Harper, the one-time commander of the famous 51st (Highland Territorial) division, and as such we were to remain until Germany was defeated. We were in goodly company, for the other divisions were the New Zealanders, the 37th and eventually the 5th, but we were never put to shame at any time. Indeed, the spirit of "Go one better" was always amplified by deeds, and by none more assiduously than the 7th Manchesters.

Hebuterne and the immediate district was the "happy hunting ground" of the division until the final grand hunt in August. As in 1914 the village stood on the high-water mark of the advancing tide of Huns. In their last effort they had captured it but the Australians had driven them out again. If a visit be paid to this part of France the reason for its importance to either side will be seen at once, for it stands near the northern end of a commanding ridge which runs north and south, and from which good observation is obtained for many miles in all directions. This was the ridge over which the Huns had swarmed in March, to be thrown back again, after a severe dispute, by the newly arrived Anzacs, so that the present position was good for us but poor for "Jerry." Hebuterne was the culminating point of a

177

very pronounced Hun salient, and our line swept round in a notice-able curve from the corner of Bucquoy to Beaumont Hamel, almost touching the south-eastern edge of the village.

Looking north was the famous ground where Gommecourt had once stood. In 1917 the French had decided that Gommecourt should be preserved in its battle-scarred state as a national monument, for the blood of many brave soldiers had there been shed during the fierce Somme fighting of 1916. Notices were put up, huge white boards with black printing in French and English, enjoining no one to in-terfere with the trenches and wire, etc., but to leave things just as they were. Oh, the irony of it! Here was the Hun again pounding, pound-ing with fierce wrath and insistent desire to smash his way through. Those self-same notices were shell-shattered, while in his zeal to de-stroy the dug-outs which he knew so well in Gommecourt, for he had made them, he dropped, in one morning, more than thirty 15-inch shells in the village.

To the right of Gommecourt could be seen the naked stumps of Rossignol Wood, a beautiful name reminiscent of delightful summer evenings. But the song of the nightingale was now gone, and the only tunes to be heard were the deadly rat-tat-tat of Boche machine guns and the fierce hissing of our shrapnel bullets through the decayed un-dergrowth, the time for this devil's music being regularly thundered out by the crash, crash, of heavy howitzers.

East of our ridge, and parallel to it, was a long gentle valley. In the old days the Germans had been content to build their trenches half-way up the eastern slope, and the French had faced them on the op-posite side, but now the Huns in the foolish arrogance of their hearts must needs swarm over the whole valley, and offer themselves and their works as targets for our searching gun-fire. On the summit of their ridge and due east of Hebuterne is Puisieux-au-Mont, in almost the same condition of devastation as Gommecourt, while further be-yond, the trees of Achiet can be seen.

During the summer months those who wished could reckon up the times of arrival and departure of trains at the German railhead at Achiet, for the smoke from the engines could be distinctly observed. Night after night our planes droned heavily over to the accompa-niment of wonderful displays of "flaming onions," parachute flares, searchlights, and anti-aircraft gun-fire, and bombed these back areas with demoralising effect. Further along the enemy ridge to the right, and closer in, was what the trench maps grimly described as "Serre (site of)."

If you want testimony of the complete destructive power of British shell-fire, go to Serre. The roads round about were marked on these maps, but ironically labelled "Damaged by shell-fire." I think the word "obliterated," openly admitted in the case of one or two, would have applied to all. In other words the whole terrain bore the traces of the thunderous days of 1916, and nothing of value was left standing. Thus, when keen observers set their maps and scanned the low ground for Mark Copse, Luke Copse, Touvent Farm, Observation Wood, or Red Cottage, there was nothing visible. It was all a myth. Further south the masses of white chalk thrown up by the historic crater at Beaumont Hamel were useful for they served as a landmark and helped to locate other points of interest.

Compared with the enemy we were in a relatively happy position. The ridge which contained the front line shielded all the immediate back area from direct observation, so that even the garrisons of the support trenches could wander about in the open, while if there was "nothing doing," the men back in reserve could lie out in the long grass and bask in the sunshine. This was all very comforting and re-lieved the strain of war very considerably, but the advantages in the matter of organisation were illimitable. Rations came up in the middle of the day, and the limbers and water carts, in singles of course on ac-count of balloon observation, trundled up the road in the afternoon to a point within four hundred yards of the front line! As the men put it "We were laughing"—especially when the enemy once or twice at-tempted a relief before darkness over their exposed ground, and were severely knocked about for their pains.

But to return to Hebuterne and the days of our first acquaintance with it. Many people were convinced that the Hun would attack again, and our higher command had found support for this gloomy prospect amongst their archives, so that we were enjoined to remain on the strictest qui vive. The first day's work consisted in re-organisation of the line, based upon the principle of defence "in depth." This meant that a battalion, for instance, did not expose the whole of its personnel in the front line to be obliterated in the first shock of attack, but they must be disposed in the best tactical positions, with a slight garrison in front and the remainder ranged along behind.

Speaking very generally a unit was made responsible for the de-fence of an area, and the principle of defence was to hold it, not by successive lines of defence, but by a series of mutually supporting posts arranged chequerwise and in depth. This arrangement was intended to break up the enemy's attack formation, to stop parts of it and to allow other parts to advance, but to advance only in such places as would make them most vulnerable to counter-attack. This principle applied also down to the company and even the platoon. It is easily seen that a good deal of organisation was demanded from the battalion commander, while the smallest unit commander, perhaps a lance-corporal, was left with much responsibility. In view of the possibly impending attack, Hebuterne was hurriedly put into a sound state of defence by the untiring energy of Gen. Henley and his subordinates.

Whilst all this was going on our patrolling was excessively active, and every night No Man's Land fell into our hands right up to the enemy posts. If possible we were to "Snaffle a Hun" with a view to identification and information about the supposed attack, and when it was discovered that the Boche was too alert in spite of persistent small attempts by the Manchesters and the L.F's. this was regarded as good proof by the attack theorists. However, nothing materialised beyond the steady arrival of Boche shells of all calibres, and we were not sorry.

When the brigade moved out into reserve the 7th had to dig themselves into the earth near Chateau-de-la-Haie north of Sailly-au-Bois. In less than twenty-four hours small groups of men had made a hole for themselves, covered it with an elephant shelter, and camouflaged it with sods. It was heavy work while it lasted, but it was necessary to work quickly because of hostile aircraft. A neighbouring battery of 60-pounders were righteously indignant at our invasion, but still the staff said we were to go there, and there we went. On the other hand it was by no means comforting to realise that once the Hun spotted the 60-pounders we should be partakers in the unwelcome attention that would probably follow, so we were quits anyhow.

Luckily the enemy did not see us, or he was displaying a lofty contempt, for after five day's residence the battalion moved up into the line at Gommecourt, having had no mishap. During this period our lists of "Bucquoy decorations" came through, and they were very gratifying. In addition to the M.C's. already mentioned, Capt. Nidd and 2nd-Lt. Harland were similarly rewarded for their work as company commanders. Sgt. McHugh, who had acted as C.S.M. of "C" company, received a bar to his M.M., and Sgt. Heath, who had died of wounds, was decorated in like manner. Twenty-four other men received the Military Medal, their names being recorded in the appendix at the end of the book.

On April 30th the new C.O., Lt.-Col. Manger, of the Durham L.I., arrived. A regular soldier of many years' standing, he was pleased to be sent again to a territorial battalion, for he had learnt the value of these troops whilst commanding the 2nd 9th King's Liverpool Regiment of the 57th Division. He joined the battalion at Gommecourt and Major Higham immediately went down for a rest. There was very little of outside interest during the succeeding days beyond the usual work of consolidation and keeping the enemy under closest possible observation. Still, the battalion was glad to be relieved on May 6th, the whole division coming out for a good period of rest.

The 127th Brigade were given camp areas around Henu, divisional headquarters being at Pas. We made the most of these May weeks, filled with delightful sunshine, and, as events worked out, it was as well we did, for it was the last long rest period we were to get until after the armistice. Important changes took place in the battalion about this time. Major Higham and Capt. Townson, both pre-war officers of the 7th, severed their active service connection with us by being invalided to England, the former's place being taken by Major Rae of the Liverpool Scottish. Amongst a draft of officers that we received from a division that had been broken on the fifth army front was Capt. Allen, M.C., whose original unit was the 6th Manchesters. He was put in command of "A" company. R.S.M. Anlezark, of the 1st battalion, was posted to us for duty, and A/R.S.M.

Clough succeeded R.Q.M.S. Ogden, who had returned to England after a long period of hard and useful work with the 7th. It was not many weeks after this period of rest that another long-standing and popular officer was lost to the 7th; this was Capt. Nidd, M.C. We had always known that his grit and determination exceeded his physical capacity, but his splendid sense of duty led him to ignore this fact, although it was common knowledge that had he so wished he could have been invalided out of the army long before. After severe trials on Gallipoli, a campaign he went through from June to the evacuation (he was one of the very few men to whom that evacuation was irksome), he had had a relapse in hospital in Egypt for some weeks.

The Bucquoy fight, however, had proved too much for him, and he never really recovered from the ill-effects of it. This was accentuated by the death of two of his near and dear friends—Lt. W. Thorp for whom, as one of his subalterns, he had a particular esteem, and Capt. Tinker. The latter was a pre-war officer of the 7th, while Thorp had gone out to the Sudan in the ranks, served through Gallipoli with distinction (*vide* Major Hurst's book) and then received a commission early in 1916. Capt. Tinker's record with the battalion was one of steady confidence. After being invalided to England from a wound received on Gallipoli, he rejoined in Egypt in Feb. 1916, and was immediately given command of "A" company. From that day he had always been amongst us, and, except when on leave or on a course, he was with his company, in the line or out of it. In fact, it was a record of "full steam ahead" until the day he was killed amongst his men.

What Tinker was to "A" so was Nidd to "B" company, and his greatest regret, when at last hospital claimed him, was in leaving the men whom he knew so well. His departure was followed by a long illness, and it was a great blow to his friends to hear of his death after the armistice in his own home at Cheadle Hulme. His name can be added to the long list of victims of the great German offensive in March.

Strict training was indulged in during these weeks, and in addition hot, laborious days were occupied by rehearsals of the manning of the Red Line in the neighbourhood of Souastre, to say nothing of skeleton counter-attacks upon Beer Trench, Rum Trench, and Stout Trench, near Gommecourt. We never knew the point of these names unless they were to act as a stimulant to the vigour of our thrusts, the troops labouring under the delusion that the trenches were filled with the liquids indicated. At all events they were not there during the rehearsals in spite of the hot weather. But if these diversions caused us to attain the boiling point of excitement, the arrival of General Byng on May 21st to witness a special stunt by the 7th almost burst the thermometer.

A source of some interest was the presence of an American battalion consisting of raw troops of three weeks' New York training, to which the 127th Brigade was acting as godfather. They worked diligently and with a keen appreciation of any hints supplied to them by their British friends. Also, not to be outdone by our frequent displays of football, they regularly utilised our ground for baseball, of which game they possessed a few brilliant exponents. We soon grew to like our new allies, and we were rather sorry when they departed to join their own division.

On June 6th the 42nd Division took over the line once more and were not relieved of responsibility of the front until Sept. 6th, sixteen days after the big offensive had commenced. The 7th occupied the part of the front which we knew so well at Hebuterne, relieving a battalion of the New Zealand Division. The "Diggers" had worked hard upon these trenches with the result that they were now in excellent condition. A good spell of weather also assisted in the comfort of the troops. Col. Manger's policy was to give the Hun no rest, and he began to put his principles into practice at Hebuterne.

As soon as we arrived, a thorough reconnaissance of the enemy positions was made, and we began to make preparation for a raid of some magnitude. This was carried out by "B" company, of which Capt. Grey Burn was now in command, and the officers selected to go over with the raiders were Lieut. Wender, D.C.M., who had previously served with the 1st Battalion in Mesopotamia, 2nd-Lt. Milne and 2nd-Lt. Goodier. Goodier had been a sergeant in "C" company, and for his excellent services at Bucquoy had been recommended for promotion in the field to the commissioned ranks, a distinction which came through while we were at Henu.

It was known that the enemy held his front line in a series of isolated posts, each armed with light machine guns. Curiously enough, whether through lack of material or not we never knew, he paid little or no attention to wiring in these days, except in utilising what old wire lay about. One of these posts was located within one hundred yards of our front line in Fusilier Trench, and this, it was decided, should be raided. At 1 a.m. on the morning of June 16th a three minutes' shrapnel barrage was opened on the enemy's trench, while a box barrage of H.E. was placed all round the portion to be raided. At the end of this time the boys leapt over in four parties, three to make for the trench and the fourth to act as support and as a covering party for withdrawal. Then it was found that the shelling had hardly been sufficient for numerous enemy flares went up, throwing daylight over the whole scene, and our men were greeted by heavy machine gun fire. Wender, who was on the right, jumped over first and rapidly dashed off for the Boche trench, leaving his men well behind. He was never seen or heard of again, and it must be presumed that he was killed in the trench.

Goodier got his men across on the left and they jumped into the trench, only to find it filled with concertina barbed wire, so they came out again and worked their way along the top to the centre, being by this time heavily bombed. They came to a party of Huns who immediately fled, but Goodier seized one and he and his now tiny party returned triumphantly with their prisoner and with fragments of bombs in their bodies. Milne, having ranged over part of the Boche trench to find no one, covered the withdrawal and then brought his party in. It was an extraordinary show in which everyone had displayed considerable pluck, and the taking of one prisoner had just converted it into a success, but we had sustained a large number of casualties, most of them, fortunately, only slight.

Of the officers, Goodier was scratched, and Milne had a bullet through his arm, whilst among those who were not actually with the raiders Lt. C. S. Wood, the signalling officer, was somewhat badly wounded, his work being taken over later by 2nd-Lt. Smith, and Lt. S. J. Wilson was slightly wounded. 2nd-Lt. Goodier was awarded the M.C., Sgt. Fleetwood and Sgt. Green the D.C.M., while five others received the M.M. for this night's work. This was the concluding page of our first chapter in the front line, for we then moved out to Sailly in reserve.

When the brigade went into the line again it was to take over the sector to the right of Hebuterne on the ridge previously mentioned. The most important feature about this part of the line was La Signy Farm, which lay just below the crest on the eastern side of the ridge. The ruins of the farm building were in Boche hands, but the eastern side of the five hundred yards square hedge that surrounded the grounds ran along our front line. North of the grounds our line was echeloned forward and then ran due north to the corner of Hebuterne. Skeletons of large trees stood up like tall sentinels over the piles of bricks and stones which had once made up the farm buildings.

At the farthest corner of the hedge was a shell-pitted patch of ground in a slight depression marked on the map as Basin Wood. This was known to be honeycombed with deep dug-outs and galleries and was therefore a frequent target for our heavy howitzers. Further south the two opposing lines were almost parallel as far as the vicinity of Watling Street—then a Boche trench. In the dead ground behind our line was Euston Dump, which had gone up with a tremendous roar in the early days of the March fighting, leaving a large hole. Stoke's mortar shells, "footballs," etc., were scattered about in all directions. Not far away from here was the Sugar Factory, which, from the attention it received, the Hun regarded as more important than we did.

The C.O. maintained his policy of worrying the Hun in every possible manner, the fullest use being made of the artillery liaison officers and the Stokes and Newton trench mortars for this purpose. Every night little strafes were planned which must have kept Fritz in a constant state of speculation as to what might happen next. To assist in these annoying tactics a special company of R.E., whose particular devilry was gas, came up and dug in 1,000 gas projectiles behind the support lines. On two separate nights, after everything had been considered favourable, they gleefully let them off at La Signy Farm and its environs, and then disappeared down their dug-outs to gloat over the picture of choking and writhing Huns. We consoled ourselves with the probability that the enemy had sustained more casualties than we had.

On July 8th Corps had a sudden recurrence of "attackitis," and, doubtless at the instigation of a junior intelligence officer, they sent out a frantic request to "all whom it may concern" to ascertain who the enemy were in front. They had feared a relief by large German soldiers who were anxious to smell the blood of the Hated English. This message, or an adulterated form of it, filtered "through the usual channels" and so reached the 7th in the late afternoon. Two hours before darkness it had been answered in the following manner.

Reconnaissance had indicated an enemy post within eighty yards of our line close to where the Serre road crossed it, but it was protected by concertina barbed wire. "D" company were holding that part of the line, and they were asked to furnish a party prepared to go over almost at once for a Hun. An enterprising artillery liaison officer, Lt. Bates, obtained permission to make use of a couple of 4.5 howitzers which he said were new and very accurate, and these, firing graze fuse shells at his correction would smash the wire. The only place from which observation on this wire could be obtained was in our front line directly opposite to it, and here a temporary O.P. with telephonic communication to the battery was rigged up, the garrison of this part being moved off left and right for safety.

It was a nerve-racking experience in that O.P., as may be gathered from the fact that we were trying to hit an object less than 70 yards away! It took over an hour to get a satisfactory result, and then 2nd-Lt. Gorst, Sgt. Horsfield and seven other men, in shirt sleeves and armed with revolvers, hopped quickly over, ran along a shallow trench or ditch, and entered the Hun post. It was empty with the exception of one dead man who had just been killed by one of our shells. He was quickly carted back, but with great difficulty for he was a big heavy fellow, while Gorst and Horsfield searched along the trench both ways for more Huns. None were to be found, however—evidently our inexplicable shelling had scared them off altogether. Still the dead man was good enough for the purpose, for he furnished the required identification, and his regiment was immediately wired to H.Q. There had been no relief, so calm reigned once more.

The spirit of "Go one better" inspired Lieut. Wilkinson and a few of his transport men to perform deeds of "derring do" in the line, for one night they came up and captured a German G.S. wagon from No Man's Land. It lay just in front of our line near the Serre Road and had evidently been abandoned during the New Zealand counter attack in March. A bridge of duck boards was put over the trench and Wilkinson and his men went out and skilfully dragged their prize back to safety. Its arrival at the transport lines next morning was naturally the occasion for great rejoicing and hero-worship, after the sensation caused by dressing up the driver in a Boche tin hat and great coat. On another night Sgt. Aldred with a small party made an exceptionally plucky effort to enter an enemy post and was afterwards awarded the M.M. After eight days of such work as this in the front line we moved out to Bus in divisional reserve to enjoy a most pleasant few days under canvas.

We lost Padre Hoskyns at this period. He had received an order which filled him with chagrin to report for duty as Senior Chaplin to the 6th Division, so he journeyed at once to the divisional H.Q. and told the major-general he would sit on his doorstep until he got permission from him to stay with the battalion. Efforts were made but they were of no avail, and a more peremptory order than the last was received, so he took a sorrowful farewell and departed, followed by the regrets of the whole battalion, and indeed of a good number of the division. *Some have greatness thrust upon them*, was applicable in his case, for he had not sought promotion but preferred to remain a "parish priest" and live amongst the men.

Much the same remark applied to the C.O. who, in the absence of General Henley at Divisional Headquarters, was called upon to take command of the brigade during the succeeding weeks, for he always expressed his preference for battalion work. Owing to the fact that Major Rae was in hospital at this time with the "flue," Capt. Creagh assumed command of the battalion, and Lt. Barratt being on a month's leave in England, Lt. Wilson was temporarily appointed Adjutant. Capt. Palmer, an old officer of the 7th, who had been carrying out important work in England since his recovery from a wound obtained in Gallipoli on June 4th, returned to us some weeks previous to this and was put in command of "C" company.

During our period in reserve the 126th brigade had continued our worrying tactics and had attempted to raid La Signy Farm. They found the place strongly held, however, and after repeated efforts to get to the Hun positions had been forced to abandon the attempt. When we took over the front line from the 10th Manchesters for a continuous spell of sixteen days, we found that we were expected to co-operate at once in a forward movement with the New Zealanders, who were in the Hebuterne sector, and who intended to occupy a shorter line across the valley. The first day, July 19th, found us making preparations for this operation at express speed ready for evening. Lieut. Edge, an old second line officer, was put in charge of a party supplied by "C" company, and they were expected to capture and hold a Boche post about 500 yards away.

It was decided that the silent method would be the best, so artillery support was declined. Edge displayed consummate skill and patience in carrying out this hazardous enterprise, and his difficulties were not lessened by disturbing events on both flanks. All along the New Zealand front, from Hebuterne to Rossignol Wood, an advance was taking place, while immediately on the left the 6th were moving forward and in the process had met with considerable resistance so that a pitched battle had arisen. To add to the troubles the Naval Division on our right had selected this night for a raid near Beaumont Hamel, accompanied with noise, with the result that the Hun put down his protective barrage all along our ridge. Our front line was packed with men who were to go over and dig a communication trench and generally assist in the consolidation when the post had been captured, and how they escaped casualties from this shelling was nothing short of a miracle.

Meanwhile, Edge and his men were creeping steadily forward, and were encountering difficulties amongst huge shell holes, loose tags of wire and a very irregular hedge which they were trying to follow as a guide. Eventually they reached the post and took the enemy completely by surprise. A short rush carried them in and one Boche was captured, but the rest got away in the darkness, leaving their gear behind them. The consolidating party followed up quickly, and covered by a protective screen who lay out well in front in the vicinity of Red Cottage, they dug L.G. positions, fire steps for riflemen and placed coils of wire out in front and on the flanks. A good deal of the C.T. was also dug—quite sufficient at any rate to enable a careful man to crawl down to the new post in daylight. It was a good night's work, and earned a well-deserved M.C. for Lieut. Edge and M.M's. for Sgt. Banahan and three others.

Next day, brigade considered the necessity for careful consolidation of the ground gained by the 6th and 7th, but Capt. Creagh intimated that he wished to make his position more secure by capturing the Triangle, a strong triangular redoubt which lay in the grounds of La Signy Farm, and which dominated the post we had just taken. Permission was granted to carry out this enterprise, and once more preparations were rushed forward and orders made out for the operation to be accomplished that night. This time "D" company, temporarily commanded by Lt. Douglas, was selected to provide the attackers. They were back in reserve, close to Batt. H.Q., and on suitable ground for carrying out a quick rehearsal. Also it was decided that the best method of clearing the Boche would be by bombing. The battalion bombing officer was Lieut. Gresty, who belonged to "D" company, and he was put in command of the attacking party, 2nd-Lt. Gorst, at his own request, being detailed to assist him.

The post captured the previous night was the "jumping off" place, and the plan was to work along the enemy trench to the right, clear it by bombing, and so get to the Triangle. The whole operation was a huge success, and never did the eager fighting qualities of the Fleur de Lys show up to prouder advantage than in the display given by "D" company that night. The unexpected direction of approach took the enemy completely by surprise, for our men had not proceeded far before they caught a working party out in the open. There was a short scrap, but most of the poor Jerries had no weapons handy, and they ran off squealing and chattering like a lot of monkeys, leaving their dead and wounded behind.

Our men pushed on quickly, anxious to make the fullest possible use of the surprise element, until the northern corner of the Triangle was reached. Here they split up into two parties, Gresty continuing the original direction, and Gorst turning along to the right. The latter party found the trench strongly occupied, but the enemy were so oblivious of what was happening that they were busy "dishing out stew" for the evening meal. When they were surprised a few of them indeed showed plucky fight, hurriedly seizing bombs and throwing them wildly in the direction of the attackers.

Others succeeded in grasping their rifles, and Gorst received a nasty bullet wound in the shoulder, but not before he had accounted for one or two Huns with his revolver. Sgt. Horsfield, who understood perfectly the meaning of "Carry on, Sergeant!" continued this part of the show, and the Huns were chased along the trench to the western apex. Here a pitched bombing battle ensued, and very soon the enemy got out and raced across the open in the direction of the farm. Meanwhile, Gresty had led his men over a sort of switch back trench, for it had been so heavily pounded by our Newton T.M's. that it was difficult to make it out at all in the dark.

Nevertheless they struggled along, and finding the far corner of the Triangle occupied, quickly bombed the enemy out of it and proceeded to consolidate. At the same time other parties, each of one N.C.O. and six men, had been detailed in the work of manning various posts *en route*, digging L.G. emplacements, and wiring and constructing of communication trenches. In fact, in a very short time the whole place, which had been a Hun strong point, was swarming with British soldiers busily working to turn round the defences.

Just as dawn was breaking a few Huns effected an entrance into one of the trenches and commenced to bomb the post at the far corner, whereupon the late Lce.-Cpl. Lockett of "C" company, who was in charge of the post at the apex, took a couple of men and promptly counter attacked them. Their leader, an N.C.O. with the Iron Cross and another man were captured, while the rest made off again. Lce.-Cpl. Lockett was awarded the D.C.M. for his sensible and courageous action.

A good many casualties must have been inflicted on the enemy during this night's work for they left a number of dead and wounded behind, whilst several others suffering from slighter wounds must have got away. They left booty in our hands, and the large number of rifles and machine guns alone indicated the strength of the garrison. Our men obtained plenty of souvenirs, but they were sensible enough to hand over anything of military value, which was returned to them after examination by competent authorities. Useful disposition maps, and intelligence reports, to say nothing of piles of letters and postcards were thus sent up for inspection, while during the next few days when visiting the area occupied by "D" company one was greeted by the unwonted scent of cigar smoke, for the Hun was ever a connoisseur on cheap cigars.

Heavy rain during the following days converting our new trenches into a quagmire, the necessity for digging and cleaning up became all the more urgent, although it entailed a heavy strain upon the men under most uncomfortable conditions. As "B," "C" and "D" companies had each "had a stunt" and covered themselves with glory, it now remained for "A" company to do likewise. Their turn came on the night of July 27th, when it was decided to push forward and occupy Cetorix Trench, about 300 yards beyond the Triangle, and so make our position even more secure. Unfortunately there was very heavy rain in the early evening, but the party went out, and after a serious dispute with the enemy, in which 2nd-Lt. Goodier, M.C., was wounded again, gained their objective. What was supposed to be a trench, however, was found to be a sunken road, frightfully shell-pitted, and in a most appalling condition of mud and water. It was not considered worth holding and the whole party was wisely withdrawn.

The La Signy Farm fighting was not yet over, for on the morning of August 3rd, while "B" company were in the front line, the enemy put down a heavy barrage on all our positions, particularly on the Triangle. Then, just as dawn broke, a party of about forty Huns rapidly started across No Man's Land, but the 7th were too much for them. They stuck to their posts and rapidly emptied Lewis guns and rifles amongst them, and when they were sufficiently close greeted them also with bombs. The Boche became disorganised and scattered, some groping about for gaps in our hastily constructed wire, but it was a hopeless business and the remaining plucky ones cleared off in disgust. Then Lt. Pell-Ilderton followed out with a small party, and finding a couple of dead brought them in. The Huns had carefully removed all evidences of identification before the venture, but one man had a black and white cockade in his cap, which proved him to be a Prussian. As the previous division was known to be Wurtemburger, we immediately notified this fact to H.Q. Further proof was afforded by a slightly wounded Boche who, having apparently got lost, had wandered into a post occupied by the 6th.

That day we were relieved by the L.F's. and went back into divisional reserve, this time to billets in Louvencourt, and there received congratulations from various people for our excellent work during the last long spell in the line. The final incident furnished Col. Manger with an extra battalion motto: "What we have, we hold." For the attack on the Triangle, Military Crosses were awarded to Lieut. Gresty and 2nd-Lt. Gorst, while Sgt. Horsfield, who had already earned the D.C.M. and Belgian Croix de Guerre when with the 9th Manchesters, received a Military Medal. Five other ranks were similarly decorated.

The battalion was augmented about this time by the arrival of the cadre of the 2nd 7th Manchesters. The 66th Division had suffered severely in March and as it was undergoing re-organisation, all the second line units, or what remained of them, were sent to the 42nd division. Capt. Nelson also returned after a long absence since his wound in May, 1915, and was given command of "A" company, Capt. Allen, M.C., having been detailed to take charge of a divisional L.G. school.

CHAPTER 9

Hammering the Hun

SERRE RIDGE AND WARLENCOURT

After a fortnight at Louvencourt the brigade went into the line again on August 18th, this time on the right of the divisional front. During our period in reserve important events had taken place south of the Somme. A lightning stroke, chiefly delivered by the Canadian Corps who had been suddenly and secretly rushed down from the Lens area, had altered the whole aspect of the war, for the German Army, which not long before had entertained such high hopes of reaching the coast and Paris, was driven to anxiously defending his line. Weak spots in the Hun armour were being sought out and pierced so that on the whole the enemy was having a bad time. Anticipating trouble on the third army front he had withdrawn his outposts to a safer line all along the Ancre and up to Puisieux, and our men had been able to walk cautiously forward several hundred yards.

Such was the situation when the 7th took over the front line, at the moment quite unsuspicious of the stirring events in which they were shortly to take a share. Major Rae commanded the battalion, the C.O. being away on Paris leave, while Capt. Barratt had resumed the duties of Adjutant. The Company Commanders for this tour of duty were Lt. C. B. Douglas, "A," Capt. Grey Burn, "B," Lt. Abbott, "C" and Capt. J. Baker, "D." Suddenly, without previous warning, operation orders were received on August 20th for a big attack to commence along the whole army front the following morning. This was rapid work indeed, and the hurried state of preparation can be better imagined than described, especially in view of the extraordinary nature of the barrage which called for most accurate timing and an elaborate barrage table. The manner in which Major Rae and Capt. Barratt swiftly dealt with all these details and communicated their wishes to the people concerned, a task of no small magnitude under more favourable conditions, calls for the keenest appreciation from all who took part in that first important battle.

The division expected to cover, in the first day's fighting, the large mass of high ground which is flanked on its western edge by Serre and overlooks Miraumont on the eastern side. A Prussian division was known to be defending this part of the line. The 7th were to take part in the initial assault in the right brigade sector, while the 125th brigade were on the left. A thick mist enshrouded the land in the early morning of August 21st, and doubtless many men on both sides thought of the similar conditions which prevailed on the 21st of another month when the Hun attacked with such terrible results. Here was the revenge and it was to take place, curiously enough, under like circumstances.

At 4.50 a.m. the attack commenced, preceded by a short but destructive barrage over the enemy position. For the Fleur de Lys "C" and "D" companies led off, their objective being a part of the sunk road running across the front from Puisieux to Beaumont Hamel. It was impossible to see more than forty yards, and this rendered control by the officers practically out of the question. The section commanders, however, in many cases Lance-Corporals and even privates, rose magnificently to the occasion, with the result that touch was maintained and the direction of advance preserved. Short, sharp struggles took place at various points, but the Boche were overpowered, and eventually a good line was established on the objective. "C" company lost 2nd-Lt. Harland, M.C., and Lt. Lofthouse, both wounded, while "D" company, although keeping their officers, had Sgt. W. Brown killed.

The next phase of the battle comprised the attack of "A" and "B" companies who passed through the first objectives and advanced to the top of the ridge. Lieut. H. N. Kay of "B" company was shot dead at close range during the clearing of a dugout in the early stages of this fight, while later on this company suffered heavy casualties, Sgt. Green, D.C.M., M.M., being killed and Sgts. Guttery and Gleeson wounded. On reaching the final objective Lt. Douglas carried out work of the greatest value in the organisation of his company. In spite of the strongly increasing enemy shell-fire he moved about amongst his men with such coolness and disregard for personal danger that his example inspired the men for the strong counter attacks which later took place. For his splendid leadership and initiative he was afterwards awarded the Military Cross. Capt. Grey-Burn and his company on the right were having an awkward time from enemy snipers, but he organised his now small numbers very carefully, and personally kept the enemy under close observation. Seeing an enemy concentration in progress, evidently for a counter-attack, he quickly gave information, and the gunners were able to disperse the enemy with a very effective barrage.

The conduct of all ranks during the counter-attack, which was launched early in the afternoon, was so splendid that it broke up the Hun effort. Later in the day the enemy made another attack with a strong body of picked storm-troops from another division brought up specially from the reserves, but the greeting they received from our rifle, Lewis gun, and machine-gun fire caused enormous casualties, and the attack collapsed. Capt. Grey-Burn was decorated with the M.C. for his share in this splendid day's work. The ground captured in the first day's fighting, representing an advance of 5,000 yards, was consolidated and held for the next two days, during which time the left of the division was executing a turning movement to encircle Miraumont from the north.

The work of the signallers, under Lt. Smith, cannot be too highly praised for their contribution to the success of this battle, because communications throughout the operation were excellent and twice served to bring down a barrage in short time, so assisting the infantry to smash the enemy attacks. The stretcher bearers nobly performed their work under most trying conditions, what with the heavy mist followed later by intense heat, the badly broken ground and the long distances they had to carry the wounded under shell fire. Lce-Cpl. Twist, M.M., of "D" company, performed prodigies of strength and valour in this way, receiving a bar to his M.M., and Pte. Greer, M.M., of "B" company, proved an able second to him. Lt. Stanier was badly wounded whilst with "A" company, losing the sight of one eye.

The next movement was the crossing of the River Ancre in the early hours of August 23rd. This was well done by "B" company, "A" company, now under the command of Capt. Nelson, being in support with "C" company. During the advance, and with the co-operation of the East Lancs. north of Miraumont, large bodies of prisoners were cut off and rounded up on the far side of the Ancre. When the ground had been made good and it was ascertained that the Hun had definitely retired, it was thought that the day's work was done. This, however, proved to be wrong, as a further advance to Warlencourt was ordered, and it was to commence as soon as possible. The 6th moved off about dusk with the 7th in support, and although the right flank was exposed this did not hinder the advance.

The greater part of the movement was carried out in darkness and over strange ground, but the leadership was very skilful and the brigade came in contact with the enemy on the outskirts of Warlencourt about 10.30 p.m. Boche M.G. nests quickly opened a terrific fire, but few casualties were caused. A rapid deployment took place and positions quickly occupied in case of a surprise. The enemy fire, however, increased in intensity, and the cover afforded being of the scantiest, it was decided to withdraw a short distance to a line of trenches and there await daylight. Fortunately no serious losses had been incurred, and when dawn broke it was found that the enemy had retired still further during the night.

At this point the division was pinched out of the line by the Naval Division on the right and the N.Z. Division on the left converging across our front in the next day's advance, and we were enabled to take advantage of a short respite from the struggle. The vigour and effectiveness of the 42nd division's attack has been since proved by an unexpected tribute from the enemy. The following extract from Ludendorf's *Memoirs of the War, 1914-1918*, Vol. 2., page 692, refers to the fighting at this time:—

On August 21st the English attacked south of Arras between Boisleux and the Ancre.... As the offensive developed, the enemy succeeded on the north in pushing us back from the Ancre. At this point a Prussian division ... given a sector covered by the river, had failed badly. This threw the whole line into confusion.... The situation there became extremely critical about August 25th.

The 7th marched back a short distance to Irles, and made themselves comfortable in the German dugouts there for a day and a half. Looking back over those days of new experiences for the battalion one realises the valuable work accomplished by Lt. Wilkinson and his transport section. When out of the line he invariably carried off the honours in the "spit and polish" transport competitions frequently held in the division, but it was on difficult occasions such as these that he showed up to prouder advantage. The transport lines had been brought up to Colincamps, and the distance from there to Warlencourt was about twelve miles. The roads were in an impossible condition so that all supplies had to be carried on pack animals, and the fact that nothing failed reflects the greatest credit upon the administrative arrangements of Capt. and Q.M. Wood and the transport officer.

Villers-Au-Flos

During our few hours' absence from the line the Naval Division had been in some heavy fighting as we saw when we arrived on the night of August 27th in the support position near Loupart Wood. Skilfully sited machine guns had taken terrible toll of the brave naval men, and their bodies still lay where they had fallen, so that one of our first jobs was to bury them. The front line ran along the western outskirts of Ligny-Thilloy, but it was suspected that the enemy would not make a vigorous stand here. His shelling was particularly beastly, however, and if he did intend to retire further he was at least taking the necessary artillery precautions. By August 30th preparations were complete for another forward move, but early morning showed us that the Hun had gone, so we were merely required to follow him up.

The pre-arranged plan was carried out, and after the 127th Brigade had made good the high ground east of Thilloy, in face of some opposition, the East Lancs. came through and took up the advance on what had now become a one brigade front. They had not gone far before they encountered the enemy in strength holding Riencourt, and they promptly attacked it. The 8th Manchesters bore the brunt of this attack and they suffered very heavily, little ground being gained. A brilliant night show by the 10th the next night, however, subdued Riencourt, and this rendered the line sufficiently straight to be able to continue the advance.

The 127th Brigade took over the front again and rapid preparations were made to co-operate in an attack which was to take place along the whole army front. It was now clear that our higher command were not disposed to allow the enemy to settle anywhere, if possible. It promised to be ding-dong work amidst ever-changing scenes, with the guns making the most of their opportunities and struggling over the torn ground behind the infantry as best they might. But the supply services experienced the biggest demand upon their wits and resources, uprooted from their comfortable and secure villages and cast out upon the shelterless land of the devastated area just like the infantry.

Their work was wonderful, however, and very rarely had Tommy occasion to grouse about either the quality or the quantity of the food that was served up to him under these trying conditions. It was common knowledge that when the Boche had come over in March, he had not been so well treated, and had been forced in the urgency of his plight to eat horses and mules killed in the fighting.

It was evident that we had now got the full measure of our foes, and were in the comfortable position of being able to give battle when and where we pleased, and be practically confident of success. The front was becoming shorter also, with the result that a divisional sector was considerably smaller than formerly, and this entailed of course longer periods out of the line for the soldier. Leave also continued to flow, and proved an important factor in keeping up the morale of the troops. How different from the old days, when we used to advertise our intentions to the Hun when a stunt was impending by stopping leave in the army concerned! Capt. Grey-Burn, M.C., went to England for a month on August 31st, and Lt. S. J. Wilson was put in command of "B" company for the coming operations, while in the continued absence of Capt. Palmer, Lt. Hammond was in charge of "C" company. Lt. Smithies, recently joined from the second line, took over the duties of intelligence officer. Col. Manger was required to temporarily command the 126th Brigade, and this left Major Rae in command of the battalion once more.

The next village in our line of advance, now practically due east, was Villers-au-Flos, and this, with the high ground beyond it, was to be taken in the first stride of the coming battle, a matter of 2,500 yards. After this the L.F.'s. would leap-frog through and exploit success as far as possible. This time the 5th and 6th were detailed to execute the first shock of the assault with the 7th in close support. As a matter of fact "C" company were sent forward to act under the orders of the 5th in view of the extra opposition which was expected on the right sector. On the night of September 1st the remainder of the battalion, in order "B," "A," "D," companies moved up close to Riencourt, to occupy old, shallow trenches, and await the needs of the brigade either during or after the assault.

Soon after dawn the barrage opened, and simultaneously the Manchesters advanced accompanied by a single tank. The New Zealanders were carrying out a similar task on the left, while the 17th Division had to get through Beaulencourt and over a large stretch of bare country on the right. The 6th Manchesters progressed in fine style, and everything went according to plan. The enemy put up a stiff fight for it and hung on to the last in the cunningly concealed machine gun posts. It was in this part of the fighting that Lieut. Welch (a one-time 7th officer) with a section of Stokes' mortar men performed a gallant deed that earned for him the D.S.O. The progress of events on the right, however, was not so clear and straightforward.

As was expected the 5th encountered strong opposition, for they advanced along a double row of old German trenches which contained a large number of dugouts, and disconcerting masses of wire at irregular intervals. It was thus difficult to maintain cohesion in the attack, while every dugout contained machine gun crews who had been unharmed by the barrage, and who, owing to the delay in getting ahead, had been able to come out and man their positions without interruption. The 5th, therefore, lost heavily, particularly on their right flank, and before very long "C" company of the 7th found themselves in the front, almost isolated, and taking a stern part in the assault.

They pushed on until all the enemy trenches had been cleared to the south-east corner of Villers-au-Flos, and then stayed in order to get in touch with the remnants of the 5th on their left, after which Lieut. Hammond reported progress. In view of the danger from this flank, for we were already well ahead of the troops on our right, "B" company was ordered forward to protect the southern and eastern sides of Riencourt, and so prevent any Hun attempt to get in behind our forward line. Later it was found that the 5th positions required more strength, and "A" company were sent up for that purpose, while Capt. Baker was ordered to take his company to form a defensive flank behind the 6th, for the New Zealanders were still echeloned to the rear.

Evening of September 2nd thus found the 6th at the tip of a sharp salient, and the enemy still very active in front, with his shelling steadily increasing in intensity. "B" company were thus ordered to continue the advance on the right and attain the final objective, slow and complicated work for it all took place in the dark. First the 1,500 yards from Riencourt to "C" company had to be traversed, and from there it was another 1,000 yards to the required position; meanwhile the enemy was continually shelling with 5.9's at important points and with whizz-bangs promiscuously. Nothing was known of the enemy in front, and the situation on the right was equally obscure. Patrols worked cautiously ahead however and fortunately no opposition was encountered, so that the final objective was made before dawn.

As daylight broke on the 3rd Sept. it was found that the next village, Barastre, had been rapidly evacuated by the enemy who had left a quantity of material behind him. Although the men were dog-tired "B" company sent out a large fighting patrol to try to get in touch with him, but they traversed well beyond Bus, the next village, and returned according to orders without seeing him. Meanwhile a squadron of cavalry (Scots Greys) had been ordered up, and they preceded the advance of the 125th Brigade who by this time were marching through in accordance with previous plans. They encountered Hun rearguards near Ytres, but the attack was resumed at once, and in the course of the next two days the enemy was pressed back into the Hindenburg system in the vicinity of Havrincourt.

The Manchesters had now the opportunity of seeing how great an organisation must follow in the wake of advancing infantry. First came the field guns, drawn by teams of mules, followed by the 6-in. howitzers, bouncing along in jolly fashion over the uneven roads behind motor lorries containing their ammunition. Then the observation balloons appeared, still observing, at a height of about 100 feet, being pulled steadily by motor conveyances. Intermingled amongst these were staff cars, ambulances, motor lorries for all purposes, infantry transport, D.A.C. wagons and various other impedimenta of a moving army. Most of these people took up their abode around Barastre, occupying old British huts, or erecting tents and bivouac sheets, so that ground which twelve hours previously had been Hun land, gingerly approached by us, had become a huge camp seething with an active soldier population of Britishers.

On September 6th the division came out for a long-delayed rest, and marched back to Warlencourt in Corps reserve. A few tents were provided, but only a small portion of the battalion could be accommodated in them, so it was necessary to dig in once more. There was quite a quantity of material about, however, and it did not take us long to make ourselves weather-proof and more or less comfortable. Fortunately, the Huns had not had time to destroy the two wells in the village, although the explosive charges had been laid, so that water did not prove the difficulty it might otherwise have done. A special order of the day from the brigadier admirably epitomised our feelings of satisfaction with our work in the war up to this date, so it would be as well to quote it at length:—

Manchesters,
You have added a new anniversary to those which your gallantry has already made famous. On 4th June, 1915, in Gallipoli,

you forced your way like a spearhead into and through line upon line of Turkish trenches. On 25th March, 1918, at Achiet and Bucquoy, you stemmed and stopped the onrush of the tide of Huns that was to have found its way to the Coast.

Yesterday, after three months of unbroken fighting in trenches and in the open, and in face of stubborn resistance by Huns more than equal in numbers, you stormed and took Villers-au-Flos with the utmost dash and determination; a feat which would have been notable if performed by battalions at full strength and fresh from a period of rest.

When Manchester hears of this new proof of your prowess, she may well be as proud of her sons as I am of commanding such soldiers.

Anthony Henley,
Brig.-Gen., Commanding 127th Inf. Brigade.

3rd September, 1918.

The fortnight at Warlencourt was spent in refitting, and intensive training in attack. One day was occupied by a demonstration of an assault by a company, using live ammunition. This was carried out by "D" company in the presence of the corps commander and large numbers of officers and N.C.O's. of the division, and was followed by educational criticism by the general.

It was obvious that all this had a specific purpose, and we were not left long to wonder what the purpose was. A tremendous battle was brewing, and rumours placed its magnitude at from three army fronts to the whole allied front. Anyhow, the chief thing that concerned us was that the 42nd was to take part in the cracking of the hardest nut in the German defence, namely, the Hindenburg system. The enemy had had three weeks in which to consolidate his already perfected ramification of trenches and dugouts, and there was no doubt as to their determination to definitely stop the British advance there. If this failed they had lost the War.

On September 22nd the division marched up, and took over the front from the 37th Division, the 125th Brigade occupying the forward positions just east of Havrincourt Wood. The 7th found themselves out in reserve just north of the Canal du Nord behind Hermies, and it was pleasing to see the old haunts again. Men thought grimly of the experiences we had been through since those happy days more than a year ago, and these sights served to call up the memory of many a pal who had since made the big sacrifice. And now, perhaps, we should get an opportunity of seeing those mysterious lands beyond Flesquieres, Marcoing and so on, that we had gazed upon so long. As far as possible training was continued and a certain amount of company re-organisation took place.

Owing to the weakness of companies they had been reduced to three platoons, some of these being much below strength. Reinforcements had been expected, but they did not materialise to an appreciable extent. However, the exigencies of the task in hand demanded that the four platoon formation should be adopted in spite of the small numbers. In view of this, therefore, it was necessary to crowd in rapid training in attack on this principle, so that each man should be well acquainted with his function. After the battle surplus had been eliminated the company commanders were as follows:—"A" company, Capt. Nelson, "B" Lt. S. J. Wilson, "C" Capt. Allen, M.C., and "D" Lieut. Gresty, M.C. Lt.-Col. Manger commanded the battalion, while Capt. Creagh had returned and was adjutant. Two days before the attack Capt. Nelson went into hospital with dysentery which had frequently recurred in a violent form during the preceding weeks. A slight re-adjustment was thus demanded amongst the officers to give every company a fair share of leadership and Lieut. Hammond was sent to command "A" company.

Briefly the plan of attack was as follows. The divisional frontage was covered by the 125th Brigade on the right and the 127th Brigade on the left, with the remaining brigade in support. As far as the 127th Brigade was concerned, the attack was to be accomplished in five bounds. The first objective, along the whole of the brigade front, was the work of the 5th Manchesters, and consisted in capturing the German front line which ran chiefly along Chapel Wood Switch. The next four objectives, called for convenience the Red, Brown, Yellow and Blue Lines, were to engage the attention of the 7th on the right and the 6th on the left of the brigade front, and were to be taken by the leap-frog method by companies.

Thus, in the 7th, "C" company's objective was the Red Line, "A" the Brown, "D" the Yellow, and "B" the Blue Line. These lines were by no means parallel to one another, their shape being largely controlled by the configuration of the ground and the German trenches. It is also important to note that the Hindenburg system was being taken in enfilade on this part of the front. Two or three great parallel trenches ran along in the direction of the advance, and they were full of deep dug-outs capable of holding thousands of men. Our main security lay

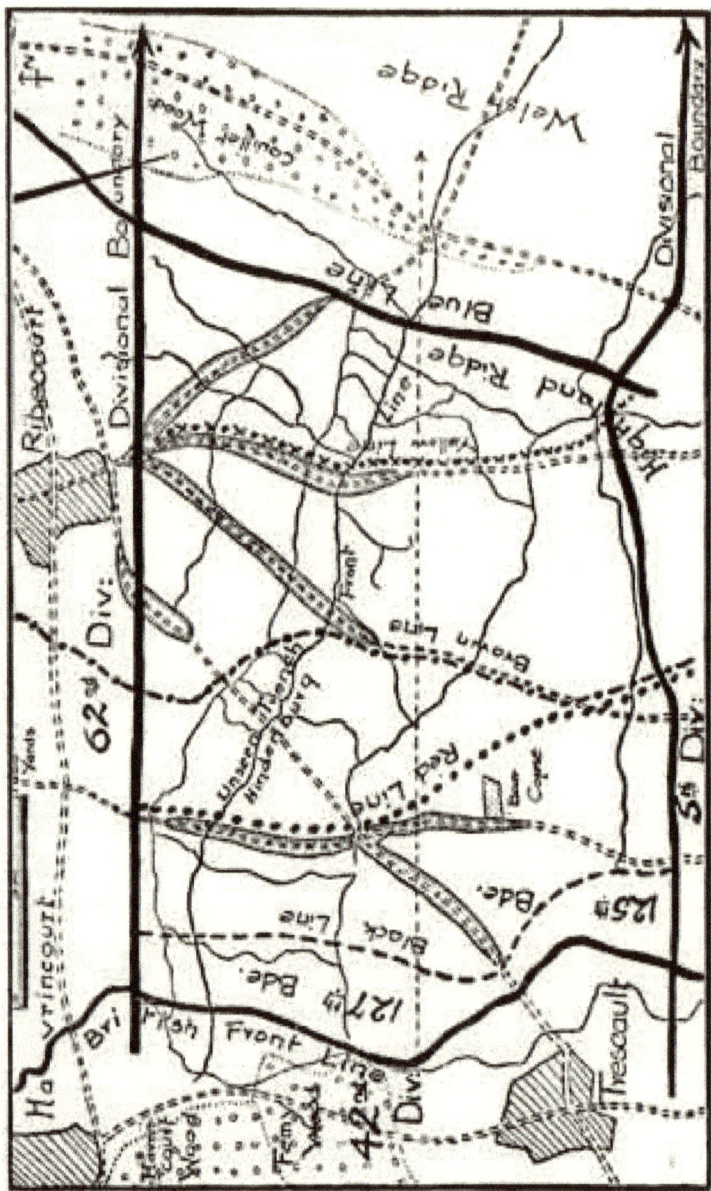

Attack on the Hindenburg Line, Sept. 27th, 1918

in the fact that a simultaneous attack was taking place along a widely extended front, and the enemy would not be able to fill these dugouts with counter-attacking troops drawn from other fronts.

Space does not allow of a detailed description of the orders for attack, but it can easily be imagined that they were pretty considerable in view of the heavy work to be accomplished by the artillery. As this portion of the German line was known to be powerfully defended by large numbers of troops, extensive trench systems, dugouts and wire, it was part of the strategy of Foch to concentrate artillery here, and records showed that on the two days September 27th and 28th shells were consumed at an unprecedented rate. In our sector alone, the programme comprised the capturing of 3,500 yards in depth of the most strongly defended ground in France, including the vicinities of the famous Highland and Welsh Ridges of terrible memory in the Battle of Cambrai.

Every yard of this ground was subjected to a continuous creeping shrapnel barrage lasting for almost three hours, while moving steadily ahead of this was a terrific bombardment by all calibres from 4.5 howitzers upwards upon the enemy's main trenches and supposed defence points. The brigade frontage, measured north to south, was 1,250 yards, and this was equally divided between the 6th and 7th. As we were going over one company behind another, each company was responsible for nearly 700 yards—a very large front considering our depleted numbers. There is no doubt, as far as we were concerned, the task looked formidably ambitious.

On the morning of Sept. 26th final operation orders were issued, and that night we moved up to our assembly positions in a huge dugout near Femy Wood, capable of holding the whole battalion. It was slow work moving along the canal and across the Trescault-Havrincourt road, and it is not surprising that eventually the intervals between platoons closed up and the four companies were strung out in one long line. The confidence felt in the success of the operations, was evident by the fact that the 6-inch howitzers were installed in front of the Trescault road within 500 yards of the enemy. Whilst we were assembling there were motor lorries on the road unloading stacks of ammunition for them!

By the time the battalion had been packed into the dugout dawn was swiftly approaching, which meant the commencement of the battle, for Zero for the third army was 5.25 a.m. The 6th corps, the 62nd Division of which touched up with our left, were to have three hours' fighting before we commenced, and for this reason we welcomed the shelter of the dugout while it was in progress. The configuration of the ground was responsible for the manner in which the battle was to grow along the whole front. The advance of the 127th Brigade was to take place along the shoulder of a long hill running broadly east to west. North of this high ground was a long valley stretching through Ribecourt towards Marcoing. Another shoulder similar to but higher than ours flanked the valley on the north, and it was this, together with the commanding village of Flesquieres, that the 6th corps were to make good before our attack commenced. Again, the 125th Brigade, who were on our right, and also on the higher part of the shoulder, were to open the 42nd divisional assault half an hour ahead of ourselves.

About 8 o'clock "C" company led the way out of the dugout and took up their assault positions near the front line. At the appointed hour, following behind the 5th, they moved forward to the attack, in the formation which we had practised so frequently, and which was the most suitable for the large frontage that had to be covered. All four platoons were in line, and each platoon was divided into four sections, the two rifle sections on the flanks, and the two L.G. sections in the middle and echeloned to the rear. This was the artillery formation useful for covering the ground previous to the actual assault, each section moving in file (*i.e.*, two ranks) well opened out.

When close to the enemy position the platoons extended and formed two lines, with a L.G. in the centre of each line, and riflemen on the flanks. Every Company went over in this formation, and strict orders were issued that no man was to enter the enemy trenches for the purpose of covering the ground, but to keep out in the open, otherwise great confusion would arise, and officers would lose control of their men.

Misfortune greeted "C" company from the start. Capt. Allen, M.C. and 2nd-Lt. Ray were killed immediately, and casualties were soon very heavy. It was evident the enemy was making the most of his superior position and the clear sweep of ground. The remnants of the company pushed on, however, and reached their objective. "A" company followed and they also suffered severely from the moment they advanced out of Ferny Wood. Then it was noticed that most of the machine gun fire was from the right flank, and our men were being subjected to a terrible enfilading fire as they moved across the open.

All the officers became casualties, Lt. Hammond wounded, 2nd-Lt.

McAlmont wounded, 2nd-Lt. T. Woods wounded, and 2nd-Lt. Carley, killed. The few men of the company, now led by C.S.M. Joyce, reached the Red Line and joined "C" company, which, Lt. Edge, M.C., having been hit, was now under the command of 2nd-Lt. Jones. It was impossible, with the small number of men, scattered over a wide front, to continue the advance for the moment. "D" company, moving up according to programme, were treated similarly to the previous two companies and men began to drop long before they anticipated meeting any resistance.

Thus, before they had gone very far 2nd-Lt. Thrutchley and 2nd-Lt. Wright were wounded, which left Lt. Gresty, M.C. and 2nd-Lt. Milne to carry on the leadership, a task which they performed in fine style. They quickly arrived at the Red Line, and then took cover for a short period. Soon after this, "B" company came along, but on nearing the Red Line, they found many men of "D" turned about firing rifles and L.G. towards their right rear. It was now obvious that the ground to the right of us had not been cleared at all, and the enemy was left free to work his will upon us from the higher ground. By this time a tank had arrived and materially assisted us in dealing with the problem. Gresty then decided to push on and his company mounted the rising ground in front. From this point they unfortunately swerved to the left, probably being influenced by a road which ran diagonally across the front towards Ribecourt, but nothing could stop their irresistible dash. As they crossed this road Milne, with a handful of his platoon, added to our already considerable number of prisoners, by capturing a large crowd of Huns.

With characteristic impetuosity, reminiscent of the La Signy Farm days, Gresty and the men of "D" following up under the barrage, rushed across the Brown Line and made for the Yellow Line. They were now only a small gallant band but they were undaunted. Prisoners captured were told to go down to the rear, which they did right gladly without an escort, so that the assaulting party who now in formation and well-nigh in size, began to resemble a Rugby football team, could preserve their strength. Two 77 m.m. guns lay in their path, and at their approach the Boche gunners spiked them and made off, leaving them an easy prey to the 7th.

After this, Gresty decided that he was on his objective, as indeed he was, but he was more or less in the 6th sector, and when he was quickly joined by a company of the 6th he began to realise it. There was trouble on his right, however, as well as from the front, and the small party of men were disposed to defend the ground they had captured, a difficult enough task in view of the fact that they had to find positions to face in two or three different directions. Touch was obtained with the 62nd Division in Ribecourt, and it was found that the 6th corps had had great success in their part of the battle, so that already the advance was proceeding towards Marcoing.

"B" company's effort was really a separate story. As soon as "D" company had disappeared over the crest in front of the Red Line they continued the advance. 2nd-Lt. Pearson was on the extreme right and he had been instructed to keep touch with the L.F.'s. From the beginning, however, he had not seen them, and his platoon was moving along "in the air," and naturally meeting with strong resistance. They had not expected to meet the enemy for another 1,500 yards if events had worked out "according to plan," but they were now fighting them at every step. Gallant deeds were performed in dealing with Hun machine guns, and many prisoners were taken, but greatest of all were the achievements of Pte. Jack White. Single-handed he rushed a machine gun post, bayoneted the man on the gun and pursued the remainder of the team with fire, inflicting casualties.

Later on he again rushed forward alone to a strongly held trench, but was killed practically on the parapet. His name was recommended for a V.C., but unfortunately nothing more was heard of it. In view of the heavy casualties, Lt. Wilson went across to Pearson and told him to close his platoon slightly towards the left, in order to keep a cohesion in the company, for it was evident that the Hun resistance promised to be strong, and there was no hope now of assistance from the right flank. In this manner the high ground near the Brown Line was reached, but the company was suffering from fire both from the front and the right flank. 2nd-Lts. Siddall and Gapp were wounded, as well as three platoon sergeants, and there was no knowledge as to what had happened to "D" company.

At this moment the Germans developed a counter-attack from the right in a manner to be expected from an intelligent and courageous enemy. The obvious thing for them to do was to cut in behind "B" company's right flank and attempt to regain a footing in "Unseen Trench" which had just been taken from them. From an offensive force we were suddenly transformed into a defensive force, and the men were still out in the open. Wilson drew back his right flank so as to face the Huns, but kept his left in touch with the 6th on the road in front of the Brown Line, and from this position, the men being disposed in shell holes, "B" company held up the enemy attack and defended the ground won. The Huns were on higher ground and when they had been finally driven to earth they kept up vigorous sniping at very close range, a form of fighting that we returned with interest. Pearson was hit in the stomach and later died on the way down, so that Wilson and C.S.M. Shields were left to control the remainder of the company.

The arrival of 2nd-Lt. Smith with signalling apparatus enabled communication to be obtained with battalion H.Q. Lt. Wilson outlined the situation and was told in return that the L.F's. had not yet reached Boar Copse, having met with powerful resistance. He was further ordered to hang on to his position and wait until the L.F's. had drawn up in line. Meanwhile a company of the 5th was sent up to strengthen the flank. Continuous touch by means of patrols were kept with the enemy, and his movements were carefully watched. Within 300 yards were a couple of German 77 m.m. guns, pluckily worked by the gunners at point blank range until our machine gunners, who had now arrived, co-operated with L.G's. from the 6th and ourselves in putting them out of action. They were taken by the 10th in the night. Meanwhile Gresty and the company of the 6th on the Yellow Line had been ordered to fall back 300 yards to a less isolated position, and a sound front and flank was thus established.

The battle had now reached a stage when the next move would be ordered by the brigade or even by the division. Careful observation of the enemy led us to suppose that he was weakening and Gresty and Wilson intimated that when the L.F's. arrived at the Brown Line, having re-organised their companies, they should be prepared to continue the advance in the 7th sector. Division had decided otherwise, however, and had ordered up a battalion of the 126th Brigade. Rapid preparations were made for a night attack to complete the divisional task, the 10th Manchesters to cover the 127th Brigade front and the L.F's. to continue on their right. Before nightfall, the enemy having withdrawn from the trenches immediately in front, "B" company pushed on again and established a good line running north and south in front of the Brown Line, and touching up with the L.F's. who had now arrived. This considerably simplified the work of the 10th, who were able to assemble in the night on an even front.

The night attack was a success. The Huns were evidently demoralised and put up no fight at all, surrendering in large batches without firing a shot when our men arrived at their dugouts, so that the Blue

Line was made good before dawn. Then came the work of exploiting success, and on the 42nd divisional front this was carried out by the 8th Manchesters, and the 5th East Lancs., the 126th Brigade having taken over the front during the afternoon of Sept. 28th. They were able to make good progress over Welsh Ridge before encountering serious resistance. Later in the day the New Zealand Division marched through to follow up the enemy, so that the 42nd could go down for a rest. Gladly did the *Fleur de Lys* pack up their traps and march back over the ground that had recently seen such stern work.

The brigadier had been up and personally thanked Lts. Gresty and Wilson for the work achieved by "D" and "B" companies, remarking that having seen the ground, and knowing the difficulties which had to be encountered, he thought all the men were heroes in having accomplished so much. Such praise coming from so sound a soldier was naturally received with gratitude and pride, and we felt that once again the name of the 7th Manchesters had been scored honourably and deeply in the records of warfare. The battalion reassembled in the big dug-out and there realised sadly the abundance of accommodation now afforded.

It had been a glorious fight but won at a terrible cost. Out of the 450 or so men who went over there had been more than 300 casualties. Of the sixteen officers who started out four only remained. 2nd-Lt. Pearson's death was particularly sad. He had gone out in the ranks in 1914 with the 7th, and had been twice wounded on Gallipoli, after which he served continuously with the battalion till the winter of 1917, when he went home for a commission. He had returned as an officer only a few weeks previously, and in this fight proved himself a courageous and skilful leader of men.

About 600 prisoners had been taken by the battalion, as well as the two field guns, large numbers of machine guns and other booty. More important was the death-blow to the German resistance. The Hindenburg Line had been smashed, the enemy was obviously demoralised, and they were in full flight for the next piece of ground which could offer a suitable position for delaying our rapid advance. The awards to the 7th for this battle included a bar to his Military Cross for Lt. Gresty, and Military Crosses for Lt. Wilson, 2nd-Lt. Milne, 2nd-Lt. Siddall, and 2nd-Lt. Thrutchley. C.S.M. McHugh, M.M., C.S.M. Tabbron, and Sgt. Mather received the D.C.M., while twenty N.C.O's. and men obtained the M.M., Pte. Greer being given a bar to his M.M.

The following Special Order of the Day indicates the value of the work done by the Manchesters in this day's fighting:—

29th September, 1918.

Manchesters,

For the second time in this month of September you have struck the enemy a heavy blow. It has brought us appreciably nearer to the complete victory which our country is determined to achieve.

I do not yet know the full amount of our booty. It can be estimated from the two miles of our advance, and from the prisoners, considerably more than a thousand in number.

I wish to record my admiration for the splendid behaviour of all ranks. The victory was won under conditions of exceptional difficulty, and, as at Villers-au-Flos, against an enemy superior in numbers to the attackers; and it was won by the magnificent determination and devotion of the troops.

Anthony Henley,
Brig.-Gen., Commanding 127th Inf. Brigade.

CHAPTER 10

Pursuing the Hun

THE SELLE RIVER

Yet again the vicinity of Havrincourt Wood was the abode of the 42nd division, and having been supplied with tents we set about the task of refitting and reinforcing. Companies once more attained a strength of about 100, and as the new men largely consisted of troops drafted from non-infantry units, principally A.S.C. from England, and men out for the first time, it was necessary to push along vigorously with training, for it was certain that we should be wanted again for fighting very soon. Returns from leave, etc., caused the following arrangement of company commanders:—Lieut. Douglas, M.C., "A" company; Capt. Grey Burn, M.C., "B"; Lieut. Gresty, M.C., "C," and Capt. J. Baker, "D"; while Capt. S. J. Wilson, M.C., was detailed to battle surplus. In the absence of Col. Manger on English leave, Major Rae assumed command of the battalion, while Capt. Barratt resumed the duties of adjutant, Capt. Creagh having gone to England on a senior officers' course.

When the division broke up camp on October 8th and marched up the line to get into closer support, the situation was roughly as follows. Since the battle on the Hindenburg Line the enemy had had no rest, and in spite of the difficulties of the ground (in one place a canal running north and south intervened) the N.Z.'s. and divisions right and left, had made steady progress, inflicting terrible casualties on the Boche who were sturdily resisting every yard of ground. To the north, Cambrai was still in the hands of the Hun, and from the continual fires seen in that direction it was obvious that he was wreaking characteristic vengeance on the helpless town.

The part of the Western Front between Cambrai and St. Quentin was recognised as the key to the whole situation so that naturally exertions were gigantic by both sides. Foch maintained his artillery concentration in this sector and undoubtedly one of the greatest wonders of that year of wonders, 1918, was the manner in which the guns obtained their never-ending supply of ammunition. The steady pounding never ceased day or night, and when infantry action took place, the noise welled up to terrific barrage speed for hours on end. When the nerve-shattered German soldier pathetically walked over to our lines one morning with hands up and exclaiming "*Kamerad*, too much shell!" he was surely expressing the enemy point of view. The line had thus been pushed on to the western outskirts of Solesmes, and troops in this area were now waiting for the fall of Cambrai and Douai to continue the pressure. When these events took place preparations were made for another battle.

During the battalion's march forward there was considerable night-bombing by enemy aircraft, and on the first night Sgt. Riley, an old member of the battalion, was killed and several men of H.Q. wounded by bombs on their bivouac. It was a fair country that the 7th were now approaching. After seven months' campaigning in the dismal devastated lands of the Somme regions the sight of whole houses with chimneys and roofs, and smoke exuding from them in the correct manner, was as welcome as an oasis to the thirsty traveller in the desert. Here were billets, a word of which we had almost forgotten to use.

But picture our excitement when we saw a real live civilian. The sight of these things probably brought home to our men the full meaning of the German defeat more than anything else. The 127th brigade spent a few days under most comfortable conditions in the village of Beauvois on the Cambrai-Le Cateau road, residing in houses, almost complete with furniture. A few of the villagers had courageously remained behind, taking cover in their cellars while the fighting and shelling took place above their heads. A good deal of wanton destruction had been carried out by the retiring Hun, but on the whole the countryside presented a normal appearance, a most welcome sight to eyes wearied with the scenes of devastation, and an important factor also in keeping up the morale of the troops.

Eventually the N.Z's. were relieved, and it was found that a very skilful and determined enemy lay in front. Subsequent events, indeed, showed that the strongest remaining division in the German army, the 25th Division, had been put into this sector. They had been conserved during the recent fighting, and on the prisoners who were captured clothing and equipment were brand new. They had a proud record extending right through the War, and claimed they had never received a beating from any British troops. (They were soon to meet their Waterloo.) The 126th Brigade were detailed to deliver the first shock of assault. Their objective included, after crossing the Selle River within point blank range of the German M.G's. and rifles, a deep Railway Cutting east of the main Solesmes road, Belle Vue Farm, and the ground immediately beyond the railway. The 127th Brigade were to go through when these positions had been made good and occupy the high ground overlooking Marou, a small hamlet on the final objective, which was to be taken by the 6th Manchesters.

The battle opened at dawn on October 21st, and after very heavy fighting, in which one exceptionally large number of the enemy stood and fought hand to hand and were killed with the bayonet; the 126th Brigade took all their objectives in splendid fashion. Then came the Manchesters, the 6th on the left, the 5th on the right, and the 7th in close support. The 6th advanced well, but the 5th quickly had trouble being held up owing to the troops on their right not keeping up. The enemy was fighting well, his infantry and machine gunners being particularly stubborn and covering their retirement very skilfully. Machine guns swept the advancing lines of the 5th, and the bare high ground to be crossed left them very exposed to exceedingly heavy enfilade fire. It was during this portion of the fight that Pte. Wilkinson of the Wiganers obtained the V.C. for message carrying. Five of his comrades had been killed within a few yards after starting on the same mission. Wilkinson volunteered to be the sixth to make the attempt. He was entrusted with the task and got through.

The 7th were now drawn into the battle, and "D" company advanced to form a defensive flank for the right company of the 5th. With this help the line was advanced, but it could not reach the final objective and so link up with the 5th who had already reached and occupied Marou. "A" company had advanced in support to the 6th and took up their allotted positions, forming four defended localities in depth ready to make a defensive flank if necessary. The 62nd division on the left had pushed through Solesmes and had made good the high ground to the east of that town, joining up with the 6th Manchesters.

At 4.30 p.m. a further barrage was put down for the 5th division and the 5th Manchesters to continue the advance. The latter, however, were very weak, having suffered heavy casualties, therefore "C" company of the 7th went forward and advanced to occupy the final objectives. The enterprise was entirely successful, and a machine gun nest, which had caused most of the trouble on the right, was captured, the garrison surrendering as prisoners. A dangerous counter-attack was repulsed by "C" and "D" companies and then the line was secured, and junction made with the 5th in Marou. Enemy artillery fire had been heavy during the day, and Battalion H.Q. in a deep ravine suffered severely from large calibre shells, so that they moved forward in the night to a healthier spot near the 6th H.Q. The positions were maintained all next day until relieved by the 125th Brigade.

Luckily in this show our casualties were light, totalling a loss of about 40 other ranks, very few being killed. The action of Capt. Baker in forming the defensive flank for the 5th undoubtedly restored an uncertain position, and materially assisted in the further advance. We were all pleased when he was awarded the Military Cross for this and general good work throughout the War with the 7th since June, 1915. The pace and power of the attack can be gauged by the fact that six battalions of the redoubtable Hun 25th Division, in spite of their proud record, were obliterated, and three days after the battle the division was disbanded and absorbed in another. The destruction of this division was an achievement of which the 42nd were justly proud. The motto of *Go one better* had been "put over" the Boche in an unmistakable manner.

On October 23rd the division marched back to Beauvois again, the N.Z. division having once more taken up the pursuit of the enemy, following him vigorously to the vicinity of Le Quesnoy. The 4th corps were going well, and all through these operations it was a noticeable feature in the situation maps of the third army front published from time to time that they always occupied the most advanced positions, and seemed to perform the function of the spear head of the attacks.

MORMAL FOREST

As the line of advance for the 42nd Division lay through the huge Mormal Forest, our training at Beauvois was largely in wood fighting. We were making preparations for what was to prove the last battle of the War. Col. Manger returned from leave and resumed command of the battalion, while Major Rae remained on battle surplus where, unfortunately, his old illness recurred and he had to go to hospital and eventually to England. His excellent work with the 7th, however, had been recognised for he was awarded the D.S.O. after the Armistice. Capt. Grey Burn, M.C., was promoted to Major and became second in command of the 5th L.F's. "B" company being taken over by Capt. Branthwaite, a recently joined 2nd line officer. Capt. D. Norbury, having returned from a tour of duty at home, was made O.C. "A" company, while Capt. S. J. Wilson, M.C., commanded "C" company.

The battalion marched out on the evening of November 3rd to take part in the work of exploiting success after the N.Z. division had smashed the enemy line. The attack commenced on the morning of November 4th, and after fierce fighting, and only after the garrison had been completely surrounded, Le Quesnoy was captured. The "Diggers" followed up vigorously and chased the Huns through a large part of Mormal Forest. Meanwhile our job was to "keep closed up" as far as possible and be ready to continue the pursuit, with the 126th leading and the 127th in support.

The first night was spent at Viesly, and the second at Pont à Pierre, just south of Salesches. The next day the weather completely broke down, and we moved forward in pouring rain, over the recently captured ground, arriving late at night in a thoroughly soaked condition at the tiny village of Herbignies on the western edge of the Forest. Here we found most of the civilians had remained through the fighting, and they told excited stories of the happenings. Small children toddled about the houses while Boche shells were still bursting not very many hundred yards away. It seemed a most extraordinary situation after the loneliness of war as we had always known it. These things had been the monopoly of the soldiers, but here were women and children trespassing upon our preserves. It helped us to realise the true tragedy of War.

That night the 126th Brigade took over the front, a sketchy business in view of the position, and the N.Z's. marched back. One of the officers, during the day, had called out to us in characteristic Colonial fashion, "Well, boys, are you going up to finish it?" whereupon one of the men replied with Lancashire directness, "Ay, we started it, so we may as well finish it." There was a good deal of peace-talk flying about. German prisoners had admitted that they could not go on much longer, while rumours about conferences were very prevalent. Still, until we got orders to stop fighting, this job had to continue, and that was the chief consideration for us, although the order to cease fire would have been keenly appreciated.

Early morning found us on trek in a steady downpour of rain

which made our already wet clothes more and more sodden. In this doleful fashion we splashed along over the muddy forest tracks to get close to the East Lancs. who were carrying out an attack. The 8th Manchesters had a particularly stern time, encountering nests of machine guns which had not been cleared from their exposed flanks, so that they lost very heavily. Nevertheless, the attack was eventually pushed home, and the Huns were dislodged.

Subsequent events revealed that from this moment the German retirement became a scurry of a disorganised rabble. The roads were blocked by their hurrying transport, and personnel simply made the best use of their legs, scampering across country where it was impossible to march on the roads. The civilians told us that utter confusion reigned everywhere. Our foremost troops undoubtedly met determined resistance from the machine gunners, but they were probably blissfully ignorant of what was taking place behind them.

As far as the 7th was concerned November 6th was one of the most miserable and trying days ever experienced. In the middle of the morning we arrived at our position, where we stayed during the whole of the day in a bitterly cold rain with no possibility of shelter. When it was ascertained that the enemy had been dislodged we made a few fires and tried to restore life to our numbed bodies. The divisional commander, having seen our condition, and realising that very few in the brigade would be fit for fighting after two such days, ordered up the 125th brigade, who had had an opportunity of getting dry and warm. We marched joyfully back in the middle of the night to Le Carnoy and there spent two days in billets.

The advance of the 42nd was now rapid. Hautmont, a fairly large manufacturing town, was captured after street fighting, and by the evening of November 9th an outpost line had been established southeast of Maubeuge. The 7th meanwhile had marched up through the forest and were billeted in the small village of Vieux Mesnil. Here we received official orders to stand fast on the morning of November 11th. At 11 a.m. the battalion paraded outside the church and there the bugles sounded "Cease fire" for the first and last time during the War.

The men took the news very quietly. We were too close to actual events to give ourselves over to the mad demonstrations of joy such as took place in spots more remote. At the same time everyone experienced a curious feeling of calm satisfaction that an unpleasant task had been accomplished. The 42nd division had taken part in two great

215

drives, the clearing of the Turk from British territory in 1916 and the clearing of the Hun from allied territory in 1918.

CHAPTER 11

Aftermath and Home

The division concentrated at Hautmont, and on November 14th the 7th marched into this town, and there occupied billets close to the Square. We now had an opportunity of realising the manner in which the Hun had delivered his last expiring kicks. Delay action mines had been placed under the railway at various points, and although one of the terms of the Armistice demanded that they should be indicated and removed, many were too near the time for explosion to allow of their being touched. As a result the railhead could not proceed beyond Caudry for some time, and it was necessary to convey supplies over a considerable distance by road. As arrangements had also to be made to feed the civilians, and repatriated prisoners of war, who now began to stream across the frontiers in an appallingly emaciated condition, some idea will be gained of the difficulty of keeping the troops sufficiently rationed. The men of the 7th, however, realised this and took a common sense view of the matter.

In the second week of December the 42nd Division marched up into Belgium to Charleroi, the 127th Brigade being quartered at Fleurus, a delightful village about six miles out of the town. Here the men of the 7th had a most happy time, for the villagers welcomed us right gladly and made us extremely comfortable in our billets. Turkeys, beer, extra vegetables and rum once more figured in the 'Xmas fare and it was with really rejoicing hearts that the Fleur de Lys spent their last Yuletide away from home. "C" company maintained the prowess of the battalion by securing the divisional prize for the best decorated dining hall. Later, chiefly through the efforts of C.S.M. Branchflower and Sgt. Aldred, M.M., we carried off the divisional cup for boxing.

On 'Xmas Eve the first of a series of events at once sad and joyful began to occur. Long-standing friendships and partnerships were rapidly broken up by the departure of drafts for demobilisation. Every few days parties went off, and one saw old faces gradually disappear from our ranks. The return, in the midst of glorious weather, of Capt. Barratt and Lt. Gresty, M.C. from Manchester, with the battalion colours was the occasion for a splendid ceremonial parade in which the Belgians took a lively interest. It was a proud moment when they were safely deposited in the officers' mess, and everyone took a share in their due honours.

The final stage in the long adventurous career of the 7th Manchesters during this great war was completed on March 31st when the cadre of the battalion, led by Brevet Lt.-Col. Manger, arrived at Exchange Station, Manchester, and amidst a tremendous and enthusiastic concourse of people proudly made their way through the city to Burlington Street, to deposit the colours in their home at the depot. The following Saturday evening a reception was held, when large numbers of men and officers with their friends united once more to do honours to the record of their battalion.

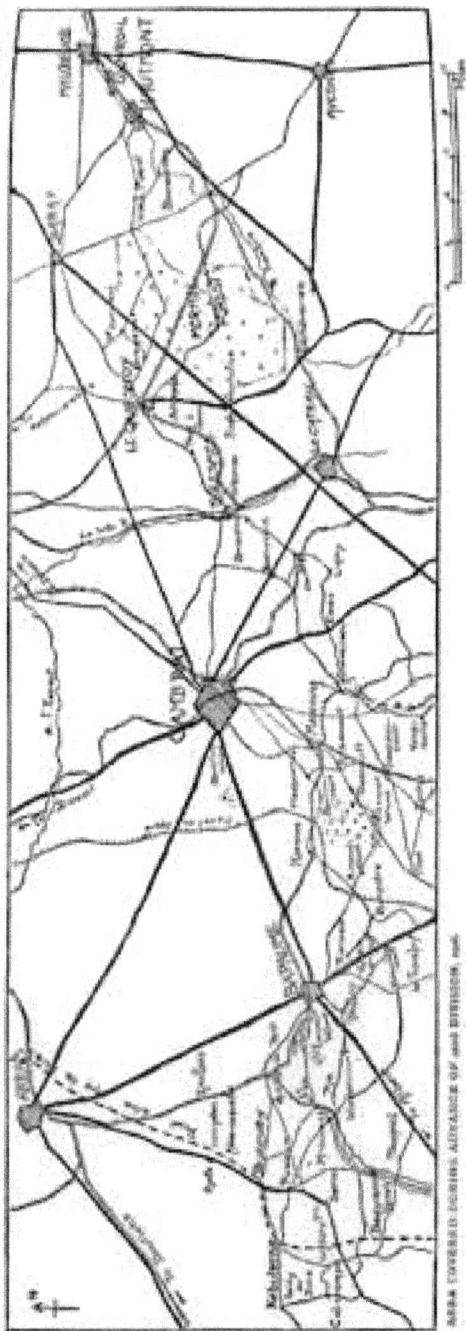

Area Covered During Advance of 42nd Division, 1918.

Appendix 1

HONOURS AND AWARDS TO MEMBERS OF THE BATTALION.

OFFICERS.

Fawcus, Major (Actg. Lieut.-Col.) A. E. F.	Distinguished Service Order.
	Military Cross.
	Legion d'honneur.
	Mentioned in Dispatches, Gallipoli (twice).
	Mentioned in Dispatches, France, June, 1918.
Manger, Major (temp. Lieut.-Col.) E. V.	Brevet Lieut.-Colonel.
	Commander of the Order of St. Michael and St. George.
Hodge, Lieut. (Actg. Lieut.-Col.) A.	Distinguished Service Order.
	Military Cross.
	Mentioned in Dispatches.
Canning, Lieut.-Col. A. (Attached)	Order of St. Michael and St. George (3rd Class or Companion).
	Mentioned in Dispatches.
Cronshaw, Major (Actg. Lieut.-Col.) A. E.	Distinguished Service Order.
	Royal Serbian Order of the White Eagle.
	Mentioned in Dispatches, France, 7.11.17.
Carr, (Actg. Lieut.-Col.) H. A.	Distinguished Service Order.
	Mentioned in Dispatches,
Brown, Major J. N.	Brevet Majority, 3.6.15.
	Distinguished Service Order.
	Royal Serbian Order of the White Eagle (4th Class).
	Japanese Sacred Treasure (3rd Class).

	Mentioned in Dispatches, 16.3.16, E.E.F. 25.9.16, E.E.F. 16.1.18, E.E.F.
Burn, (Actg. Major) F. G.	Military Cross.
	Mentioned in Dispatches, France, 6.7.17, and Egypt, Dec. 1917.
Creagh, Major P. H.	Distinguished Service Order.
	Mentioned in Dispatches, 26.8.15, E.E.F. 11.12.15, E.E.F.
Scott, Major & Quartermaster J., D.C.M.	Order of the British Empire.
	Mentioned in Dispatches, Gallipoli, E.E.F., 10.4.16.
Rae, Major G. B. L.	Distinguished Service Order.
	Mentioned in Dispatches.
Staveacre, Major J. H.	Mentioned in Dispatches, 26.8.15.
	(Killed in Action).
Creagh, Capt. (Actg. Major) J. R.	Mentioned in Dispatches, 7.11.17, 18.11.18.
Chadwick, Capt. G.	Royal Serbian Order of the White Eagle (4th Class).
Hayes, Capt. F.	Military Cross.
	Mentioned in Dispatches, July, 1916; July, 1917.
Nasmith, Capt. G. W.	Order of the British Empire.
	Mentioned in Dispatches.
Thorpe, Capt. J. H.	Order of the British Empire.
	Mentioned in Dispatches.
Whitley, Capt. (Act. Lt.-Col.) N. H. P.	Military Cross.
	Croix de Guerre, France.
	Crown of Italy.
	Mentioned in Dispatches, Gallipoli, E.E.F.
Farrow, Capt. J., R.A.M.C.	Military Cross.
Nidd, Capt. H. H.	Military Cross,
	(Died).
Williamson, Capt. C. H.	Military Cross.
	(Killed in Action).
Baker, Lieut. (Actg. Capt.) J.	Military Cross.
Collier, Capt. H.	Mentioned in Dispatches.
Kirby, Capt. E. T. (C.F.)	Military Cross.

Hoskyns, Capt. E. C. (C.F.)	Military Cross.
Norbury, Capt. C.	Mentioned in Dispatches, 24.5.18.
Norbury, Capt. M.	Mentioned in Dispatches, 16.1.18.
Branthwaite, Capt. R. H.	Mentioned in Dispatches, 7.11.17.
Douglas, Lieut. C. B.	Military Cross.
Edge, Lieut. N.	Military Cross.
Goodall, Lieut. J. C.	Military Cross.
Goodier, 2nd-Lt. A.	Awarded Commission in the Field.
	Military Cross.
Gresty, Lieut. W.	Military Cross and Bar.
Harris, Lieut. L. G.	Military Cross.
Siddall, 2nd-Lt. J. R.	Military Cross.
Wilson, Lieut. (Actg. Capt.), S.	Military Cross.
	Mentioned in Dispatches, 8.11.18.
Franklin, Lieut. H. C.	Military Cross.
	Mentioned in Dispatches, 10.4.16.
Allen, Capt. C. R	Military Cross.
	(Killed in Action).
Bagshaw, Lieut. K	Military Cross.
Welch, Lieut. (King's Own)	Distinguished Service Order.
	Mentioned in Dispatches.
Gorst, 2nd-Lt. H.	Military Cross.
Milne, 2nd-Lt. J. H.	Military Cross.
	Mentioned in Dispatches.
Harland, 2nd-Lt. J. A.	Military Cross.
Thrutchley, 2nd-Lt. F. D	Military Cross.
Woodworth, Lieut. F. T. K.	Mentioned in Dispatches, 8.11.18.
Thorp, Lieut. W. T.	Mentioned in Dispatches, 24.5.18.
	(Killed in Action).

NON-COMMISSIONED OFFICERS AND MEN.

Abbreviations:

M.M. = Military Medal.

D.C.M. = Distinguished Conduct Medal.

M.S.M. = Meritorious Service Medal.

276236	Aldred, Sgt. J.	M.M.
1070	Anlezark, R.S.M. W.	M.S.M.
275726	Bailey, Pte. S.	M.M.
275782	Banahan, Sgt. J.	do.
275021	Bamber, Sgt. F.	D.C.M.
		M.S.M.
275039	Booker, L/c F. W.	M.M.
276702	Botham, Pte. W. E.	do.
275889	Bowman, Pte. J.	do.
276845	Boydell, Pte. J.	do.
276327	Bradshaw, Pte. W.	do.
276418	Braithwaite, Pte. T.	do.
276264	Broughton, Cpl. A.	do.
280	Calow, Sgt.	Mentd. in Dispatches.
275125	Clavering, Sgt. H.	M.S.M.
275103	Clough, R.Q.M.S. S.	Croix de Guerre (Belgian)
276047	Collinge, Pte. H.	M.M.
1536	Connelly, Pte. J.	Mentd. in Dispatches
275724	Conry, Pte. R. E.	M.M.
276151	Craven, L/c A.	do.
303461	Daley, Sgt. W.	M.M.
51167	Davies, Pte. W. T.	do.
276842	Dearden, Pte. R.	do.
275141	Downs, Pte. A.	do.
300991	Eastwood, Cpl. W.	M.M.
276856	Edwards, Pte. R.	do.
275173	Fidler, Sgt. W.	M.M.

105	Fielding, Sgt. W.	Mentd. in Dispatches
275161	Fleetwood, Sgt. A.	D.C.M.
1904	Franks, L/c J.	Mentd. in Dispatches.
275201	Gammond, A/Sgt. T. A.	M.M.
375395	Green, Sgt. J. W.	D.C.M.
		M.M.
		(Killed in Action.)
277007	Greer, Pte. A.	M.M. and Bar.
276028	Gregory, Cpl. B.	M.M.
276254	Goffey, Sgt. W.	do.
275218	Hadfield, Sgt. A.	M.M.
57548	Halfhide, Pte. C.	do.
295015	Hand, Sgt. A.	D.C.M.
5211	Hartnett, R.S.M. N.	*(Died of Wounds.)*
		Mentd. in Dispatches.
276486	Hayhurst, Pte.	M.M.
42732	Heasman, L/c A.	D.C.M.
275524	Heath, Sgt. F.	*(Died of Wounds.)*
		M.M. and Bar.
275256	Holbrook, Sgt. J.	D.C.M.
550239	Horsfield, Sgt.	D.C.M.
		M.M.
		Croix de Guerre (Belgian).
276171	Hyde, L/c L.	M.M.
276424	Jackson, L/c E.	*(Died of Wounds.)*
		M.M.
276973	Jennions, Pte. H.	do.
376666	Jolley, Sgt. J.	do.
275281	Joyce, C.S.M.	M.M.
		Gold Medal of St. George of Russia (2nd Class).

276640	King, Cpl. A. W.	D.C.M.
276648	Latham, Pte. H.	M.M.
275319	Lockett, Cpl. S.	*(Died of Wounds.)*
		D.C.M.
276719	Lyons, Pte. C.	M.M.
276482	Lynn, Sgt. H.	do.
275326	Lievesley, Sgt. J. L.	do.
275705	Macguire, Cpl. A.	M.M.
275822	Mather, Sgt.	D.C.M.
2409	McCartney, L/c H. S.	*(Killed in Action.)*
		Mentd. in Dispatches.
275935	McClean, Pte. T.	M.M.
275355	McHugh, C.S.M.	D.C.M.
		M.M. and Bar.
400535	Moore, Pte. T. C.	M.M.
276020	Morris, L/c G.	do.
40	Mort, L/Sgt. W.	D.C.M.
275365	Mottram, L/Sgt. G.	M.M.
275704	Mullin, Pte. C.	M.M.
275426	Parker, Sgt. G.	M.M.
40849	Parkin, Pte. I.	do.
12782	Pickering, Pte. W.	do.
276932	Quinn, Pte. J.	D.C.M.
49738	Reeves, Pte. E.	M.M.
2263	Richardson, Pte. M.	D.C.M.
276535	Riley, Pte. J. G.	M.M.
275468	Riley, Sgt. R.	do.
		(Killed in Action.)
48576	Rotham, Pte. J.	M.M.
37647	Rourke, Pte. A.	do.

275509	Sanderson, Pte. G.	M.M.
57229	Shaughnessy, Pte. W.	M.M.
275495	Shields, C.S.M. J.	M.S.M.
		Mentd. in Dispatches.
275513	Snadham, Cpl. J.	Mentd. in Dispatches.
376453	Standring, Cpl. W.	M.M.
233	Stanton, Sgt. J.	Mentd. in Dispatches.
57216	Stubbard, Pte. R.	M.M.
275571	Tabbron, C.S.M.	D.C.M.
276540	Thorpe, Sgt. H.	M.M.
303634	Titchener, Pte. E.	do.
275883	Titterington, L/Sgt. H. L.	M.M.
277020	Twist, L/c T.	M.M. and Bar.
275590	Walsh, Pte. J.	M.M.
275604	Walton, Pte. F. G.	do.
275646	Warrington, Pte. W.	do.
277635	Wisken, Pte. A.	do.
		(*Died of Wounds.*)
275627	White, Cpl. F.	D.C.M.
		Mentd. in Dispatches.
275632	Wilkinson, Pte. H.	M.M.
51624	Wilkinson, Pte. J.	do.
275952	Wilmer, Pte. R.	do.
295025	Wood, Cpl. T.	D.C.M.

Appendix 2

MEMBERS OF THE BATTALION KILLED IN ACTION, DIED OF WOUNDS, MISSING, Etc.

As these lists may not contain the names of all those members of the battalion who made the supreme sacrifice, I tender my apologies to the friends and relations of those whose names have been omitted. Some difficulty has been experienced, however, in making the lists as full as they are.

S.J.W.

OFFICERS.

Allen, Capt. C. R., M.C.	Killed in Action	27.9.18
Bacon, Lieut. A. H.	Killed in Action	7.8.15
Brown, Lieut. T. F.	Killed in Action	30.5.15
Carley, Lieut.	Killed in Action	27.9.18
Cooper, Lieut. C. M.	Killed in Action	20.10.18
Dudley, Lieut. C. L.	Killed in Action	4.6.15
Freemantle, Lieut. W. O.	Killed in Action	4.6.15
Granger, Lieut. H. M.	Killed in Action	29.5.15
Grant, Lieut. R. W. G.	Killed in Action	25.5.17
Kay, Lieut. H. N.	Killed in Action	21.8.18
Lomas, Lieut. F.	Killed in Action	4.6.15
Ludlam, Lieut. E. W.	Killed in Action	28.3.18
McLaine, Lieut. D.	Died of Wounds	2.4.18
Nidd, Capt. H. H., M.C.	Died of Sickness contracted during the war	4.3.19
Pearson, Lieut. H.	Killed in Action	27.9.18
Philp, R.A.M.C., Capt.	Killed in Action	27.3.18

Ray, Lieut. H. M.	Killed in Action	27.9.18
Rylands, Capt. R. V.	Killed in Action	29.5.15
Savatard, Capt. T. W.	Killed in Action	29.5.15
Staveacre, Major J. H.	Killed in Action	4.6.15
Sievewright, Lieut. M. J.	Killed in Action	2.11.17
Thewlis, Lieut. H. D.	Killed in Action	4.6.15
Thorp, Lieut. W. T.	Killed in Action	28.3.18
Tinker, Capt. A. H.	Killed in Action	28.3.18
Ward, Lieut. G. H.	Killed in Action	4.6.15
Williamson, Capt. C. H., M.C. (R.F.C.)	Killed in Action	27.3.17
Wender, Lieut., D.C.M.	Killed in Action	16.6.18
Wood, Lieut. A. S.	Died of Wounds	29.3.18

NON-COMMISSIONED OFFICERS AND MEN.

Killed in Action.

1533	Abercrombie, Pte. E.	16.12.15
5204	Adamson, Pte. C.	27.9.18
1665	Adderley, Pte. E.	4.6.15
275740	Alman, Pte. T.	14.9.17
490	Anderson, Cpl. R.	4.6.15
2045	Anderton, Pte. F.	
1740	Ayres, Pte. W. A.	4.6.15
1355	Bailey, Pte. W.	4.6.15
2348	Bain, Pte. T. P.	4.6.15
2403	Balon, Pte. E.	29.5.15
2215	Banks, Pte. A.	4.6.15
1968	Bannan, Pte.	4.12.15
3014	Barber, Pte. S.	10.8.15
1888	Barks, Pte. F. C.	7.12.15
27504	Barnes, Pte. J. H.	8.9.17
1347	Barnett, Pte. I.	29.5.15
52996	Barratt, Pte. R.	21.8.18
275059	Barrow, L/c T. E.	8.9.17
74429	Barry, Pte. R. J.	21.8.18
276522	Bedford, Pte. F. A.	27.9.18
2009	Bell, Pte. A.	4.6.15

275823	Bennett, Cpl. C.	27.9.18
276100	Bennet, Pte. R.	5.4.18
1941	Bent, Pte. W.	16.9.15
1228	Berry, Cpl. J.	4.6.15
275956	Beswick, Pte. R.	27.9.18
2438	Billington, Pte. H.	4.6.15
59824	Bincliffe, Pte. A.	27.9.18
276693	Bland, Pte. H. W.	28.3.18
980	Bleasdale, Pte. W.	30.5.15
2018	Boardman, Pte. A. H.	19.9.15
2143	Bouchier, Pte. G. C.	4.6.15
896	Bowe, Pte. G.	4.6.15
49841	Bowling, Pte. T.	27.9.18
277064	Boyd, Cpl. H.	2.9.18
1873	Bridge, Pte. E.	7.8.15
3456	Bright, Pte. W.	18.9.15
1009	Bromley, L/c E.	31.5.15
276676	Brookes, Pte. A.	28.10.17
1617	Brookes, Pte. J.	4.6.15
275929	Broughton, Pte. V.	28.3.18
1534	Brown, Pte. E.	4.6.15
2290	Brown, Pte. G.	4.6.15
	Bruce, Pte. W.	31.5.15
1730	Buckley, Pte. W.	5.6.15
1712	Burgess, Pte. A.	5.6.15
1197	Burgess, Pte. J.	4.6.15
276966	Burns, Pte. R.	28.3.18
2336	Callaghan, Pte. H.	9.6.15
275111	Calardine, L/c J.	25.3.18
2192	Callon, Pte. J. W.	4.6.15
76918	Carr, Pte. A. E.	21.8.18
276657	Castrey, Pte. E.	28.10.17
1431	Cavanagh, Pte. F.	4.6.15
1402	Cawley, Pte. B.	8.8.15
2255	Chadwick, Pte. C.	4.6.15
1277	Chadwick, Pte. W.	18.9.15
275968	Chappell, Cpl. J. H.	25.8.15

2070	Chappell, Pte. L.	4.8.15
2363	Clare, Pte. H.	4.6.15
2125	Clarke, Pte. E. E.	4.6.15
2311	Clime, Pte. J.	4.6.15
276697	Colley, Pte. W. J.	27.9.17
275110	Collier, L/c C.	27.8.17
1662	Collins, Pte. R. C.	4.6.15
2011	Collins, Pte. W.	31.5.15
4084	Connor, Pte. J.	1.9.16
164	Cookson, Sgt. S. R.	29.5.15
1948	Cott, Pte. T.	4.6.15
1897	Cousell, Pte. J.	4.6.15
1212	Cox, Pte. J.	31.5.15
24754	Croughan, Cpl. C.	27.9.18
3033	Cunnington, Pte. R.	8.8.15
276265	Darbyshire, Pte. H.	6.5.17
2333	Davies, Pte. C.	13.5.15
74436	Davies, Pte. G.	20.10.18
1931	Davies, Pte. T. A.	4.6.15
2098	Dawson, Pte. T. B.	29.5.15
275130	Day, Pte. H. G.	18.8.18
2831	Dean, Pte. H.	7.8.15
1772	Dillon, Pte. H.	4.6.15
2247	Ding, Pte. W. H.	30.5.15
61024	Dodd, Pte. J.	27.9.18
1301	Dodds, Pte. J. E.	4.6.15
1145	Doolen, Pte. R. J.	4.6.15
2315	Draper, Pte. J. E.	4.6.15
2457	Driver, Pte. R.	18.9.15
74406	Duckley, Pte. L.	8.10.18
275140	Dyehouse, L/c W. H.	27.9.18
74435	Dyke, Pte. F. G.	20.10.18
268	Eardley, Pte. G.	4.6.15
77445	Edgerton, Pte. G. J. A.	10.6.18
276670	Elphinsone, Pte. R. J.	28.3.18
276593	England, Pte. E.	8.9.17
2077	England, Pte. W.	4.6.15

277013	Evans, Pte. G.	29.10.18
2478	Farrar, Pte. A.	7.8.15
275910	Farrington, Pte. A.	2.9.18
1921	Fawdrey, Pte. G.	4.6.15
2432	Finch, Pte. H. B. L.	4.6.15
2364	Fitchett, Pte. F.	4.6.15
2130	Fisher, Pte. B.	29.5.16
2217	Fisher, Pte. J.	4.6.15
1700	Fitzsimmons, Pte. J.	4.6.15
37736	Fletcher, Pte. E. H.	27.9.18
275171	Foden, Sgt. W.	27.9.18
275163	Ford, Pte. P.	27.9.18
276513	Ford, Pte. R.	14.9.17
276602	Forester, Pte. J. H.	3.5.17
275970	Franklin, Pte. L.	11.9.17
2302	Gamble, Pte.	4.6.15
275190	Gardener. Pte. W.	27.9.18
38692	Garratt, Pte. J.	11.9.18
276558	Garrett, Pte. A.	6.1.18
2176	Gibbons, Pte. J.	4.6.15
1926	Gillibrand, Pte. A.	4.6.15
39393	Gilbert, Pte. R.	27.9.18
2212	Goulding, Pte. P.	4.6.15
2362	Graham, Pte. J. A.	31.5.15
276999	Graham, Pte. W. H.	8.9.17
2397	Grainger, Pte. H. M.	29.5.15
	Green, Pte. J. D.	4.6.15
375395	Green, Sgt. J. W., D.C.M., M.M.	21.8.18
1313	Gresty, Pte. F.	13.7.15
1397	Hall, Pte. C.	13.7.15
41749	Hall, Pte. H.	14.6.18
1352	Hallam, Pte. F.	4.6.15
275981	Hamilton, Pte. G.	26.6.15
3205	Hammersley, Pte. J.	19.9.15
276861	Hampson, Pte. J.	29.3.18
1720	Hargreaves, Pte. H.	4.6.15
2450	Harling, Pte. J.	4.6.15
2378	Harrison, Pte. E.	13.5.15

3416	Harrison, Pte. H. N.	16.9.15
1369	Harrison, Pte. T. S.	9.11.15
1259	Heath, Pte. G.	4.6.15
2401	Hewitt, Pte. W.	4.6.15
57162	Higham, Pte. T.	27.9.18
1627	Hinchliffe, Pte. W.	4.6.15
1799	Hilditch, Pte.	4.6.15
49513	Hills, L/c G. G.	21.8.18
60404	Hindly, Pte. J. B.	21.8.18
2164	Hobbs, Pte. T.	31.5.15
2386	Holland, Pte. J. H.	4.6.15
238	Holdercroft, Pte. F.	4.6.15
275264	Hodgkins, Pte. W.	23.5.17
49511	Hodgkinson, Pte. J. D.	9.6.18
1178	Hodson, Pte. F.	4.6.15
3287	Hollingworth, Pte. D.	7.8.15
1856	Holmes, Pte. S.	4.6.15
275013	Holt, Cpl. J.	27.9.18
54400	Hope, Pte. J. W.	27.9.18
2413	Horrocks, Pte. W. E.	7.8.15
1358	Horrox, Pte. W.	29.5.15
25300	Hughson, Pte. G.	27.9.18
2351	Hunt, Pte. F.	4.6.15
1922	Hunt, Pte. S. A.	4.6.15
276634	Ikin, Pte. J. W.	6.5.17
275876	Ingram, Pte. H.	6.1.18
276054	Jackson, Pte. J.	18.4.18
276433	Jackson, L/c J.	4.6.15
203	Jackson, Pte. J. S.	4.6.15
2313	Jennings, Pte. W. G.	12.6.15
1520	Jepson, Pte. W.	8.8.15
276659	Johnson, Pte. J. H.	30.3.18
750	Jones, Pte. H.	4.6.15
1823	Jones, Pte. J.	4.6.15
50338	Judge, Pte. M.	26.9.18

3669	Kaufmann, Pte. S.	5.12.15
1118	Kearney, Pte. A. D.	
51893	Keeber, Pte. H.	27.9.18
1935	Keeble, Pte. F.	29.5.15
1841	Keegan, Pte. G.	29.5.15
1663	Kellett, Pte. W.	4.6.15
1674	Kelly, Pte. H.	29.5.15
2026	Kelly, Pte. J.	4.6.15
1331	Kenyon, Pte. A.	31.5.15
74471	Kerfoot, Pte. F.	1.7.18
2360	Kershaw, Pte. J. H.	4.6.15
2125	Kidd, Pte. T.	3.8.18
1748	Lamb, Pte. R.	4.6.15
1807	Laver, Pte. H.	8.8.15
275318	Lawton, Sgt. C. H.	8.11.17
1570	Lee, Pte. J. M.	13.8.15
3207	Lee, Pte. W. H.	24.12.15
1898	Lees, Pte. W.	4.6.15
3532	Leigh, Pte. W.	18.8.16
44370	Livesley, Pte. W.	27.9.18
2282	Lomas, Pte. F.	4.6.15
275330	Lomas, Pte. G.A.	28.3.18
1296	Longshaw, Pte. R.	4.6.15
2374	Lowerson, Pte. H.	4.6.15
2160	Lyons, Pte. J.	4.6.15
2416	Lyons, Pte. T.	9.10.15
1923	Lythe, Pte. F.	8.8.15
1945	Maley, Pte. E.	4.6.15
1282	Manley, Pte. J. N.	16.8.15
40717	Mallis, Pte. G. W.	12.9.17
275360	Martin, Pte. W. H.	23.5.17
	Marvin, Pte. G.	4.6.15
42547	Mason, Pte. J.	27.9.18
275865	Master, Pte. E. H.	28.3.18
276302	Mates, Cpl. J.	23.8.18
2409	McCartney, L/c H. S.	7.8.15

1361	McClure, Pte. E.	8.8.15
19434	McKeown, Pte. E.	22.7.18
1647	McKie, Pte. W. K.	4.6.15
276874	McVey, Pte. J.	5.4.18
1442	McWilliam, Pte. R.	4.6.15
276175	Mellor, Pte. G.	5.4.18
1681	Merriman, Cpl. R.	4.6.15
276096	Metcalfe, Sgt. F. E.	9.9.18
275887	Milligan, Pte. A. J.	26.6.18
2408	Milligan, Pte. J.	31.5.15
276612	Milward, Pte. K.	18.4.18
42526	Mitchell, Pte. H.	27.9.18
252	Molyneux, Pte. H. S.	7.8.15
85281	Morrell, Pte. J.	27.9.18
1874	Morris, Pte. A.	4.6.15
1906	Moisey, Pte. J.	4.6.15
74459	Myers, Pte. R.	21.8.18
42166	Nevin, Pte. J. S.	27.9.18
2455	Newbold, Pte. S.	28.5.15
1485	Oarkinson, Pte. A. C.	29.5.15
2428	Oates, Pte. L.	30.5.15
3298	O'Brien, Pte. A.	18.9.15
276431	Oldham, Pte. W.	1.9.18
276288	Ormerod, Pte. A. E.	29.3.18
1695	Page, Pte. A.	4.6.15
295017	Parsons, Cpl. F. N.	23.7.16
1278	Passant, Pte. R.	31.5.15
48	Peacock, Pte. W. H.	4.6.15
891	Pearce, Pte. F.	4.6.15
51741	Pearson, Pte. G.	27.9.18
2454	Phillips, Pte. J. P.	31.5.15
2300	Pickles, Pte. W.	4.6.15
2119	Pope, Pte. W.	4.5.15
2132	Raper, Pte. A. E.	4.6.15
275481	Rawlings, Pte. H.	9.10.17
2044	Rawlinson, Pte. W. R.	4.6.15

1671	Rawson, Pte. W.	21.5.15
1258	Rhodes, Pte. J. W.	4.6.15
2805	Rideal, L/c J. H.	8.8.15
275468	Riley, Sgt. R., M.M.	8.10.18
1991	Roberts, Pte. A.	18.8.16
1283	Robertson.	29.5.15
276473	Rogers, Pte. S.	27.8.19
10788	Rogerson, Pte. W. H.	27.9.18
276039	Rosewell, L/Sgt. A.	21.8.18
2355	Royle, Pte. F. E. H.	4.6.15
1689	Russell, Pte. W. H.	30.5.15
276630	Salter, Pte. H.	30.4.17
2003	Sanderson, Pte. J.	13.5.15
276241	Scraton, Pte. C.	27.9.18
276888	Shaw, Pte. B.	21.8.18
276551	Shearere, Pte. G.	30.3.18
2033	Shepherd, Pte. J. E.	30.5.15
2243	Shipley, Pte. J. E.	16.10.15
276533	Sidebottom, Pte. H.	29.11.17
275506	Smith, Pte. H.	4.4.18
3018	Smith, Pte. M.	16.9.15
1673	Smith, Pte. R. S.	31.5.15
2245	Smith, Pte. W. H.	29.5.15
1657	Smith, Pte. W. H.	29.5.15
1187	Stanton, Cpl. W.	7.8.15
1956	Starkie, Pte. C.	4.6.15
275489	Steel, Pte. R.	6.5.17
29421	Stott, Pte. A.	20.10.18
2369	Super, Pte. C.	26.5.15
276967	Sweeney, Pte. J.	21.8.18
275903	Tanner, Sgt. A.	27.9.18
275550	Tanner, Sgt. E.	13.5.18
277005	Tardoe, Pte. P.	29.3.18
57266	Taylor, Pte. H.	27.9.18
276421	Taylor, Pte. J.	24.10.18

276240	Taylor, Pte. J. H.	10.6.18
1846	Taylor, Pte. S.	31.5.15
	Thomas, Pte. J. A.	18.8.17
57453	Thompson, Pte. S. E.	21.8.18
1040	Thompson, Pte. T.	29.5.15
275558	Thornily, Pte. B.	13.5.18
57442	Timothy, Pte. E.	27.9.18
275866	Titterington, Cpl. F.	27.9.18
3021	Twigg, Pte. F. A.	7.8.15
1943	Vardon, Pte. C.	31.5.15
1413	Verity, L/c J.	4.6.15
277759	Vickers, Pte. J. H.	5.4.18
1835	Walker, Pte. R.	4.6.15
2057	Walker, Pte. S.	29.5.15
275606	Wallace, L/c E.	7.1.18
1775	Walley, Pte. H.	4.6.15
275597	Ward, Pte. J.	5.4.18
2322	Watmough, Pte. A.	4.6.15
275793	Watmough, Pte. W.	5.4.18
2270	Webb, Pte. S.	4.6.15
521	Webster, Sgt. H.	29.5.15
276962	Welsh, Pte. R.	3.5.17
1893	Whelan, Pte. J.	4.6.15
1725	White, Pte. R.	29.5.15
202152	White, Pte. J.	27.9.18
2261	Whitely, Pte. J. B.	7.8.15
55933	Whittaker, Pte. A. T.	27.9.18
276605	Wilbraham, Pte. T.	30.4.17
2335	Wild, Pte. G.	21.7.18
2226	Wilde, Pte. H. J. R.	29.5.15
1573	Williams, Pte. A.	4.6.15
295119	Williams, Pte. J.	1.6.17
1354	Williams, Pte. R.	29.5.15
2458	Williams, Pte. W. V.	4.6.15
1311	Wilson, Pte. L.	4.6.15
2406	Winter, Pte. D.	29.5.15

714	Winterbottom, L/c G.	31.5.15
57246	Wittle, Pte. F.	27.9.18
1939	Wood, Pte. A.	31.5.15
3642	Woodward, Pte. H.	1.12.15
298004	Wookey, Pte. A. J.	27.9.18
1924	Worrall, Pte. S.	29.5.15
275716	Young, Pte. G.	
8002	Young, L/c H.	27.9.18

Dead—Presumed Killed in Action.

1976	Duffy, Pte.	4.6.15
1903	Haydock, Pte. J.	4.6.15
1535	Hunt, Pte. H.	4.6.15
1603	Makin, Pte. A. W.	4.6.15
1965	Moore, Pte. G.	4.6.15
2079	Newman, Pte. G. E.	4.6.15
1960	Newman, Pte. G. E.	4.6.15
69	Plan, Pte. R.	4.6.15
1434	Tearsley, Pte. A.	4.6.15
1646	Williams, Pte. S.	4.6.15

Dead—Sickness.

2515	Ashton, Pte. C. B.	16.10.15
2274	Boden, Pte. G. C.	5.11.15
2554	Clare, Pte. H.	18.8.15
3271	Couper, Pte. G.	30.7.16
3275	Edwards, Pte. J.	8.8.15
275252	Hardy, L/Sgt. A.	1.3.19
37791	Leach, Pte. R.	14.11.18
3051	Oldfield, Pte. W. F.	12.10.15
1701	Redford, Pte. S. F.	27.5.16

Died in Egypt.

1180	Beckett, Pte. R.	8.2.16
4361	Hind, Pte. W.	26.9.16
2099	Kenyon, Pte. F.	26.12.14

4176	Stocks, Pte. T.	29.5.15
932	Williams, Pte. F.	21.1.15
2368	Wood, Pte. E.	4.6.16

Died.

276353	Berry, Pte. J.	28.1.18
275051	Blackledge, Pte.	6.2.18
275083	Brewer, Pte. M. C.	18.9.18
3325	Ebourne, Pte. W.	22.1.17
276587	Haslewood, Pte. T.	23.3.18
2326	Keogh, Pte. F.	22.5.15
276559	Norton, Pte. J.	20.8.17
276297	Vipond, Pte. A.	7.10.17

Died of Wounds.

74412	Baker, Pte. H.	10.10.18
276623	Bamber, Pte. M.	19.4.18
1958	Bancroft, Pte. J. W.	23.9.15
1738	Barton, Pte. T.	25.5.15
275035	Beckett, Pte. J.	3.11.17
2178	Boaley, Pte. A.	29.5.15
74408	Bridson, Pte. R.	25.7.18
275068	Brown, Sgt. H.	22.8.18
2402	Brown, Pte. J. W.	30.6.15
1780	Burr, Pte. H.	14.5.15
756	Butcher, Pte. H.	7.8.15
2436	Byrne, Pte. T.	17.6.15
2268	Carpenter, Pte. C.	
275109	Carroll, Sgt. J.	27.3.18
275108	Cavanagh, Pte. J.	29.3.18
2381	Chantler, Pte. J.	21.4.15
276626	Clegg, Pte. H.	4.11.17
275104	Cliffe, Pte. G.	6.4.18
1479	Connell, Pte. A.	27.8.15
276595	Cookson, Pte. W.	23.7.18

3080	Dale, Pte. H.	24.7.15
275133	Davidson, Pte. S.	1.6.17
276974	Davies, Pte. G.	5.9.17
3035	Davies, Pte. H.	31.7.15
276434	Doherty, Pte. T.	11.11.17
295030	Daley, Pte. A.	14.4.18
277565	Earnshaw, Pte. N.	22.8.18
275937	Fairhurst, Pte. F.	28.3.18
276960	Finch, Pte. S.	25.3.18
53904	Forbes, Pte. W.	25.8.18
276680	Gibson, Pte. F.	26.4.17
27515	Gibson, Pte. J.	3.4.18
42683	Goddard, Pte. T.	23.8.18
275188	Golton, Pte. J.	25.5.17
48689	Greenhalgh, Pte. J.	30.7.18
1455	Gregory, Pte. J.	14.10.15
276345	Harrop, Pte. W.	2.9.18
5211	Hartnett, R.S.M.	19.10.17
2014	Hazeltine, Pte. J. R. H.	29.5.15
275254	Heath, Sgt. H., M.M.	24.4.18
295073	Heyward, Pte. S.	10.6.17
2655	Hunt, Pte. W.	2.6.15
276424	Jackson, L/c E., M.M.	27.3.18
1858	Jacques, Pte. G.	8.8.15
295038	Johnson, Pte. A.	5.1.18
276286	Johnson, Pte. R.	28.3.18
275791	Jones, Pte. J.	6.4.18
275307	Kay, Pte. R.	6.4.18
295	Leigh, Pte. E.	8.8.15
275319	Lockett, Cpl. S. E., D.C.M.	27.9.18
1179	Lowrey, Pte. H.	31.5.15
3662	Marshall, Pte. R.	13.12.15
1821	McCleod, Pte. A.	27.5.15
1500	McHugh, Pte. H.	28.6.15
276350	Midgeley, Pte. T.	28.9.18

2433	Milligan, Pte. A.	28.5.15
2002	Millington, Pte. T.	15.6.15
276414	Minns, Sgt. W.	28.3.18
1761	Minshall, Pte. F.	5.6.15
3038	Mitchell, Pte. H.	17.9.15
2269	Moran, Pte. J.	4.6.15
1598	Morris, Pte. E.	29.5.15
1265	Morris, Pte. H.	19.7.15
38	Munday, Sgt. F.	10.6.15
276519	Norman, Pte. E.	25.8.17
429	Nuttall, Pte. H. W.	29.5.15
1561	Pannell, Pte. T.	9.8.15
1821	Parsonage, Pte. A. F.	4.6.15
1438	Pease, Pte. W. S.	30.6.15
277763	Pender, Pte. W.	16.4.18
176	Percival, Pte. J.	15.6.15
	Platt, Pte. W. C.	25.8.18
276432	Prendergast, Pte.	25.8.18
2316	Powell, Pte. A. E.	29.5.15
1401	Reid, Pte. J.	30.10.15
276645	Roberts, Pte. J.	5.5.17
2067	Ross, Pte. C.	25.8.15
2965	Salt, Pte. G.	5.11.15
1929	Slowe, Pte. J. W.	4.7.15
276368	Sparling, L/c P.	22.8.18
1937	Sowden, Pte. W. P.	15.6.15
276321	Stahler, Pte. J.	20.10.17
2375	Thomas, Pte. E.	20.7.15
276987	Treadway, Pte. T.	22.12.17
275566	Taylor, Pte. J. W.	5.4.18
275790	Wakefield, Pte. G.	29.9.18
275603	Walker, Pte. J. W.	4.4.18
1357	Walsh, Pte. M.	11.6.15
295023	Ward, Pte. A.	12.11.17
1788	Ward, Pte. J.	1.6.15
2296	Wilde, Pte. J. F.	15.9.16

1699	Winstall, Pte. H.	13.8.15
276635	Wisken, Pte. A., M.M.	22.8.18
2347	Wolstencroft, Pte. R. K.	29.5.15
2121	Wrigley, Pte. J.	22.6.16

Reported Dead.

| 1441 | Downey, Pte. O. | (no date) |
| 275223 | Hilton, Pte. W. | (no date) |

Missing.

1148	Balf, Pte. C.	4.6.15
2323	Bracegirdle, Pte. L.	7.8.15
1793	Harrison, Pte. W.	4.6.15
276230	Johnson, Pte. W. A.	16.6.18
569	Kirkby, Pte. H.	4.6.15
2206	Krell, Pte. J.	7.8.15
3231	Stoddart, Pte. L.	7.8.15
2007	Tracey, Pte.	
1614	Wakefield, Pte. A.	4.6.15
2172	Wallace, Pte. G.	4.6.15
1262	Williams, Pte. H.	4.6.15
267	Worrall, Pte. J. E.	4.6.15